Fathers and Sons
in Cinema

FATHERS AND SONS IN CINEMA

Gershon Reiter

McFarland & Company, Inc., Publishers
Jefferson, North Carolina, and London

Library of Congress Cataloguing-in-Publication Data

Reiter, Gershon, 1945–
    Fathers and sons in cinema / Gershon Reiter.
        p.   cm.
    Includes bibliographical references and index.

    ISBN 978-0-7864-3788-7
    softcover : 50# alkaline paper ∞

    1. Fathers and sons in motion pictures.   I. Title.
PN1995.9.F42R45   2008
791.43'65251— dc22   2008013240

British Library cataloguing data are available

On the cover: John Wayne (left) and Montgomery
Clift in *Red River*, 1948

Manufactured in the United States of America

McFarland & Company, Inc., Publishers
    Box 611, Jefferson, North Carolina 28640
    www.mcfarlandpub.com

For my father and son,
Avraham and Ziv Reiter

For my daughters,
Ella and Lia

Acknowledgments

I wish to thank those whose contributions and support helped with the writing of this book.

First and foremost, my profound gratefulness to John David Ebert, whose good will, frank criticism and invaluable insight helped me shape a rambling manuscript into a book.

My heartfelt gratitude to Ziva Garbi and George Delany, who were with me from start to finish, offering their insightful comments, unending support and encouragement.

I would like to express my gratefulness to all the others who contributed to the completion of this book: Barry Spector, Lesley Brill, Tom Leitch, Dr. Herbert Stein, Professor Arthur M. Eckstein, Joan and Bill Schwanger, Bob Gould, Ann Hafften and Franz Schemmel, Anna Goldstraw, Yudit Halivney, Dalia Goldberg, Tzvi Keren, Miriam Elman, Ora Dvir and Ester Broide.

Table of Contents

Preface: The Ties That Bind
Fathers and Sons and
the Dragon Between Them

Then God said, "Take your son, your only son, Isaac, whom you love, and go to the region of Moriah. Sacrifice him there as a burnt offering on one of the mountains I will tell you about."

Genesis 22: 2

My first glimpse of the dragon must have been when I heard the opening verse of Bob Dylan's "Highway 61 Revisited." In this verse Dylan retells the Binding of Isaac, placing it on Highway 61. The father's readiness to sacrifice his son was powerful and mysterious. It encapsulated the dark ties that bind fathers and sons. What's more, placing the event on the "Blues Highway" (which stretches from New Orleans, birthplace of jazz, through the Mississippi Delta, cradle of the blues, up "Ol' Man River"'s muddy waters by way of Memphis in the South to Chicago in the North, and further north to Dylan's hometown of Duluth, Minnesota), Dylan was bringing it all back home. He didn't call the album *Highway 61 Revisited* for nothing.

If placing the Binding of Isaac on Highway 61 suggested something about Dylan's relationship with his father, what was I to make of finding that his father's name was Abraham, and that he married a woman named Sara and named two of their sons Samuel Isaac Abraham and Jakob? This telling disclosure turned the song into a personal statement. The dialogue is between the biblical God and the First Patriarch, but the son tells the tale. He is the victim. From his point of view, the opening verse of the album's title song isn't so much about God testing Abraham's faith as it is about the son's anxiety about being his father's son, about his fear of the father's retribution. After such a traumatic event, surely no son would ever see his father as before.

Only upon learning Dylan's father name did it occur to me that Abraham was also the name of my father, which probably explains the song's initial grip on me. Of course, I knew it all the time. But I didn't think of it too much. I didn't make the connection. I didn't recognize (admit) that this was my story, that I was also the victim of Abraham. Not the actual Abraham, not my real father, who died when I was seven and whom I remember fondly, but the father I had internalized, split off from the pain that had accompanied his death, the father I had introjected. This introjected father, and Dylan's marriage to a woman named Sara, must have been in the back of my mind when I had the most momentous dream, my own *Highway 61 Revisited*.

In the dream I enter a primitive Indian reservation where everyone seems to be able to read my thoughts. The Indians are supposed to be menacing, but as it turns out, once you get closer and get to know them, they're quite friendly, even helpful. The dogs are the ones I should be aware of. They are the creatures I'm really afraid of, since they can sense my fear. I have to weave through them and not show my fear. It seems I have entered a forbidden enclosed reservation.

Somehow I become the chief's son and am wearing his golden robe. Then I feel I have to escape through a fence to the outside from where I came, as my real identity (as someone from the outside) seems to have been exposed. I get by the dogs and climb a huge tree whose branches reach over the barbed-wire fence that surrounds the reservation. But as I climb down the other side, my robe gets caught in the barbed wire. I know that I can make a quick and clean getaway if I take the robe off, but I also know that I must keep wearing it, as if it is a ceremony, a rite I have to undergo. As I near the ground outside the reservation, someone (a big dog or the chief?) discovers my escape. Once outside the reservation, I become more muscular and am half-naked.

Then, as I climb a hill overlooking the reservation (at my back now), the sun is going down, its red glow reflecting on my skin, making it seem reddish-brown, not unlike the Indians I've left behind. As I reach the top of the hill, located in the back of my real house, I meet a woman I know. Her name is Sara.

I knew this dream was important, but I only began to appreciate it some months later when reading *The Hero in Hemingway's Short Stories*, by Joseph DeFalco, a book that revealed the underlying meanings in Hemingway's stories by focusing on their mythic structure and the journey motif they employed. The opening story, "Indian Camp," was too much like my dream for me not to turn to it and try to understand what it was telling me — what I was telling myself. In his reading of the story, DeFalco seemed to explain my dream.

In Hemingway's story the young Nick Adams accompanies his father, a doctor, to an Indian village where an Indian woman is about to give birth. The story is essentially about a son's birth and a father's death, the mother giving life and the father taking his life. Beneath the narrative, however, in the story's subterranean landscape, Hemingway is dealing with the relationship between Nick and his father. Considering that the drama Nick witnesses is "staged" by the Indians, who are more primitive, more connected to the elements, it might be a projection of his place in the family triad.

What struck me about DeFalco's reading of the story was the pattern of the hero's journey — departing, initiation and return. This was the pattern of my dream. I enter the reservation, get past the dogs, obtain the robe and go with it over the fence. But more than that, like Dylan's Johnny mixing up the medicine in the unconscious basement (in "Subterranean Homesick Blues"), in my dream I was *mixing up the myths.* I was the biblical Isaac; meeting the father's wife, I was the mythological Oedipus. Coming back with the golden robe I was also Jason with the Golden Fleece. Just as Jason had to get the Golden Fleece guarded by the sleepless dragon in order to get King Pelias' crown, I was telling myself what I had to do, what I had to seek and retrieve. I was telling myself that to grow as a man I had to obtain something belonging to the father.

Not only did DeFalco explain my dream, but he also introduced me to Joseph Campbell's *The Hero with a Thousand Faces,* the book on which he based his reading of Hemingway's stories. Campbell's book deepened my appreciation of the journey's universal pattern, which, as I soon discovered, wasn't only in myths and dreams. It was also in many of our movies. I first noticed it in its entirety in *Back to the Future,* where Marty McFly, the movie's young hero, was on his own hero's journey. It was all there, and it fit so perfectly. Movies, after all, have an uncanny ability to convey mythic stories. Coming as close to reality as any other medium, and dealing mostly with images, both "real" and metaphoric, movies are truly projections of our collective dreams and private myths. They are our filmmyths.

In time, the more I looked at movies as filmmyths (as I came to call movies that combine the universal pattern that underlies *myths* with the modern medium of *film*), the more I discovered the recurring theme of fathers and sons. Then, in an epiphany of sorts, I envisioned the dragon. In one clear flash, I realized that many of these cinematic heroes were dealing with what Campbell called "the ogre aspect of the father," the very dragon that comes between fathers and sons. Just as Dylan had retold the Binding of Isaac, these filmmyths retell dragon-slaying myths. Unlike myths, however, in which heroes slay dragons that guard golden treasures and captive princesses, the heroes of these filmmyths "slay" characters who personify the dragon, figures embodying the introjected ogre father that thwarts the heroes' potential for growth and independence. The cinematic hero's slaying of the dragon, his coming to terms with the ogre aspect of the introjected father, I came to see, is in such classics as *Red River, North by Northwest* and *The Searchers,* and in such modern filmmyths as *Fields of Dreams, Stand by Me, E.T.,* and *The Lion King.* They all envision how heroes slay the dragon, how they untangle the dark ties that bind fathers and sons.

Introduction:
Myths and Filmmyths

The original departure into the land of trials represented only the beginning of the long and really perilous path of initiatory conquests and moments of illumination. Dragons have now to be slain and surprising barriers passed — again, again, and again.

— Joseph Campbell, *The Hero with a Thousand Faces*

What Are Myths?

For a definition of myths, particularly as they figure in films, we need look no further than John Ford's western *The Man Who Shot Liberty Valance* (1962). From his first talking western, *Stagecoach* (1939), which set the standard for westerns to come, Ford had used the backdrop of the American West to deal with the myths of America. Only towards the end of his career, however, when examining the western through *Liberty Valance*, did he deal directly with the subject matter of myths and their elusive meaning.

Like many mythical westerns that open with the advent of the hero, from *Shane* to the westerns of Clint Eastwood, Ford's western opens with the arrival of Senator Ransom Stoddard (James Stewart) and his wife in the western town of Shinbone, where he started his political career. The senator's return, as the town newspaper's reporter sees it, is too important an event to go uncovered. The reason for the visit, told in a flashback, takes up most of the movie. It tells the truth behind the myth of the man who shot Liberty Valance.

The flashback story starts with the young Stoddard, a romantic lawyer from the East bound for Shinbone, on a stagecoach which is held up by the town's arch villain, Liberty Valance (Lee Marvin). He whips Stoddard for trying to stand up for a woman passenger and rips up his law book, teaching him "western law." The man who finds the beat-up lawyer and brings him to town is the same Tom Doniphon (John Wayne) whose death brings Senator Stoddard and his wife back to town at the start of the movie. It is revealed that while Stoddard's political career was built on the myth that he was the man who shot

Liberty Valance, the real shooter was Doniphon, who shows Stoddard the truth behind the shooting in a brief flashback within the flashback.

The reporter's concluding line at the end of Stoddard's story — "When the legend becomes fact, print the legend" — both defines Ford's mythical western and offers a clear-cut definition of myths. As this famous line confirms, and as the movie illustrates, the legend is what is important. Ford underscores this point by having the man who in fact shot Liberty Valance die in virtual oblivion, while the man who allegedly shot him is remembered and hailed as a hero. What really happened does not matter so much as what is *believed* to have happened. And because the townspeople believe that Stoddard, who stands for law and order, did the shooting, he becomes a hero, bigger in legend than in life. The belief that he killed the evil Valance blows up the event to mythical proportions, until, in time, it becomes myth — a western myth of the hero slaying the dragon.

Contrary to the way it is presented in *Liberty Valance*, myth nowadays is generally used to describe an event or a person as untrue or unreal, as a falsehood. By "myth" we usually mean there is a pervading belief in something or someone that never really existed. "It's just a myth," we dismiss it. But as *Liberty Valance* demonstrates, fact or fiction has little to do with myths and the role they play in our lives. If myths did not capture our imagination, as Stoddard's legendary shooting did, they would disappear into oblivion much like Doniphon. But myths are still part of our lives because they are first and foremost stories we tell ourselves about ourselves. More than literal tales that convey the true events of an historic event or facts about a person's life, myths are metaphoric stories that reflect who we are and what we could be. In the same sense that it is not the dream's "intention" to convey an event that really happened, but rather to project the inner workings of the dreamer to make the unconscious conscious, so is the "intention" of myths: to reveal the inner workings of our collective psyche. "The mythologizing propensity of the psyche," as James Hillman calls it, "is a basic psychological movement that, try as we will, is never overcome; the psyche never fully yields to the delusion of an only literal, only factual reality. Mythmaking, like dreaming, is always going on."[1]

The western in general, and *Liberty Valance* in particular, are classic cases of "mythmaking" in movies. This mythmaking explains, however partly, the western's popularity from the early years of cinema. It answered our need for myths and for mythical heroes. These bigger-than-life characters were certainly more accessible, and easier to identify with, than the greats of Greek mythology. Where the Classical heroes are mostly left to our imagination, the cinematic heroes are experienced with our eyes. And yet, the heroes are alike in that, while solving real problems, they resolve inner conflicts. John Ford underscores this in *Liberty Valance* by having Ranse Stoddard embody the two conflicting sides represented by Tom Doniphon and Liberty Valance, the two sides of the law ruled by the six-gun. In closing with Stoddard, who, after revealing the truth of the legendary shooting, is ironically told, "Nothing's too good for the man who shot Liberty Valance," Ford emphasizes the import of myths. The legend, the myth, is what people remember. Like the western itself, it assures us that good triumphs over evil, that the hero slays the dragon.

Myths and Metaphors

To understand myths, we need to understand metaphors. The two not only originate in our creative imagination, but we create the mythic narratives, the messages, and the metaphors with which to convey them. That is why myths, when taken literally, are perceived as fantastic tales that never really happened; when taken metaphorically, as one thing meaning another, myths take on new meanings, becoming metaphoric tales through which we reveal our shared psyche. Much as a diver's mask helps us see underwater, metaphors reveal what lies beneath the literal, as when revealing the underlying (unconscious) journey in the hero's outer adventure. Suddenly we see much more of what lies beneath the surface. We start understanding the messages we are sending ourselves through myths.

A well-known example of myths and metaphors, and a great revealer of our shared psyche, is the myth of Oedipus, who solved the riddle of the Sphinx. In seeing the creature that in the morning walks on four legs, at noon on two and in the evening on three, as a metaphor for the three ages of man, Oedipus saves the city of Thebes from the famine and disease brought about by the Sphinx, another name for the dragon. Of course, the Oedipus myth, as initially interpreted by Freud, is one of our timeless self-addressed messages, conveyed through metaphors.

Another brilliant illustration of the use of metaphors to convey the underlying message, and an ingenious cinematic take on the Oedipus myth to boot, is Roman Polanski's *Chinatown*. Even the movie's title is a metaphor that harbors a number of meanings. More than a place, Chinatown is a state of mind. It is a metaphor for the *other*, for what Freud called the *uncanny*. As "Chinatown" suggests, and as the movie bears out, there is a dragon loose on the town. Noah Cross (John Huston) is a monster who hoards the life-giving "water and power," threatening to turn Los Angeles into a lifeless desert. Under Cross's ruthless greed, Los Angeles is much like Thebes under the Sphinx's reign of terror. And despite what he may think, the movie's hero, J. J. Gittes (Jack Nicholson), is not up to the task of slaying the dragon. "You may think you know what you're dealing with here," Cross warns Gittes in their first encounter, "but believe me, you don't." In fact, as suggested in the opening, the movie itself, like the town of the same name, is not what it seems. The black-and-white Paramount logo the movie's sepia-toned credits, together with the black-and-white photos in the opening shots, lead us to believe we are seeing a black-and-white film noir. But as the camera pulls back to show the private eye's office, we see that the movie is in color. We are shocked into recognition right from the start, just as Gittes's client, Curly, is shocked by what he sees.

When he looks at the pictures of his wife fornicating with another man, which are not unlike a son's mental images of his mother and father, Curly, the betrayed husband, sees more than he wants to. Like Oedipus who saw too much and blinded himself as a result, the bald-headed Curly takes out his rage on the private eye's new blinds. "All right, Curly. Enough is enough. You can't eat the Venetian blinds. I just had them installed Wednesday," the white-attired Gittes says, putting a stop to Curly's display of emotions. But for Gittes, enough is not enough. His self-satisfaction, his hubris, drives him back to Chinatown, where, like Oedipus, he fulfills the oracle's prophesy. He repeats the past mistake of "trying to keep somebody from getting hurt and ended up making sure that she was hurt." Only then does he heed the advice one of his operatives tells him in the movie's closing line: "Forget it, Jake, it's Chinatown."

In hindsight, Gittes's same advice to the woman posing as Mrs. Mulwray — "Go home and forget everything" — suggests that he is also talking to himself, much as Oedipus unknowingly investigates himself. And like Oedipus, who thought King Polybus was his father, Gittes is led to believe that "Mrs. Mulwray" is who she seems. He tries to dissuade her from learning about her husband "*seeing* another woman." ("Do you *know* the expression 'Let sleeping dogs lie'? You're better off not *knowing*.") But Gittes can surely use some of his own advice. Like the curious "kitty cat" that he is (according to the Polanski character before he slashes Nicholson's character's nose, warning him, "Next time you lose the whole thing!"), when Mrs. Mulwray insists that she has "to *know*," Gittes takes on the investigation. Despite the many warnings, despite being over his head, he has to know.

An early warning that he is over his head comes when Gittes learns the name of the man Mrs. Mulwray wants investigated. It is the man from "Water and Power." Gittes gets another warning in the very next scene, in Hollis Mulwray's closing line at the public hearing about Water and Power: "I'm not going to make that mistake twice." But just as he does not see that the real Mrs. Mulwray (Faye Dunaway) is standing behind him when he tells the boys (who try to warn him) the Chinese joke he just heard, Gittes does not foresee that she will take him back to Chinatown, where he makes that mistake a second time. He neither heeds his own advice to let sleeping dogs lie nor his barber's observation that "the heat's murder." Even when Mrs. Mulwray offers to drop the lawsuit, saying, "You know all you need to know," Gittes refuses. "Is this a business or an obsession with you?" she asks the persistent Gittes.

All in all, the Oedipus myth is never mentioned in the course of the movie, though the incest between Evelyn Mulwray and Noah Cross is a strong tip-off. The movie's metaphors make *Chinatown* another retelling of the Oedipus myth. With all the *see*s and *know*s that come up throughout the movie, not to mention the prominence of the private eye's "castrated" nose and the femme fatale's flawed iris, "a birthmark of sorts," *Chinatown* can be subtitled *The Eye Nose.* We see the whole movie from Gittes's nosy point of view, through his private eye. Moreover, considering the numerous images of "one" eyes and various lenses that turn up, *Chinatown* can be seen as the private eye's (one eye's) knowing by seeing, which recalls the Oedipus myth and is what movies are all about.

Filmmyths

Nowadays there is no better way to get in touch with myths than through the movies. Movies, after all, are a natural and effective medium for conveying myths, and when they tell myths they function as "productions and projections of the psyche."[2] In effect, they are filmmyths, films that project our modern-day myths, films through which we tell ourselves about ourselves. These self-addressed messages, these projections of our psyche, give filmmyths their special appeal. It is what makes filmmyths so fascinating and so successful at the box office. It is why movies such as those in the *Star Wars* saga, and the *Lord of the Rings* and *Matrix* trilogies, have created such a following. Other than being great cinematic achievements, they all are filmmyths. They tell us, as never before, who we are and what we could be.

With their uncanny ability to project the psyche in a most entertaining and accessible manner, filmmyths (and movies in general) provide an emotional experience that is hard to come by in the real world. That is why when we have a great emotional experience, or witness a "super" realistic event, we say that it is just like the movies, as if movies are more real than reality. And in a way they are. In the darkness and comfort of the theater, which for the most part eliminates reality and renders the spectator in a relaxed state, movies convey stories in a way that vividly resembles reality. The images on the movie screen recall the images we project on our "mindscreen" in our dreams. And as in dreams, for the duration of the viewing, we are in a semi-somnambulist state, believing that the images are real. This is another facet of filmmyths' magical power. In the theater, the images on the screen mirror our shared psyche, our collective unconscious.

Probably the most "notorious" example of a screen mirroring the hero's unconscious is Hitchcock's *Rear Window.* Somewhat like Dorothy Gale's *back*-yard, the neighboring rear windows that the hero, Jefferies (James Stewart), watches through his own rear windows are screens onto which he projects images of his unconscious fears and desires. This point is suggested by his girlfriend (Grace Kelly), who tells him, not unlike a therapist, "Let's start from the beginning, Jeff. Tell me everything you saw and what it means." What Jefferies watches obsessively are various man-woman relationships, which mirror what Lisa wants from their relationship and what he would rather look at from afar. Confined to a wheelchair, Jefferies scratches his leg inside the cast like someone might abuse himself while watching a titillating movie from the safe distance of a theater seat. Jefferies is a voyeur to such an extent that he only gets excited about the stunning Lisa when she crosses the courtyard and enters the "window screens" while assisting him in investigating the tenant Thorwald (Raymond Burr). Likewise, as spectators watching the action from the comfort of the theater seat, we are captivated by the cinematic heroes who personify our fears and desires, our hopes and dreams. We may not always see it, because it is usually not as obvious as in ancient myths, but more than a few cinematic heroes are engaged in slaying dragons.

Dragons Dead or Alive

Like the mythical Theseus, Perseus and Jason, many of our cinematic heroes today have their share of dragons to slay. Only unlike the dragon in ancient myths, the cinematic dragon is not a dragon as such. Just as in dreams psychic forces are embodied by persons or animals, the cinematic dragon is personified by a menacing figure who taunts and obstructs the hero from obtaining his Golden Fleece. The dragon is such an inherent creature that oftentimes it is envisioned in early childhood stories. "The child identifies itself to a varying extent with the young hero of the story. It has an unconscious apprehension of the difficulties that stand 'twixt cup and lip' ... and magnifies them into dragons and monsters."[3] Similarly, in filmmyths that deal with the difficulties between fathers and sons, the son's "unconscious apprehension" of the father, both his dread and his perception, makes the father something akin to a dragon. In such filmmyths as *Back to the Future* and *Stand by Me*, for example, the young heroes project their "unconscious apprehension" of the fathers (the introjected fathers) on menacing figures that personify the dragon. A more concrete example of the dragon, albeit in its feminine form, is presented in *The Wizard of Oz*, where Dorothy Gale projects her introjected mother on the witch of her dream. In all three filmmyths, the protagonists resolve their difficulties with the parental figure by slaying the dragon.

The defining moment in *Back to the Future* comes when George McFly lays out his nemesis with one clean punch, thus becoming George the Dragon Slayer. With one swing of his hand the man "not good in confrontation" slays the brute who has hounded him all his life. With this heroic deed, George removes the obstacle that stands in the way of his getting the young woman he wants and becoming a man. "I never knew he had it in him," Marty comments on his father's heroics. "He never stood up to Biff in his life."

Gordie Lachance's moment of truth in *Stand by Me* comes when he stands up to the evil Ace with a gun like one of his Western heroes. "What are you gonna do, shoot us all?" Ace taunts Gordie. "No, Ace," Gordie says, standing his ground in the showdown with his dragon, "just you." Backing off, Ace tries to save face: "We're not going to forget this, if that's what you're thinking. This is big time, baby."

In *The Wizard of Oz*, Dorothy eliminates the witch with one splash of water from a nearby bucket, melting the witch's wickedness into oblivion. With the life-restoring water she "slays the dragon" that has been after her since she first crossed the threshold to Oz. "Who would've thought a good little girl like you could destroy my beautiful wickedness?" The witch is surprised by Dorothy's resourcefulness. She did not think the girl had it in her.

Much as the dragon is the magnified "unconscious apprehension" of the father, at least in tales of fathers and sons, the slaying of the dragon is the release from the clutches of the introjected father. For the most part, each culture may portray the dragon and its slaying according to its beliefs and way of life, but it is same metaphoric tale of the hero dealing with some part of his unconscious "The dragon, let us remember, is not a snake, not an animal at all. It is a fictitious animal, an imaginal instinct, and thus the instinct of imagination or the imagination as a vital, instinctual force."[4]

Perhaps what makes the dragon such a ubiquitous figure in both myths and filmmyths is the fact that it is a creature comprised of many creatures—a sort of composite archetype. It is at once a gigantic reptile with a lion's claws, with the tail of a serpent, bat-like wings, scaly skin and a mouth with fiery breath. But whatever shape it assumes, the dragon is generally a symbolic manifestation of an archetypal force that obstructs our path to ourselves. That is why it is often portrayed as guarding a precious treasure, a golden object that represents the self. In Greek mythology, for example, the dragon guards the golden apples of the Hesperides' gardens and the Golden Fleece. In Norse mythology, the dragon Fafnir guards the Rhinegold.

In Christian legends, the dragon is the formidable beast against which the knight must prove himself, most notably seen in the myth of Saint George the Dragon Slayer, where Saint George represents the ego and the dragon the unconscious. This dragon is best represented in modern Western literature by the white whale Moby Dick, whose cinematic counterpart is the huge shark in Spielberg's *Jaws*. Once again, as in Shinbone and Chinatown, there's a dragon loose in the seaside town of Amity. Whether from the labyrinth or from the ocean's depths, it is the same monster of the unconscious. Like Theseus freeing the town of Athens from sacrificing its youth to the Minotaur, *Jaws'* hero slays the leviathan shark, freeing Amity of the underwater menace attacking the town's youth. Only then does he overcome his inner obstacle, his fear of water, the same water in which the dragon dwells.

Of course, as a metaphor, the introjected father is not necessarily a dragon. It is called by other names, but the role it plays in the psyche is the same. In his book *Finding Our Fathers*, Samuel Osherson calls it "the wounded father." He defines it as "the internal sense of masculinity that men carry around within them. It is an inner image of father that we experience as judgmental and angry or, depending on our relationship with father, as needy and vulnerable."[5] One way or another, this "inner image" of "the wounded father" is what the heroes of *Back to the Future*, *Field of Dreams* and *Lone Star* "carry around within them."

Theseus and the Minotaur

Among other things, Theseus and the Minotaur is a prototype of the dragon slaying myth, which perhaps explains its prominence in Western culture. It illustrates how the dragon comes to be and what is required to slay it. But more than that, as suggested by its opposite pairs of fathers and sons, the myth is an early expression of the two sides of the father and of the father-son relationship. One father disowns the son whose birth he initiates; the other takes care of his son's future and acknowledges him when the time comes.

Minos indirectly begets the half-man, half-bull Minotaur by letting his hubris get the best of him. In his struggle with his brothers for the rule of Crete, Minos prays to Poseidon (Neptune), the god of the seas, to send him a bull as a sign that he is the rightful heir to the throne, and promises to sacrifice the bull as a sign of his subservience. Poseidon obliges by having a white bull emerge from the sea, but Minos covets it for himself, sacrificing another bull instead. Upon learning of Minos' deceit, Poseidon settles the score by causing Minos' wife, Pasiphae, to fall madly in love with the white bull. Pasiphae has Daedalus, the legendary architect, build a hollow wooden cow for her with which she tricks the bull into mating with her. This second act of deceit sires the Minotaur. Seeking to hide his wife's bestial adultery and its hideous consequences, and probably his own dark deeds, Minos also turns to Daedalus, petitioning him to construct an elaborate labyrinth in which he confines the Minotaur.

King Aegeus, the father of Theseus, may be an absent father who departs for Athens before his son is born, but in contrast to the self-centered Minos, he leaves his son in the caring hands of his grandfather and mother. He also leaves his son the sword and sandals he will need when he comes of age. When he is strong enough to lift the rock that hides the sandals and his father's sword, Theseus goes to meet King Aegeus, who recognizes his son by the sword that he had left him. Hearing of the sacrifice that the Athenians have to make because his father is held responsible for the inadvertent death of Minos' own son, Theseus volunteers to go as one of the sacrificial youths, his mind set on slaying the Minotaur. With Ariadne's help, the noble son of a noble father slays the monster, thus freeing the Athenians from sacrificing their youth.

As suggested by the black and white sails that play a key role in Theseus' return to his father (he promised to raise a white sail if he succeeds in slaying the Minotaur, replacing the black one), the myth is about the battle between light and darkness. The mere figure of the monster calls attention to the two sides of man, the human and the animal, the conscious and the unconscious. The Minotaur, as its name Minos' Taurus intimates, is the unacknowledged dark side of the father, confined in the labyrinth, metaphor for the unconscious. And as happens when it is repressed in the unconscious, it becomes a dark force with a will of its own. It takes a hero like Theseus, armed with his father's sword, to brave the labyrinth and slay the monster.

A fascinating cinematic rendition of the Theseus and Minotaur myth is Kubrick's horror movie *The Shining*, which shows how a father gradually becomes a monster. Even when he is supposed to present his best side in the job interview, the dark side of Jack Torrance (Jack Nicholson) comes through in the glint of craziness in his eyes and the expressions on his face. Just as Poseidon helped Minos become king by sending the white bull, the hotel manager gives Jack the job of caretaker. He is to do whatever is necessary "so the elements can't get a foothold." Like Minos, who believed he could deceive Poseidon by sacrificing a substitute bull, Jack believes he is not susceptible to the elements.

As the movie progresses, as the elements get a foothold in his psyche, it becomes clear that Jack's aggression is mostly directed toward his son Danny (Danny Lloyd). At first it is unconscious, as when Jack dislocates Danny's shoulder, but gradually the ogre side takes over. It is apparent the first time we see the family together, driving up to the hotel, when Danny turns to his father and says he is hungry. "You should've eaten your breakfast," Jack chastises him. In contrast, Danny's mother, Wendy (Shelley Duvall), assures him, "We'll get you something as soon as we get to the hotel." But upon their arrival, it is the *black* cook, Dick Hallorann (Scatman Crothers), the provider of food, who is shown giving Danny *chocolate* ice cream, a sign of dark things to come.

Actually, much of what Danny (and the audience) is in for is suggested by the movie's incredible opening shot. With ominous music playing in the background, the camera moves in over a body of water, passing over a small island of green growth of bushes and trees, just as Jack moves into the labyrinth of madness. In a film of many doubles and mirrors, the opening frame is divided horizontally and vertically. Just as mirrors are used to reveal the unconscious throughout the movie, the upper half of the frame is reflected in the bottom half's waters, suggesting the unconscious and the conscious. The two sides, the light right side and the dark left side, are the two sides of Jack. At the very center of the frame, where the four sides converge as in a four-sided labyrinth, the island anticipates the Overlook Hotel in the midst of the elements, shown in the opening sequence's final shot. These bookend shots are the only ones in the opening that do not follow Jack's yellow Volkswagen as it climbs up the Sidewinder Road to the Overlook Hotel. Moreover, the hotel itself houses a model labyrinth and sports both a real labyrinth and a pictured one outside in the elements, not to mention its labyrinthine corridors and Native American carpet designs.

In the mother's first tour of the hotel, with her son and the black cook, the good father, she notices that it is like a labyrinth, alluding to herself as

Ariadne, the role she plays in this retelling of the ancient myth. "This whole place is such an enormous maze. I feel like I'll have to leave a trail of bread-crumbs every time I come in." As it were, the last time the father and son are shown together is when Jack chases Danny into the labyrinth. Like Theseus following Ariadne's string, Danny gets out by following the trail of his footsteps in the snow, leaving his father trapped, raving and howling, to freeze to death in the labyrinth.

The Shining's combination of the myth of Theseus and the Minotaur with the father-son relationship illustrates what the ancient myth is all about and how it is still relevant today. In both myth and filmmyth the son deals with the dark side of the father by slaying the dragon.

Fathers and Sons in Filmmyths

If we go by such book titles as *Fatherless America, Society Without the Father* and *Absent Fathers, Lost Sons*, America has become a society lacking fathers. As these books and others point out, the father's status in the family and the father-son relationship, or lack of relationship, have become pressing problems. Far too many fathers are absent in their sons' lives and far too few act as initiating agents for their sons' passage into the larger world. This sorry situation, this clash between the son's need for a father and the father's increasing absence, sets the stage for the dragon, the figure that represents the negative father in the son's psyche. When the father does not meet the son's needs and expectations, he is all too often introjected, becoming a negative figure who thwarts the son in pursuing his calling in the larger world, the world beyond the mother. This psychological recourse is pointed out by Robert Bly by way of Alexander Mitscherlich's *Society Without the Father*.

> After thirty years of working with young German men, as fatherless in their industrial society as young American men today, Alexander Mitscherlich ... developed a metaphor: a hole appears in the son's psyche. When the son does not see his father's workplace, or what he produces, does he imagine his father to be a hero, a fighter for good, a saint, or a white knight? Mitscherlich's answer is sad: demons move into that empty place — demons of suspicion.[6]

In our modern society without the father, instead of a father-initiator, the son gets a dragon-obstructer, the same archetypal ogre found in many myths and fairytales. "In mythology there stands beside the creative, positive father the destructive, negative father, and both father images are as alive in the soul of modern man as they were in the projections of mythology."[7]

The prototype of the positive and negative father (albeit in its feminine form) is *The Wizard of Oz*'s Good Witch of the North and the Wicked Witch of the West. The two are projections of Dorothy's introjected mother. In melting the witch, Dorothy slays the introjected dark side in her unconscious that had become an autonomous being with a life of its own. That is why Miss

Gulch, who is the "wicked witch" in Dorothy's Kansas, is not part of the family portrait at the end of the movie. Having integrated the dark side of Auntie Em in her consciousness, Dorothy no longer projects it onto Miss Gulch, who ceases to be the menacing figure of her everyday life just as the witch ceases to hound her in her dreams.

Walt Disney's animated *Peter Pan* (1953) is a sort of twin brother to *Oz*. Comparable to Em and the Witch in *Oz*, Peter Pan represents the light side of the father while Captain Hook represents the dark side. That is why the first picture of George Darling, the father of the family, shows him literally split in half; he is half real, half shadow. This image not only recalls the half-goat, half-human Greek god Pan, but the shadowy upper part, shown behind a window shade, is also a silhouette of Captain Hook, the dominant force in the grown-up George. Underscoring this point, both characters are voiced by the same actor (much as Miss Gulch and the Witch are played by the same actress). What's more, when introduced, George is looking for his pair of cufflinks (which his son, Michael, uses as the "buried treasure" in playing Peter Pan), just as Peter Pan himself is looking for his shadow. And just as Peter has his shadow sewn back, before the night is over George finds much more than the pair of cufflinks.

With Peter Pan's slaying of Hook in Neverland, the father recovers the treasure buried inside himself, returning to his London home as George the Dragon Slayer. In a movie that starts and ends with the father, the symbolic transformation George undergoes in Neverland through Peter Pan is much like Dorothy's dream journey in Oz. Both take place in the fantastic realm of the unconscious. And just as *Oz* shows what Dorothy must undergo to feel at home, *Peter Pan* shows what George must undergo to become a better father.

Disney's movie, adapted from J. M. Barrie's 1904 play, also mirrors the change that the father's role has undergone in the past century or so. As the movie suggests by the enmity between Hook and Pan, it is work, the antithesis of play, which is behind much of the father's diminishing role in the family. In what seems like "once upon a time," before the industrialization of society, before the shift from the farm to the city and all the accompanying changes, the father was around where the son could see him work and join forces with him in daily chores and manly endeavors. But with the growing separation of workplace from home, and with the demands of work constantly on the rise, the father's traditional role in the family has progressively diminished. As David Blankenhorn notes in his book *Fatherless America*, "in some respects it has been all downhill for fathers since the Industrial Revolution."[8] Ironically, because work took him away from home, the father was less available to initiate his son into the work world, the world where many men are measured and defined.

Steven Spielberg, "the perennial Peter Pan," who was a young boy when his parents divorced and "lost" his father, makes the father's absence and workaholism the central subject matter in *Hook* (1991). The father has forgotten how to play with his children, but he undertakes a fantastic journey of transformation. In *Peter Pan* it is Peter Pan's win over Captain Hook that changes the father; in *Hook* it is the father's recapturing his Pan-ness and getting rid of his Hook-ness. As the two movies demonstrate, to become better fathers, the conflict between the archetypal figures of Peter Pan, the eternal boy who eludes fatherhood at all costs, and Captain Hook, the villain who represents the absent workaholic father, must be resolved.

In many ways, this battle between the two archrivals, these two archetypes, has come to represent what growing up is all about: exchanging the freedom of *play* for the responsibility of *work*. Only after a journey to Neverland do the two fathers (and husbands) of the Peter Pan movies bring play into their life of work. At the movies' end, the fathers are less demanding, more forgiving and playful. They have succeeded in integrating the conflicting parts of work and play, achieving their own sewing of the shadow. As role models who recover the Peter Pan attitude in themselves and integrate it in fatherhood, George Darling (voiced by Hans Conried) and Peter Banning (Robin Williams) become better fathers, better initiating agents to their children. They achieve this only after banishing Hook from their lives, after slaying the dragon.

Of course, Peter Pan gets his name from the half-goat, half-god Pan of Greek mythology. Just as Peter Pan deflates the father's gravity by teaching him to fly (in *Hook*), part of the mythical Pan's role was to deflate the pomposity of the gods whenever they got too full of themselves. Like another half-and-half figure in Greek mythology, the half-bull, half-human Minotaur, Pan is often associated with the darker side of human nature. But where the Minotaur's lower half is man and its upper part bull, Pan's upper half is man and its lower part goat. This transposition is not without significance. It highlights the different aspects each figure represents. Where the Minotaur represents the bestial part of human nature, the bullheaded monster, Pan represents the instinctual energy needed to slay it.

In their own way, Disney's *Peter Pan* and Spielberg's *Hook* illustrate what measures the father must take in order to become a more accessible and real role model for his children. As the two movies show so entertainingly, it is mostly about attaining a healthy balance between work and play, the conflicting attitudes represented by the archetypal figures of Peter Pan and Captain Hook. In other words, slaying the dragon, slaying the ogre side of the father that prevents men from becoming what Peter Pan refuses and what the castrated Hook cannot, helps them become fathers, or as the case may be, better fathers.

Both Disney and Spielberg continued exploring fatherhood in two of the early 1990s' blockbusters, *The Lion King* (1994) and *Jurassic Park* (1993). Together with John Ford's *The Searchers* (1956), the two movies are examined in this book's closing section, "Becoming a Father." As in all the filmmyths covered by the book, in all three movies the hero must slay the dragon. In two of the three, *The Lion King* and *The Searchers*, the dragon, the dark side of the father, even has the same name.

Much as "Mythology helps us to see the dark side of our own fathers vividly, unforgettably,"[9] so do filmmyths. This is what this book aims to do— to track down the dragon's footprints, to show the dark side of the father in some of our more popular filmmyths. Whether obvious, as in *Field of Dreams* (1989) and *Red River* (1948), or subtle, as in *North by Northwest* (1959) and *E.T.* (1982), the book examines the dark side of the father through the metaphoric slaying of the dragon in each of its dozen filmmyths. *The Wizard of Oz*, which deals with the dark side of the mother, is the exception. But as the presence of the Witch makes plain, and as the book shows through the other filmmyths it covers, the dragon is still a force to be reckoned with. It is still a monster that the hero must slay.

Part I

RITES OF PASSAGE

Even if traditional initiations no longer appear to be objectively necessary, the psychological function they once served is still very real.

— Ray Raphael, *The Men from the Boys*

Between the pattern of birth, life and death that we all undergo, and the smaller cyclical patterns of years, seasons, months, weeks and days, there are other less obvious patterns that make up our lives. One such pattern, discerned in ceremonies of indigenous peoples by the Belgian anthropologist Arnold van Gennep, is rites of passage. Found in traditional and collective rites of initiation, it is a pattern of transformation that outlines the transition from one phase of life to another, in which the initiate undergoes the three stages of separation, initiation and return.

Unfortunately, in our modern Western culture these rites of passage are all but gone. Most of the rites we do have revolve around births, marriages and death — three basic events of our modern life that, interestingly enough, are like the three parts of the rite of passage. Unlike the "primitive" rites, however, our modern events are generally more ceremony than rite. They are mostly social get-togethers bereft of spirit, with little or no substance. One such ceremony is graduation, particularly high school graduation, if only because more young people graduate from high school than from higher learning institutions. Much like Dorothy Gale's three companions receiving symbolic objects for their achievements from the Wizard of Oz, in graduation we are recognized for our new status by receiving a diploma in a public ceremony, which celebrates and acknowledges our moving beyond our parents' authority. The event marks our *graduation* from dependence to independence. But unlike Dorothy's three companions, who risk their lives in a life-renewing journey, most of us do not undergo anything resembling a true rite of passage in attaining our diplomas. The "commencement" marks a new phase in our life, but for most of us the event is more *hollow* than *hallowed*. And for boys much more than girls, if only because they are called to assume the roles of men in what is largely a patriarchal world. But because they have not been properly initiated, the outer world in which they are expected to function as men is not matched by an inner sense of manhood. There is a wide gap between what is provided and what is expected.

In the "gap between our rapidly evolving social forms and our internalized, old fashioned images of manhood"[1] thrives the dragon. Its way is paved by a double dose of "bad medicine": the decline of traditional rites of passage and the rise of absent fathers. When the father does not provide what the son needs, when he does not initiate him into the outer world, the father becomes introjected. In time the introjected image of the father turns into what is commonly depicted in fairy tales and myths as a dragon, the beast that guards the golden treasure and holds the princess captive. Ironically, though considered the family's *provider*, the father seldom provides what his son (and daughter) really need: meaningful rites of passage into adulthood.

As often happens in our modern life, this decline in the father's role as initiator is explored in many of our most popular filmmyths. These filmmyths, which have largely replaced the myths and fairy tales of the past, compensate us for what we lack in everyday life. They may not provide what we really need, but in showing the rites the cinematic heroes undergo, the trials they undertake, filmmyths provide an illustration, a model, of the rite of passage. Through them we reveal ourselves to ourselves.

The three movies covered in this section, *The Wizard of Oz*, *Back to the Future* and *Stand by Me*, all have the three-part rite of passage running through them. They all follow the general pattern of separation, initiation and return. Each adolescent hero/heroine undergoes a rite of passage in a special world, a world where he confronts and resolves his fundamental problem. In all three filmmyths the hero/heroine's fundamental problem is with the parent of the same gender. In *Oz* Dorothy is unhappy with Em, in *Back to the Future* Marty's father is a "major embarrassment," in *Stand by Me* Gordie feels invisible in his father's eyes. And as in myths, in each movie there are figures that advance and obstruct the heroic quest.

In *The Wizard of Oz*, the advancer is the Good Witch of the North, the obstructer the bad Witch of the West. Dorothy's rite of passage takes place in the colorful Land of Oz, a complete contrast to the dreary Kansas countryside which makes up her ordinary world. And being Dorothy's dream, her rite is unconscious. It is in the unconscious of her dream that Dorothy resolves her problem with Em by confronting and slaying the Wicked Witch of the West.

The blatant unconscious of *Oz* is only latently suggested in *Back to the Future*. But it is there nonetheless. Like Dorothy, who leaves Kansas for Oz, Marty (by going back in time) leaves his ordinary world of 1985 for the special one of 1955. He time-travels to change history, to undo his parents' past mistakes. In doing so Marty changes the future. The turning point of this change is when his father slays the dragon, after which Marty slays his own, both of them literally taking the future in their hands.

In the more realistic world of *Stand by Me*, Gordie's quest to find the body of a boy his age is no less a rite of passage. At the rite's end he slays the dragon by confronting the malevolent Ace, who represents all that his dead brother is not, and all that his angry father is. Unlike Dorothy and Marty, who have the Good Witch and Doc Brown to help them, Gordie only has the memory of his dead brother and the nagging questions of the benevolent grocer (the provider of food). As in the real world, in Gordie's world there are few mentors to initiate the boys into adolescence and adulthood. Without initiators, the boys turn to one another. While each one deals with his central problem, his personal dragon, the four stand by one another throughout the journey. As the movie so aptly demonstrates, at a time when fathers are largely absent in their sons' lives, and where rites of passage are not to be had, there are many "small" rites of passage. Of course, while some boys undergo true rites of passage, others go through the motions. Where some, like Gordie and Chris, confront the dragon that embodies the introjected father, others, like Teddy and Ace, unleash their anger and aggression at what for them represents the dragon in the outer world. They mistake their projections of the dragon for the introjected father.

The fact that Vern and Teddy remain in Castle Rock, the town where they grew up, demonstrates that they did not really grow up. They never *got out* because they did not undergo a true rite of passage. They never confronted the dragon, let alone slay it, the very beast that obstructs them from *getting out*. We may identify with Gordie and Chris, as we do with Dorothy and Marty, with their heroic journeys and slaying of the dragon, but this heroism is a far cry from what most of us experience in our modern culture, where meaningful rites are hard to come by and the dragon lurks in the dark recesses of our psyches.

Chapter 1

The Wizard of Oz
Follow the Metaphor Road

Dreams are the royal road to the unconscious.

— Sigmund Freud

The Ozyssey

In examining *fathers and sons in* filmmyths, aside from a polite "ladies first," it is best to heed the Good Witch's advice to Dorothy at the outset of her journey, "It's always best to start at the beginning," and start with *The Wizard of Oz*. The 1939 classic may not be the beginning of filmmyths, but it is surely the first important one. More than any other movie, *Oz* is to American filmmyths what *The Odyssey* is to western myths. Just as the *Odyssey* has become synonymous with the mythological journey, *Oz* is the prototype of filmmyths. What is *Oz* if not Dorothy's *odyssey* back home, or, if you will, her *Ozyssey*?

Dorothy's dream journey, her symbolic attempt to resolve an unconscious problem, not only best exemplifies what filmmyths are about, her melting the Wicked Witch of her dream best exemplifies dragon-slaying filmmyths, albeit in their feminine form. Just as the dragon embodies the denied dark side of the father, *Oz*'s witch personifies all that Dorothy refuses to accept about her Auntie Em. Not ready to see Em as anything but benevolent, she projects her malevolent side on the neighboring Miss Gulch and on the witch of her dream.

To appreciate *The Wizard of Oz* and the unconscious subtext of Dorothy's dream, which conveys its messages through metaphors, it is best to keep in mind Glinda's other advice and follow the *metaphor* road, "the royal road to the unconscious." Seen metaphorically, Dorothy's dream journey is her coming to terms with the two sides of Em, the two that are one.

Two That Are One

Dorothy's problem with the malevolent mother is suggested both by *Oz*'s opening shot and by her very first words. Running away from the camera on a desolate country road with the accompanying Toto, with fences on either side, she constantly looks back, as if pursued. While the road anticipates the Yellow Brick Road of her dream, and the two fences the two sides of the Mother, Dorothy's "She isn't coming yet," which refers to Miss Gulch, foreshadows the coming of the malevolent side of the Mother. The two sides of the mother are suggested throughout the first part of the movie to such an extent that it leaves no doubt as to what *Oz* is essentially about: Dorothy dealing with the benevolent and malevolent sides of the mother, the two that are one.

Going by Dorothy's words to Toto, "Come on, we'll go tell Uncle Henry and Auntie Em," she still looks to her "parents" to deal with her problems. But as demonstrated by the dysfunctional incubator, the maternal womb, the all-benevolent mother of her childhood is no longer as she was. Just as the incubator can no longer contain the newly hatched chicks, Dorothy's benevolent mother can no longer protect her from her growing sensibility. This is underscored by the way her two guardians are presented. The ineffective Uncle Henry, who pities Dorothy as a "poor little orphan" who "ought to have somebody to *play* with," is rather motherly (benevolent); the no-nonsense Aunt Em, who talks of work and adult responsibility ("We all got to *work* out our own problems"), seems the harsher of the two, if only because she expects Dorothy to grow up and solve her problems by herself.

As if there is no escaping the coming of the she, it comes up again in the very next sequence with the three farm hands that Dorothy turns to, which opens with "How's she coming?" The question is too much like the movie's opening line to be without meaning or intent. Perhaps sensing the coming of the malevolent mother into her life, Dorothy tries to offset her one-sided view of Em, to *work out* her problem, by balancing herself while walking on the fence. Her falling off the railing and into the pigsty epitomizes her present predicament. With Miss Gulch threatening to take away Toto, who represents her natural innocence, the *home*ostasis of her childhood has been drastically disturbed. Her *fall* is just as much her *Fall*.

At this stage in her life, rather than "solve her problems for herself," Dorothy prefers to daydream of "a land that I've heard of once in a lullaby," where "trouble melt like lemon drops." But as underscored by an abrupt change of music that accompanies the coming of Miss Gulch, rather than "melt like lemon drops," Dorothy's troubles are just beginning. Dorothy's main problem is evoked by the symmetric *mise-en-scène* that has Dorothy standing between the seated Em and Miss Gulch, not unlike a scale's fulcrum, weighing the two sides of the mother.

In the confrontation with Miss Gulch, suddenly Em is not as assertive as she was before the spinster's appearance. Her handling the situation "gently" does not deter Miss Gulch, who came fully prepared with an order from the sheriff, the representative of patriarchal authority with the power to determine Toto's fate. The only one who stands up to the "wicked old witch" is Dorothy ("I won't let you take him!"). Her explanation of Toto's mischievous behavior ("He didn't know he was doing anything wrong") suggests the unconscious, where there is no discrimination between good and bad, between what is permitted and what is forbidden. As such, Miss Gulch is an agent of repression who wants to do away with the creature that represents Dorothy's irrepressible freedom to roam and play. That Toto is part of her is suggested by Dorothy's, "I'll bite you myself."

Disappointed once again with her guardians, this time for their lack of courage to stand up for her and Toto, Dorothy leaves the room in frustration. With Dorothy out of earshot, Em speaks her mind. "Almira Gulch, just because you own half the county doesn't mean you have the power to run the rest of us. For twenty-three years I've been dying to tell you what I thought of you." Em's refusal to express what she really feels, under the excuse of "being a Christian woman," underscores the autonomous power of Miss Gulch. As an unconscious force, when not confronted and incorporated in the whole personality, the other "half" that has "the power to run the rest of us" assumes a shadowy autonomy.

Miss Gulch rides off with Toto in her basket, but being the irrepressible creature that he is, he escapes at the first opportunity, demonstrating that you can't hold a good dog down. At this point in her life, Dorothy does not have the power (the brain, the heart and the courage) to stand up to the dark force that threatens what is dearest to her. Unable to deal with Miss Gulch in Kansas, Dorothy relegates her to her unconscious as the Wicked Witch of the West. As suggested by the same actress playing both roles, the two are one and the same. One is part of Dorothy's everyday consciousness, the other a shadowy figure of her unconscious.

States of Kanscious and Un-Kanscious

On the metaphor road, in the associative language of Dorothy's dream, the Kansas mentioned in her well-known line, "Toto, I've a feeling we're not in Kansas anymore," may very well be read as "Kanscious." Oz, after all, exists in Dorothy's state of unconscious (un–Kansas). Perhaps that is why Kansas is only mentioned in Dorothy's dream, why it is the first sentence in her state of unconscious. Dorothy even "repeats" this line ("Now I *know* we're not in Kansas!") with the appearance of the "benign power," personified by Glinda, the Good Witch of the North. This change from *feeling* to *knowing* is what Dorothy's journey is ultimately about. She comes to know, becomes conscious, of what home truly means.

The first intimation of *un–Kansas* comes from Em, when she urges Dorothy to "find some place where you won't get into trouble," initiating her fantasy song about a place far away from Kansas, a fantastic place over the rainbow. As suggested by the rainbow-shaped wheel of the cultivator that Dorothy holds while singing, she does not see that her "heart's desire" is already there in her backyard, in her self. At this point in her life, in the gray reality of Kansas, her wish for a rainbow-colored world, where "the dreams that you dare to dream really do come true," only comes true in dreams, in her unconscious.

The far-away world that Dorothy daydreams about, the *un–Kanscious*, is further evoked by her meeting with Professor Marvel. That is why she spots his carnival wagon that promises faraway places only after crossing the threshold of the wooden bridge (that looks like a weighing scale) that bridges the mundane and marvelous. As his name suggests, Marvel represents the not–Kansas, the *un–Kanscious*. But like the Wizard of Oz that he portrays, he is a sham, a false Oracle. His gift for intuiting what is "inside" Dorothy only works on the third try. And yet, in trying to convince her that he can read her mind, by "divining" that "they don't understand you at home," Professor Marvel gives voice to Dorothy's unconscious. The picture from which he "divines" his knowledge from the "infinite," of Dorothy and Em standing by the gate to their home, mirrors Dorothy's picture of Em. It is a symmetric (balanced) picture, taken before Miss Gulch and all that she represents became part of the picture.

With all this, perhaps the professor is more clairvoyant than he seems. Informing Dorothy that "someone has hurt" Em, "someone has just about broken her heart," he certainly knows how to play on her sense of guilt. Much like a therapist, he sends Dorothy back home to deal with her conflict about the two most important figures in her life. Once again Dorothy has to weigh between two possibilities. "If we go home, they'll send you to the sheriff," she tells Toto. "And if we don't, Aunt Em — well, she may die."

As one who can read what is inside Dorothy, the "past, present and future," in his "hope she gets home all right," the professor foretells her quest. The storm he sees coming is the turmoil that has been building up *inside her*. This is the Gale-force unleashed with the coming of the malevolent mother. Just before she is knocked unconscious, Dorothy keeps calling for Em, for the all-bestowing mother that is no longer available. In this, in her second "getting home," her way back is blocked. The cellar where her guardians and the three farmhands took shelter is locked from the inside. Like all children who must leave their childhood world behind, Dorothy has crossed the bridge of no return. Her feeling of "home" is swept right from under her feet by the all-powerful twister.

When the uprooted window *frame* renders Dorothy unconscious, the unconscious comes into play. As happens in dreams, the framed images Dorothy sees on the window-screen are borrowed from her Kanscious life. Except for Miss Gulch, who appears as herself (probably because of her forcefulness), the rest of the figures are thinly disguised projections of Dorothy's unconscious. The first woman to appear, knitting in her rocking chair, is much like Aunt Em, the most dominant person in Dorothy's life. Her knitting may very well represent Dorothy's need to be protected from the threatening forces that have entered her life. Or it may mirror her dreamworks, interweaving the myriad of everyday experiences with the fabric of her unconscious. That the unconscious is coming into play is suggested by Miss Gulch, an easy target for Dorothy's projections in her state of Kanscious, turning into the witch that hounds her throughout her unconscious dream journey.

The only persons from Kansas who are not displaced in Dorothy's dream are Aunt Em (and Uncle Henry). The ambiguous feelings she has towards them are too powerful to be represented directly. The only time Em appears is at Dorothy's deepest hour of despair. She materializes in the crystal ball, only to be driven out by the Wicked Witch of the West, just as she was overcome in Kansas by Miss Gulch. But though Em does not appear as a character in Dorothy's dream, she is represented by Glinda, the Good Witch of the North. As Dorothy's wish fulfillment, her compensation for reality, Glinda is a powerful benevolent mother who has no problem standing up to the Wicked Witch. Unlike Em, she provides Dorothy with the red slippers that protect her from the Wicked Witch. Being a "walking" journey of integrating the dark side, it is most fitting that Dorothy wears the slippers of the Wicked Witch of the West's sister. Just as it's best to start at the beginning, it's best to begin at the bottom and work from the feet on up.

In following the Yellow Brick Road from the center of the spiral, an image of psychic development, and ending where she started, Dorothy completes one circle in the spiral of psychic development, a development initiated by the spiral of the cyclone, a force that tears her away from the childish state of mind she tries to cling to. In the course of her journey, along with freeing herself from the witch, Dorothy, like a true heroine, frees everyone she encounters. She frees her three companions from their fixed (fixated) states: the Scarecrow from being stuck on the pole, the Tin Man from corrosion of rust, and the Cowardly Lion from being petrified by fear. Moreover, by freeing the broom from the Witch, Dorothy frees the flying monkeys from her dominion and the Wizard from a role too big for his britches. Even the killing of the Witch of the East, which frees the Munchkins (the displaced chicks) from her tyranny, is attributed to Dorothy.

Gathering Her Wits About Her

In her journey to Oz, Dorothy befriends three companions, assimilating the three functions they represent, the three functions she needs to free herself from the Witch's threat and achieve self-reliance. The fact that her meeting and taking along the three "helpers" are presented the exact same way underscores their similarity. In each case we first see Dorothy come into view towards the camera, where she stops to chat with the hung-up character. Each one does a song and dance routine (using the same melody), revealing what is missing in his (her) life. Each sequence ends with Dorothy walking away from the camera together with the new companion.

Thinking

At the first crossroad, where Dorothy meets the Scarecrow, there are fences on both sides of the Yellow Brick Road. As another visual metaphor for the two sides that Dorothy must bring together, one side is a flourishing cornfield, the other an arid wheat field. In answering Dorothy's question, "Which way to go?" the Scarecrow, who *thinks* himself brainless, first points to the right, then the left, finally adding, "Of course, people do go both ways," another reminder of the two sides Dorothy must integrate into one. After all is said and sung, Dorothy and the Scarecrow take the middle road, between the pair of opposites, between the benevolent and the malevolent.

At each station, with each addition of another ally, the Witch tries to sidetrack Dorothy and her companions with ever-mounting determination. On the first station she silently hides behind an apple tree, following Dorothy's progress. Under her magic spell, the apple trees turn hostile, refusing to have their apples picked by Dorothy and her companion. But at the first opportunity, the Scarecrow, using the intelligence he does not *think* he has, outsmarts the trees by taunting them into throwing their "forbidden" fruit, a sign of Dorothy's growing awareness of evil, her "using her head."

Feeling

Before the Tin Man makes the pair a threesome, and just after the naïve Dorothy remarks, "We've come such a long way already," the Witch tries once again to impede Dorothy's progress. "You call that long? Why you've just begun!" she taunts Dorothy from the roof of a wooden cabin in the middle of the woods. The woods are not as bright as the crops in the first station, but they are also not as dark as the forest of the third. The Witch tries to scare off Dorothy's "helpers" by hurling a fireball at the Scarecrow; this backfires, giving the Tin Man an opportunity to show his usefulness (to prove his mettle) by putting out the fire with his metal body. Dorothy's words to her new companions, "I feel as if I've known you all the time," suggest that the two companions are archetypes that have been around "all the time," in her psychic backyard.

Courage

At this stage of the journey, Dorothy and her two cohorts must pass through a dark forest, a common symbol of the unconscious, where brains and hearts are not enough for a safe passage. The way they are shown crossing the forest reveals what they and the Lion sorely lack: courage. Dorothy's dislike of the forest, because "It's dark and creepy," is another allusion to the dark unconscious. The animals that the three fear, "lions and tigers and bears," are projections of their fears, shadowy creatures they are not yet ready to deal with. The psychological theme is underscored by the Lion baring what is inside him, not unlike a patient to an analyst. "My life has been simply unbearable ... It's been in me so long. I just gotta tell you how I feel."

Revealing his feelings in the song "If I Only Had the Nerve," the Lion joins the trio, making them a foursome. Together they think and feel brave enough to successfully traverse the dark forest and approach the next stage of their journey. But once again, the Witch hinders their progress, this time by planting narcotic poppies in their path. The fact that the first to fall unconscious are Toto and Dorothy, suggests that this is the Witch's attempt to keep Dorothy in a state of unconscious. Likewise, the Lion falling unconscious is the Witch's attempt to keep Dorothy from gathering courage. Dorothy's functions of thinking and feeling, however, do not succumb to the Witch's scheme, as if they are already part of her consciousness.

Glinda coming to the rescue, for the second time, underscores the role each witch plays in Dorothy's rite of passage. Whereas the Wicked Witch tries to prevent Dorothy from reaching her objective by rendering her unconscious, demonstrating her function to keep Dorothy in a childish unconscious state, the Good Witch breaks that spell, thus helping Dorothy obtain a higher state of consciousness. And having regained consciousness, the Emerald City appears "closer and prettier than ever" to Dorothy and her companions. A chorus wraps up this part of the journey with three short phrases, once again alluding to the unconscious: "You're out of the woods. You're out of the dark. You're out of the night."

The Dragon's Lair

Out of harm's way, the four approach the gates of Oz arm in arm, as one. The road comes to an end, but not the journey. They're not home yet. Like the three stations on the Yellow Brick Road, Dorothy must traverse three more stations: the Wizard's chamber, the haunted forest and the witch's castle.

Primed as Dorothy and her companions are for their *appearance* before the Wizard, who sounds somewhat familiar, they are not yet thoroughly tested. Before Dorothy can return home she must venture into the dragon's lair and obtain the object of power. This is commonly the most dangerous part of the journey, the part where the hero descends to the underworld to retrieve a loved one or some other object of importance, as when Odysseus descends to Hades to obtain the direction home from the blind Tiresias, or when Theseus enters the labyrinth and slays the Minotaur. This "small task" requires much more courage than they (Dorothy) presently possess, as illustrated by the Lion's literally flying out the window.

Finding themselves in the Haunted Forest, Dorothy and her friends are no match for the Witch. But the Witch only wants Dorothy and Toto. Matching the Wizard's command to the foursome, "Now go!" the witch unleashes her army of winged monkeys with "Now fly!" They descend upon Dorothy and Toto, carrying them off to the Witch's castle.

"What are you gonna do with my dog?" Dorothy asks when the witch puts him in a wicker basket just as did Miss Gulch. Insisting "Give him back to me!" she stands up to the witch as she stood up to Miss Gulch. In fact, the whole exchange between the two is a re-enactment of the first confrontation. Faced with Toto's impending drowning (his repression), Dorothy is prepared to relinquish the slippers and their protective power, only not to lose what is most dear to her. Her willingness to surrender her protective shoes suggests that she is ready to surrender her infantile image of Em, her guardian and protector.

Once again, Toto takes care of himself, escaping at the first opportunity. Without him, however, as a bartering item and as her *raison d'etre*, Dorothy's life is in danger. For the first time in the dream she is alone with the Witch, at the mercy of her shadowy nemesis. Resorting to her most familiar source of security, she cries out for her maternal protector, who appears in the Witch's crystal ball. But Dorothy has ventured too far beyond Em's maternal haven. However much she wants Em back, she has undergone too much to go back to her familiar image of Em. "I'll give you Auntie Em, my pretty!" says the Witch; by her appearance, she *gives* Dorothy the other side of Em, the full picture. The materialization of the two aspects of the Mother in her divining device is the coming together of the two in one sphere, not unlike the circle that contains the yin and yang. This is the manifestation of the two sides that are one, the good and bad, the benevolent and malevolent.

In seeing both sides in the crystal ball, Dorothy has brought the neglected part of the Mother to where she can see it. With "I know you'd *see* reason," the Witch echoes Miss Gulch's words to Em ("Now you're *seeing* reason"), pointing to what Dorothy is beginning to see. Having attained this awareness and rid of her childish view of Em, Dorothy is finally freed from her fixation on the all-good M. She has overcome her obstacle, her refusal to see Em's other, less perfect, side. Now she can come to terms with the denied dark side of her mother and dissolve her as an autonomous force of her psyche.

One again, it is Toto who initiates this change in Dorothy. His spontaneity brings about her release from the clutches of the Witch in more ways than one. He leads her three companions to their biggest challenge, where each one musters the most of what he represents. Beyond that, just as he initiated the whole ordeal when he "didn't mean to" go into Miss Gulch's garden, now Dorothy, after not meaning to kill the Witch of the East, does not mean to melt the Witch of the West. Nevertheless, this time it is her doing. Whereas in the two previous instances it was initiated by Toto and the twister, two aspects of her psyche, now it is Dorothy herself who commits the unintentional act. Aptly enough, her *intention* is to save the Scarecrow, who represents her ability to think, to "see reason." The water that melts the Witch is the same life-retrieving element that can turn an arid "gulch" to a blossoming garden. As happens in several turning points of her journey, Dorothy's action is a spontaneous reaction, unintentional but not out of character. "Who would have thought a good little girl like you could destroy my beautiful wickedness?" says the Witch, surprised by Dorothy's resourcefulness. "I'm going," her autonomous power "melts like lemon drops." Her symbol of power, the broom, falls into Dorothy's hands like ripe fruit. Having assimilated the Witch's dark power, Dorothy attains a unified state of mind, beyond the pairs of opposites.

Home All Right

Their heroic task completed, the four have demonstrated their worthiness to receive their reward. But the Wizard is powerless to give them what he promised. True to his intuitive temperament, Toto exposes the Wizard's deception and reveals him for what he is, thus shattering the myth of the Wizard of Oz. In his true size, all the Wizard can do is give them *symbols* of the qualities they had "all the time." "What about Dorothy?" her three companions want to know. The Wizard's reply, "The only way to get Dorothy back to Kansas is for me to take her myself," if carried out, will deprive Dorothy of realizing the aim of her quest on her own. But once again it is Toto who gets her on the right track. As they are about to "return to the land of *E Pluribus Unum*" (out of many, one), which refers to both the United States and Dorothy's "united" state of mind, Toto jumps from the air balloon after a cat before takeoff, causing Dorothy to miss her flight home just as his chasing Miss Gulch's cat set off the whole quest. Once again his incorrigible impulsiveness gets Dorothy into trouble but also advances her on her journey. This time he brings about her realization of the power she always had but did not know, what was yet unconscious.

In Glinda's third and final appearance, Dorothy once again turns to her for help. "You don't need to be helped any longer," the Good Witch enlightens her. "You always had the power to go back to Kansas."

"Then why didn't you tell her before?" Dorothy's "brain" asks.

"Because she wouldn't have believed me. She had to learn it for herself."

"What have you learned, Dorothy?" her "heart" asks her.

"Well, I think that it wasn't enough just to want to see Uncle Henry and Auntie Em, and it's that if I ever go looking for my heart's desire again, I won't look any further than my own backyard. Because if it wasn't there, I never really lost it to begin with!" Accepting what is in her backyard, her unconscious, as part of her, Dorothy is ready to return home, and her magic slippers have the power to take her there. And Toto too. "I'm ready now," she tells the Good Witch.

The first shot of Dorothy's return, her return to *Kansciousness*, showing

Em's two hands putting a wet towel on her forehead, serves as a visual metaphor that sums up what the dream journey has been about — the coming together of Em's two sides in Dorothy's mind. Dorothy's first words upon waking up in her bed, "Oh, Auntie Em, it's you," express her relief and joy to see Em. But as suggested by Em's two hands (and the two braids) on either side of Dorothy's head, and as fits the metaphoric nature of the dream, she sees Em as she really is, the two sides as one. Her "it's you" can very well mean "the whole you." Having obtained the Witch's object of power and developed her three functions, Dorothy returns to the place where it all started and recognizes it for the first time. Unlike the beginning, when she was turned away by all those who inhabited her Kansas farm, now everyone is around her. Professor Marvel's words, "she seems all right now," recall his parting words on their first meeting, "I hope she makes it home all right." With his intuitive powers, he acknowledges Dorothy's feeling at home with her surroundings and herself.

"This was a real, truly live place," Dorothy tries to tell Em about her dream just as she tried to tell her about Miss Gulch in the movie's beginning. "Home! And this is my room, and you're all here," Dorothy shares what was formerly her unconscious with her enlarged family. All are with her, integrated in her personality. The only one missing is Miss Gulch, who is no longer an autonomous force in Dorothy's life. Dorothy's perception of her home, represented by Aunt Em, has undergone a change. No wonder her last words, "Oh, Auntie Em, there's no place like home," are addressed to her. In letting go of her childish and illusory picture of the benevolent Em, in accepting her malevolent side as part of the picture, Dorothy's picture is unified. In her "return to the land of *E Pluribus Unum*" with Toto, whose life was threatened at the movie's opening, Dorothy has returned home *in toto*.

Chapter 2

Back to the Future
A Rematch Made in Time

The time is out of joint; O cursed spite, That ever I was born to set it right!
— *Hamlet,* Act I, Scene V

Back to the Wizard

Like everything else in *Back to the Future*, the Ozy Wizard graffiti on Marty McFly's high school wall is not without meaning or intent. The "writing on the wall" clearly refers to *The Wizard of Oz* and the special role it plays in *Back to the Future,* pointing to the many elements of the 1939 classic that come up throughout the 1985 sci-fi movie. In fact, considering the many parallels and similarities shared by the two movies, *Back to the Future* is easily read as an '80s *Oz*. Marty's opening words, "Anybody home?" even take up where Dorothy's "There's no place like home" left off. Or better yet, they repeat Professor Marvel's very words when he pops his head through the window as Dorothy wakes up from her dream.

Despite the unreal element of time travel, *Back to the Future* may seem too authentic to suggest the inner journey that runs through the fantastic *Oz*. As if *Back to the Future* is too entertaining to harbor anything else. True, the movie does not have *Oz*'s clear archetypes, symbolic objects or unconscious characters. And yet, its tight screenplay, the cinematography, its double entendres and use of metaphors, all suggest a healthy dose of the unconscious. Just as Dorothy meets the displaced characters from her sepia-toned reality in her Technicolor dream, Marty meets his parents as they are his own age, thirty years back in time. His 1955 is Dorothy's Oz. Where Dorothy's journey is in mother *space*, the maternal container, Marty's is in father *time*, the masculine progenitor of the future. Dorothy undergoes a journey in an unfamiliar place in the brief time of her dream; Marty undergoes a journey in a familiar place but in a different time period. Likewise, upon regaining consciousness, Dorothy imparts that she had been in "a real, truly live *place*." Upon regaining consciousness in his mother's bed, Marty remarks, "I had a horrible nightmare, dreamed I went back in *time*."

The two movies' outer adventures may be different, but the inner journeys are the same. In both cases the protagonist resolves his inner problem with the dominant parent in his/her life. Just as Em advises Dorothy to work out her problems with Miss Gulch, the dark side of the mother, Principal Strickland, reminds Marty of his problem. "You got a real attitude problem, McFly. You're a slacker. You remind me of your father when he went here. He was a slacker too." This message must strike a major chord in Marty, for he soon catches himself talking just like his father. "Jesus, I'm beginning to sound like my old man."

Much like the picture of the three McFly children he carries in his pocket, which recalls the picture Dorothy carries in her basket, Marty's negative picture of his father is his chief problem. Even his girlfriend points out the exaggerated way he sees his father: "Come on, he's not that bad." In fact, just as Oz is essentially about Dorothy coming to see and accept both sides of Em, *Back to the Future* can be read as Marty's transformation in the way he *sees* his father. "I never knew he had it in him," he confesses to Doc after his father becomes George the Dragon Slayer. "He never stood up to Biff in his life." As these words suggest, Marty's negative picture is more his introjected father than the father himself. That it is in the eyes of the beholder is underscored by the fact that, with the exception of the "night of the storm," George is always pictured from Marty's point of view. Only on the night that he liberates himself from his tormentor, his dragon, is he seen "objectively," not through Marty's eyes. This negative picture of his father is the problem Marty must work out; this is the dragon he must slay. As Robert Bly points out in "Iron John," Marty's problem with his father is not uncommon for boys his age.

> In our time, when the father shows up as an object of ridicule ... the son has a problem. How does he imagine his own life as a man? Some sons fall into a secret despair.... Without actually investigating their own personal father and why he is as he is, they fall into a fearful hopelessness, having fully accepted the generic, diminished idea of father. "I am the son of defective male material, and I'll probably be the same as he is."[1]

In this *filmmyth*, Marty gets a chance to investigate (see) what makes his father tick, and the father changes before Marty's eyes from "an object of ridicule" to one of admiration. Ironically, it is Principal Strickland, the strict side of the father, who initiates Marty's change in the way he sees his father by reminding him that "No McFly ever amounted to anything in the history of Hill Valley." Marty's reply, given as a comeback on the spur of the moment ("History is gonna change") initiates his journey back in time. Typical of fairy tales, once the words are said they take on a power of their own. They become deeds.

Again like Dorothy, and like many other heroes, Marty does not embark on his journey, let alone complete it, without help from a wise paternal figure. Strickland, who represents the status quo, tries to dissuade Marty by dismissing this paternal figure, who represents the future. "Now let me give you a nickel's worth of advice, young man. This so-called Dr. Brown is dangerous, he's a real nutcase. Hang around with him, you'll end up in big trouble." Of course, the warning comes true, but not in the way he intends it. Whereas Strickland is Marty's obstructer, the dragon, Doc, as his name suggests, is his instructor. Strickland may dub Doc "dangerous" and a "nutcase," but he is the only one who can take Marty on his journey and back. Like Oz's two witches, the good and the bad, the two represent the two sides of the father. While Strickland, like Marty's defeated father, discourages him from pursuing his destiny in trying out for the school dance, Doc provides the means and sacrifices himself so that he may make his life-changing journey back in time.

The cultural shock of recognition that awaits Marty in Hill Valley of 1955 is nothing less than what Dorothy discovers in the Land of Oz. "It's all a dream. Just a very intense dream," Marty says, trying to convince himself that what he encounters is only in his head. And it may very well be, as suggested by the song "*Mr. Sandman* (Bring Me a Dream)," which accompanies Marty's arrival in his hometown thirty years back in time. As in a dream, everything is displaced—at once strange and familiar. The '80s self-service Texaco station becomes a TV commercial of the '50s. More subtly, the '85 Burger **King**, located next door to Doc Brown's lab, has its double in *Cattle **Queen** of Montana*. The double motif continues when, like a western hero who heads directly to the saloon upon arriving in town, Marty heads to Lou's Café, looking for his surrogate father, the one who got him into "trouble" and the one who can get him out, only to run into his real father. The two are shown in matching positions, like father like son, just as Principal Strickland said they were. This picture, of the "defective male" he is to become in the future, is what troubles Marty. On the bright side, the picture of the two holding their heads with their right hand is also an image that combines the movie's two most famous slogans—"The future is in your hand" and "If you put your mind to it you could accomplish anything." It points to Marty's quest and what he must do to complete it.

The double motif comes up again in the very next scene when Marty literally takes his father's place. Like Dorothy knocked unconscious by the window frame, Marty is knocked unconscious while saving his father from being hit by his grandfather's car. His first interference with the time continuum is physically saving his father, which is what his journey in time is all about—to redeem his father and his whole family. His shoving him out of the way, which lands him in his mother's bed, is surely the workings of the unconscious. After all, what son does not wish to find himself in his mother's bed? And what is more, at his own age? His question upon regaining consciousness, "Mom, is that you?" echoes Dorothy's surprise upon waking up from her dream journey, "Oh, Auntie Em, it's you." His waking in '55 anticipates his waking back in '85. And as he is in the same position and clothes he was in when Doc's phone call to adventure woke him up, for a minute both Marty and the audience think, as was actually in *Oz*, that it was all a dream. When he says, "What a nightmare," it is all but certain. Walking into the living room, however, he is just as shocked as when arriving in '55. If the first experience was a nightmare, then this is a dream come true. Especially when Lorraine and George return from a game of tennis, "incidentally" talking about what was essentially Marty's quest. "I think we need a *rematch*," Lorraine says to George. "Oh, a *rematch*. Why? Were you cheating?" The icing on the cake is the timely arrival of George's first published science fiction book, *A Match Made in Space*. Where the book is about the matching of Lorraine and George, the movie is about *a rematch made in time*. Where the father writes his story, the son re-writes history. Interacting with the past, he reshapes the future.

As in the closing scene of *Oz*, all the characters of Marty's life are at hand. Unlike *Oz*, however, where Miss Gulch is absent, her counterpart in *Back to the Future* is part of the picture. Like a shadow that has been assimilated, Biff is no longer an autonomous force that hounds George wherever he goes. Now he is working for George, who is in full control. Where in the beginning Biff wrecked George's car and refused to pay for the damage, now he is waxing it. But like the shadow that he is, he still tries to cheat his way.

When Biff gives Marty the keys to his dream machine, the *black* four-by-four ("You're all waxed up, ready for *tonight!*"), this is truly too good to be true. Seeing the look on Marty's face, Jennifer asks him, "Is everything all right?" "Yeah," he answers, looking at his parents framed by the screen door, recalling Dorothy's "movie" framed by the window. "Everything is great." Like Dorothy, Marty is "home all right."

Back to the Future does not only go back to *Oz*. Just as in her dream journey Dorothy develops her thinking and feeling functions and becomes more courageous, as symbolized by her three companions, journeying back in time Marty rewrites three of our culture's foremost myths. Intended or not, the latent presence of these myths bears out the mythical nature of the movie, its being a *filmmyth*. Like the subject matter of *Back to the Future*, the three rewritten myths are about the father-son relationship. Marty's dysfunctional father is the maimed Fisher King, with Hill Valley his kingdom, that comes *back* to life. Like Telemachus in *The Odyssey*, Marty gets *back* his father and his home. He rematches his mother and father, putting them *back* together again, according to his heart's desire, resolving the problematic Oedipal triad.

The Fisher King: Time to Change

In a movie where time plays such a key role, it is only fitting that it opens with what sounds like a metronome — especially considering that music, which we hear in time, is one of the movie's central *leitmotifs*. Only things are not as they sound. What we hear is in fact the ticking of a clock, immediately followed by other tickings of what seem like infinite keepers of time. Among this display of clocks, all reading the same time (which leaves us to believe that it is the correct time), there are three clear groups of threes. Threes, of course, suggest fairy tales, which more often than not open with the number three, alluding to the family triad. The first three is actually *one* "digital" clock with *three* consecutive odd numbers that read 7:53. Next we see three clocks with human figures. The third one, coming after Christopher Lloyd's name appears on the credits, shows a man hanging by his arms from the hands of a clock, which both recalls Harold Lloyd in his most memorable scene from *Safety Last* and anticipates Doc Brown (*Lloyd*) hanging from the hands of the clock tower towards the end of the movie. This three within a three, this clock within a clock, introduces the hero's surrogate father, who at this point in time is more a father to Marty than his own father. The third group is a trio of animal clocks.

In keeping with the movie's theme of time, the radio commercial for a pickup truck, Marty's dream machine, stresses that it is time to change. "*October* is inventory *time*. So right *now* Statler Toyota is making the best deals of the *year* on all *1985* model Toyotas." Being inventory time, it is a good time to take stock of one's life and see what needs to be changed, what needs to be gotten rid of to make place for the new. Just as it is a good time to get a good deal on last year's model, it is a good time to get a new model of parents and family. And as Doc informs Marty when all the clocks chime together at eight, "They're all exactly twenty-five minutes slow," it is later than it seems.

Though he has "no concept of time," Marty is called to tamper with time, to save the clock tower and Hill Valley from the terrible spell which fell upon it when "thirty years ago, lightning struck the clock tower and the clock hasn't run since," but not in the way the lady asking for donations intends. The group she represents, the Hill Valley Preservation Society, who "think it should be preserved *exactly* the way it is, as part of our history and heritage," like Principal Strickland, wants to preserve the status quo. Against these voices of paralysis, Marty's mission is to change the future by changing history and thus lift the spell that fell upon Hill Valley on that fateful night, when time (progress) came to a standstill.

This seemingly trivial information brings to mind the well-known myth of the Holy Grail, where Marty is the knight chosen to redeem the Fisher King and his kingdom. The Fisher King, of course, is his father, the crowned head of the McFlys, who live at the "regal" Lyons Estate, if to judge from the two lion statues on both sides of the entrance to the estate. He is a "wounded" king. Whereas in the well-known myth the Fisher King's wound brings desolation upon his kingdom, in *Back to the Future* the towering symbol of patriarchal authority, the keeper of the collective time, has ceased to function, suggesting a paralyzing spell over the whole town. True to the Grail myth, the young Marty, with his orange "life saver" as his armor, his "axe" as his sword, saves the clock tower from ever having been struck. In this way he restores vitality to the dysfunctioning Fisher King and rejuvenates his kingdom, getting a father he formerly could only dream about.

When we first meet the father he is all he was cut out to be. By his own words, he is "not very good in confrontations." When Biff grabs him by his necktie, a common symbol of masculinity, George, like the maimed Fisher King, is impotent. This portrait of the father is reinforced in the very next scene's opening shot, showing George pouring Peanut *Brittle* breakfast cereal into his unholy chalice. He offers some Brittles to Marty, but Marty declines, as if he does not want any part of his father. With all the McFlys around the dinner table, Marty, who does not utter a word throughout the scene, gazes at his father with disgust. When his mother talks about her brother, Jailbird Joey, saying, "We all make mistakes in life," it is also about her marriage to George, in which she feels more like an inmate than a mate. In Doc's explanation, she too is under a spell, under the "Florence Nightingale effect."

With parents under such a debilitating spell, change comes only when the sons take the initiative. The older David, late for his job at McDonald's, may tell his dad, upon kissing his *head*, that it is "time to change that oil," but it is Marty, the youngest of the three siblings, who rouses his father from his impotence and redeems himself in the process, becoming a successful son to a successful father.

Much as the Grail Knight was taught not to ask questions, Doc warns Marty not to interfere with events. But just as the Grail Knight ultimately asks the right question that redeems the wounded Fisher King, Marty redeems his father by tampering with time, by changing history. He brings his father to the time and place, but it is George, a knight in white tuxedo, who redeems himself with one blow, becoming George the Dragon Slayer. Subsequently, he is elevated to a position where someone asks him about running for class president. But there is one more deed that needs doing, a deed that tests the father-son relationship. If Marty does not play at the "Enchantment Under the Sea Dance," then his future parents do not kiss and he is "history"; if his father does not kiss in the destined time, then he cannot play, and he is "history."

As in the Holy Grail, both father and son come through. Marty, playing the kind of electrifying music that matches his heroic stature, not only brings new strength to his father, but also new spirit to the young people of Hill Valley. The way he rocks "Johnny B. Goode" at what Doc calls the "rhythmic ceremonial ritual," with an "axe" borrowed from his "dark" double, is proof enough. Even the black musicians, whose rhythm and blues was the bedrock of rock 'n' roll, are taken back. By bringing rock 'n' roll to Hill Valley, as the King of rock 'n' roll himself had brought it to the world, Marty injects new energy and restores life. As another of Chuck Berry's songs puts it, he delivers all concerned from the days of old. But Mary must also deliver himself from the days of old, from 1955. And as a sign of his transformation, for the first time in the movie, Marty is right on time for his one and only chance to return back in time. He is not a second late. And when the time machine does not start, Marty literally uses his head to get it going. By the car absorbing the lightning's electricity, Marty saves the clock tower from ever having been stopped.

On his return back in time, at first Marty seems to have returned to his old world as if nothing has changed. Seeing the homeless Red Thomas, Hill Valley's mayor of 1955, the drunk who comments on his return to 1985, "Crazy drunken drivers," Marty is relieved. "Wow, Red, you look great. Everything looks great." The third time he says "look great," it is about his redeemed home and family. This redemption is signaled by three physical signs of resurrection. On the bench where Red Thomas makes his bed, a sign advertising California Raisins (all we see is Raisin) suggests *raisin' the dead*, especially as the two other signs read "Salvation is Free" and "Assembly of Christ." The signs point to George's redemption from death in life and to Doc's resurrection from the dead as a result of his own interference with history, "screwing up future events, the space time continuum."

All in all, in his journey back in time, Marty undergoes what Samuel Osherson discusses in his book *Finding Our Fathers.* "Ultimately it is the internal image of our fathers that all men must heal. All sons need to heal the wounded fathers within their own hearts, on their own. The process involves exploring not just the past but also the present and future — ways of being male that reflect a richer, fuller sense of self than the narrow images that dominated the past."[2] This is Marty's quest — to heal the wounded Fisher King by exploring the past and heal the wounded image of his father. His quest is to re-set time. Or as another young man, who plays out his oedipal drama to tragic results, has so eloquently put it, "The time is out of joint; O cursed spite, That ever I was born to set it right!"[3]

Oedipus: The Future Is in Your Hands

In the Oedipus myth that runs through *Back to the Future,* Marty is a comical and reluctant Oedipus. Where Oedipus's future was determined by the hand of fate before he was born, Marty goes back in time to change his future before he is born. Where Oedipus goes from triumph to defeat, Marty moves from misfortune to redemption. Rather than kill his father and marry his mother, he saves his father from being hit by his mother's father and from becoming a man whose wife wants his son more than her husband. Appearing before his father as the "dark father," Marty even instructs him to take his place as his mother's object of desire.

That *Back to the Future* is about the father is first suggested by the three pictures of historical *fathers of inventions* (Thomas Edison, Benjamin Franklin and Albert Einstein) whose scientific ingenuity, like Doc's time machine, contributed to man's future. Unlike Marty's negative picture of his father, the three must be forefathers that Doc, Marty's surrogate father, admires and respects. Together with the many *threes* in the exposition, as well as the countless threes that turn up throughout the movie, this trio suggests the oedipal triad, "the child himself in relation to his parents."[4]

In something that alludes to Oedipus blinding himself, the first time we see the father he is arguing with Biff about a blind spot. "Now, Biff, I never noticed that the car had any blind spot before when I would drive it." When Biff shoots back, "What are you, blind, McFly?" it is Marty who is shown, as if the question is addressed to him, suggesting he has a "blind spot" to the father he "sees" before him, that he is blinded by the oedipal situation. On the other hand, unlike Oedipus, who was blinded by pride and punished himself by physical *blinding*, pride is not Marty's strong side. Hubris is not his tragic flaw. As a member of "The Pinheads," he is a far cry from the bigheaded Oedipus. When meeting them in '55, Marty is clearly not blind to the fact that Lorraine and George are his future parents. Just as Biff's question about blindness can be taken to address both McFlys, Mayor Red Thomas's re-election campaign, "Remember fellas, the *future* is in your hands," is meant for both father and son. The twin *re*-election campaigns, of *Red* in '55 and *Goldie* Wilson in '85 (the third man in this *colorful* threesome, of course, is Doc *Brown*), announce what both father and son must do. Along with George's *re*typing Biff's report in '85 and *re*copying his homework in '55, not to mention the *re*run of *The Honeymooners*, the re-election prepares us for the *re*match at the end of the journey, for Marty's *re*writing his-story.

Just as Oedipus took the future into his hands, and just like the re-election slogans, the future of father and son is in their hands. This motif is introduced by Hill Valley's future "King," the man who claims, in 1985, that "progress is his middle name," when he addresses the young George McFly about taking a stand against his oppressor. "Stand tall, boy. Have some respect for yourself. Don't you know that if you let people walk all over you, they'll be walking all over you for the rest of your life?" As stated by a black man in late 1955, whose own liberation was just beginning at the time, these words can be read as voice of the oppressed demanding its rights. Especially considering that on December 1, 1955, Rosa Parks refused to give up her seat to a white man in Montgomery, Alabama, an event that ignited the blacks, who were led by their own King, and started taking their future into their hands. If in the '80s the star of *Cattle Queen* can become president, Goldie Wilson can surely become mayor (king) of Hill Valley. Likewise, George McFly can become head of the McFly household, providing he stands up to Biff and takes the future in his hands. Presently, however, George is shackled by fears and doubts. He needs more convincing to overcome his oppressor, his dragon. Only when push comes to shove in his confrontation with Biff, the third such confrontation (after Marty's first two), does George literally take the future in his left hand.

The first sign of George using his hand is in his writing, what turns out to be his future vocation. "What are you writing?" Marty asks his father. "Stories," George briefly comes to life as he talks about his writing. "Science fiction stories about visitors coming down to Earth from other planets," George describes his first published book and Marty's visit to 1955. "Get out of town," says Marty, incredulous. His saying, "I didn't know you did anything creative" foreshadows his "I never knew he had it in him," after George literally takes the future in his hands, resolving the Oedipal situation once and for all. But for now, when Marty asks to read his father's story, George's lack of confidence does not allow it. He cannot bear the rejection. "I guess that would be pretty hard for someone to understand," he tells Marty, who does not find it "hard at all." As it were, his pen matches Marty's guitar. Both are put to use by hands.

This information, together with George's "I'm just not ready to ask Lorraine out to the dance and not you or anybody else on this planet is going to change my mind," gives Marty what he needs to get his father to use his hands to change his future. In using what he brought with him from the future to change the present, his Walkman and the music of Van Halen, and borrowing from three sci-fi movies of the 1970s and '80s, *Star Wars*, *E. T.* and *Star Trek*, Marty wakes up George from his sleep and from his spell. The next day, George literally starts using those hands that hold his future, even if it is only to open a Pepsi bottle. His change is underscored by Marty asking, "What made you change your mind, George?" Of course, what changed his mind was his close encounter of the third kind.

Subsequently, in Lou's Cafe, in a parody of a typical western saloon scene, George gets into the role of a hero by ordering a stiff one to build up his courage. "Lou, gimme a milk. *Chocolate.*" He grabs the glass with one hand, taking one shot of the dark brew before going into action. But as he informed Marty the night before, George is not yet ready for the showdown. He needs a more potent potion and a tougher approach. At this point in time, he uses his hand to hold the text that he reads to Lorraine. But even then he botches his line. He only gets it right the third time, informing his future wife that, as in the Oedipus myth, *destiny* has brought him to her. However, when Biff enters the picture, as he always does when George is at Lou's Cafe, it is Marty who lays him out with one punch, showing his father how it is done, how you take the future into your hands. This theme is reinforced by the billboard showing a pair of hands and the caption, "You're in good hands with Allstate," when, in his escape, Marty borrows a skateboard from a little kid to outrun (and outsmart) Biff and his cohorts.

In his endeavor to turn George into a man who "can stand up for himself and protect the woman he loves," Marty has his hands full. Not only does Lorraine want him to take her to the dance, George hardly fits her idea of a hero. As always, the oedipal knots are not easily untied.

On the night of "Enchantment Under the Sea Dance," a topsy-turvy night when the one sure thing is when lightning is going to strike, the oedipal situation comes to a climax inside Marty's parked car. What was merely suggested in '85 is now plain to see. Lorraine wants Marty, and even though he knows she is his mother, Marty cannot keep his eyes from wandering to her partly exposed breasts. "Have you ever been in a situation," he asks her, "where you know you had to act a certain way but when you got there, you didn't know if you could go through with it?" Of course, Marty's words can also allude to his concern for George's ability to overcome his self-doubt and play his part in their melodrama. But as in the Oedipus myth, destiny, much stronger than anything Marty can come up with, plays its unpredictable hand, coming up with a fairy tale ending beyond Marty's wildest dreams.

The first sign that things are not going as planned comes when, kissing Marty on an impulse, Lorraine wakes up from her spell, from her fixation on her "dreamboat." "This is all wrong. I don't know what it is, but when I kiss you, it's like I'm kissing my brother." Then, when she informs him that "someone's coming," and Marty is certain that George has not missed his cue and is about to save him from this awkward (taboo) situation, we are just as surprised as he is when it is Biff's hand (that is all we and Marty see) that reaches in and yanks him out of the white car's uterine interior. Instead of being saved by his father, it is the revenge of the father's nemesis, what is commonly embodied in myths and fairy tales as a giant or a dragon. "You cost three hundred buck's damage to my car, you son of a bitch," Biff informs Marty, recalling George's "assumption" that his "insurance is gonna pay for the damaged car" back in 1985. This brute does not need a lawyer to get his money back. "I'm gonna take it out of your ass."

Biff's three "right *hand* men" carry out his command to "take him in back" by shoving Marty in the trunk of the black musicians' black car, a dark womb from which Marty emerges reborn. While the black musicians send Biff's thugs to their "mammas," Marvin acts as the midwife for Martin's rebirth when he opens the locked trunk, wounding his playing hand in the process. Simultaneously, George walks up to Marty's car, ready to recite his line. This time he does not botch it, but his co-star in the drama has been replaced. "Just turn around, McFly, and walk way," Biff orders him. But this time George does not walk away. "No, Biff, you leave her alone," he says, trying his best to confront Lorraine's tormenter. Lorraine tries to get Biff to let go of George by repeating that he is "breaking his *arm*." But only when Biff pushes Lorraine to the ground does George muster his will to deal with his archrival, the dragon that holds the princess captive.

The juxtaposition of George's energized left hand and Marvin's bleeding left hand suggests that George gets his new power from the blood of his son's dark double. Just as one kiss frees Lorraine from Marty, one punch on the kisser frees George from Biff and turns him into Lorraine's object of desire. As he looks down at Lorraine, she looks up to him with love and admiration. He did exactly what she had said a man should do.

This happy ending ends abruptly with Marty's looking at his fading picture together with Doc's looking at the clock tower. It is a reminder that George may have slain the menacing "dragon" and redeemed himself momentarily, but he still has to "interact" and kiss Lorraine on the dance floor. He still has to win the princess. And he does not have much time in which to do it.

On stage, Marvin looks at Marty playing the guitar, seeming to say, "He's all right—for a white boy." Marty is too preoccupied with George's sealing his future with a kiss to really play his best. His playing is *handi*capped by George's lack of resolution. Looking at the picture stuck at the end of the guitar neck, where musicians usually stick cigarettes, he sees that time is running out. Only he is left in the picture. On the dance floor, replacing her former words to her son ("Come here and kiss your mother"), Lorraine asks George, "Aren't you going to kiss me?" "I don't know," George is momentarily his old self again. In his moment of self-doubt, as another student cuts in, Marty's playing breaks down completely. He begins to fade from the picture and his playing hand momentarily disappears. But once again, when push comes to shove, George comes through. And once again it is the man*hand*ling of Lorraine that gets him going. He shoves the intruder with the same left hand that punched out Biff, and kisses Lorraine in time to save Marty from literally vanishing into history.

As in fairy tales, when the prince kisses the sleeping beauty, the kiss resurrects Marty. He springs up, able to play the guitar once again. Having come out of this ordeal renewed, having joined forces, George and Marty signal to one another with their hands. Marty is shown moving the playing fingers of his right hand. His playing hand is back.

On his return to the future, accompanied by "Back in Time," Marty is taken back by the changes he sees before him. The biggest change is in his parents. His father is king of the house and his mother has had a change of heart towards Jennifer, her former rival. She is cured of her Oedipal fixation on her son. "Oh, I sure like her, Marty. She is such a sweet girl." Unlike the blinded Oedipus, Marty keeps his vision and gets a pair of parents who "*look* great," and a girlfriend who is "a *sight* for sore eyes."

The Odyssey: The Power of Rock 'n' Roll

Out of the three times Marty gets to perform with his electric guitar in the course of the movie, his first one comes right at the beginning, before we even see his face. It takes place in Doc's lab, the place Marty calls home. In his father's absence, Doc is to Marty what Mentor was to Telemachus. In a ceremonial rite of sorts, Marty picks up his "axe" and turns on three amplifiers, all described in automotive terminology. Just as the souped-up DeLorean, *Doc's ex machina*, transports Marty back in time, it is his guitar that transforms him into a successful son of a successful father. Only after he is hurled *back* by the speaker's blast and takes off his sunglasses do we see Marty's face. He looks *ahead* through the torn speaker, thus creating a visual metaphor of *Back to the Future.* Taking off his dark glasses, Marty has an epiphany. "Whoa, rock 'n' roll." He sees the explosive power of rock 'n' roll. As suggested by the shiny fret, the electric guitar is his modern sword with the power to slay the dragon.

Like his flying backwards, Marty goes back in time when rock 'n' roll first became popular. Curiously enough, a huge hit in 1955 was Bill Haley and the Comet's "Rock Around the *Clock*," one of the songs that launched the new music that excited youngsters and horrified their parents. Moreover, the mix of cars and music (the eighty-eight keys of the piano and the eighty-eight miles per hour the "newmobile" must reach in order to cross the time barrier) recalls another historical song that played a key role in launching rock 'n' roll, Ike Turner and the Kings of Rhythm's 1951 hit "Rocket 88." The song refers to the Oldsmobile model *Eighty Eight* that had its most successful year in 1955.

The nightmare Marty experiences in finding himself in 1955 gives new meaning to the line by the "Irish McFly" (or "Irish Bug," as Biff calls George), in James Joyce's *Ulysses,* "History is a nightmare from which I'm trying to awake,"[5] especially when recalling Marty's line to Strickland about changing history. As it were, *Back to the Future* has other parallels with Joyce's *Ulysses* and Homer's *Odyssey.* While George can be seen as Leopold Bloom, Doc Brown is Athena in the guise of Mentor. In 1985 Marty is both Stephen Daedalus and Telemachus; in 1955 he is mostly the cunning Odysseus, repeatedly outsmarting the movie's Cyclops Polyphemus, whose father is the figure of Neptune at the "Enchantment Under the Sea." (Biff's role as Polyphemus, whose one eye was blinded by the cunning Odysseus, recalls his first words about not knowing George's car had a "blind spot.") Like the detained Odysseus, Marty has to be at his cunning best with a '50s model of Circe and Calypso rolled into one.

Whereas Telemachus was repeatedly reminded he was his heroic father's son, Marty is reminded by Strickland, who connects his ability to play the guitar with his "old man." "I noticed your band is on the roster for dance auditions after school today. Why even bother McFly, you haven't got a chance. You're too much like your old man." Actually, Marty is far from the failure (loser) his father is. The three "failures" presented at the beginning of the movie are his first and last. Besides, the three are not really his fault. Blowing the speaker is caused by "a slight overload," his lateness is due to Doc's tampering with time, and his dismissal from the audition owes more to the judge's squareness than to his ability to play. As Jennifer tells him, "You're good, Marty. You're really good," which anticipates his rock 'n' roll success with "Johnny B. Goode." Presently all he lacks is self confidence, which seems to be mostly due to his lack of a good role model. But like Johnny B. Goode, school is not Marty's calling. Music is.

Revisiting his alma mater with Doc to show him his father, much as Telemachus ventured to find out about his father, like a Mentor, Doc explains to Marty his situation. "According to my theory, you interfered with your parents' first meeting. If they don't meet, they won't fall in love, they won't get married, and they won't have kids. That's why your older brother is disappearing from that photograph. You sister will follow, and unless you repair the damage, you'll be next."

In his task to "repair the damage," Marty is on his own. Like Odysseus, he has to do it by his own wits and cunning. Typical of the novice at the start of his journey, Marty's initial attempt, the direct approach, is a complete failure. Like Penelope meeting the disguised Odysseus upon his return, when Marty introduces George, Lorraine does not recognize him as her future husband. But as happens in the slaying of the suitors, all this changes on the night of the "Enchantment Under the Sea Dance," where George is initially singled out in the swarm of dancing couples, the only one jitterbugging by himself. This is the part where he rescues Lorraine as Odysseus rescued Penelope. Perhaps that is why the Poseidon statue, holding his trident, looks at him askance. As lord of the deep dark water, he seems to know something about George that is still unconscious. He is everything Lorraine wants in a man; he just doesn't know it yet. Just as Odysseus was magically transformed from the old beggar, in one heroic act he is transformed to George the Dragon Slayer.

On his return to the dance with Lorraine, George is tested again when a suitor interrupts their dancing. "Scram, McFly. I'm cutting in." For George, overcoming his self-doubt and shoving the guy down to the floor under the gaze of Neptune is just as heroic as Odysseus slaying the suitors. Up on stage, Marvin approves of his replacement's playing. "Yeah, man, that was good." And as fits the movie where many things are redone, he suggests, "Let's do another one." But Marty has other things in mind; he has a rendezvous with Doc and destiny. Or else he is still nursing the fear of rejection. "C'mon, man, let's do something that really cooks"; the shadow does not give up so easily.

Seeing the crowd's warm response, Marty reconsiders. For a young man worried that he will "never get a chance to play in front of anybody," this kind of opportunity does not come often. Coming from '85, he surely knows that rock 'n' roll was born when a white man finally started singing and playing the blues, when the blues of the blacks and the country music of the whites had come together, the two into one, in such stars as Elvis Presley and Chuck Berry, the movie's Marvin Berry's legendary cousin. Armed with his darker half's axe, and seeing his father and mother together on the dance floor, gives Marty the confidence he so desperately needs to do what he is good at. "All right," he speaks into the microphone, as Marvin looks at him just as Neptune had looked at George. "It's a blue riff in B," he instructs the Starlighters. "Watch me for the changes, and try to keep up," Marty seizes the guitar with a confidence he never knew he had. In no time the band and the crowd begin to move to the rhythm. Now we get the full meaning of Marty's "rock 'n' roll" at the opening of the movie and what Doc meant when he called the dance "a rhythmic ceremonial ritual." This is a rhythmic rite of passage, a coming together of the two sides, the white and black, the hero and his shadow. And as in the *Odyssey*, it celebrates the coming together of father and son

Marty's playing "Johnny B. Goode," the quintessential rock 'n' roll song, brings all the loose ends of the movie together. It is where Marty, who gets to play with black musicians, becomes the "good" guitarist Jennifer knew he was, where he becomes Marty B. Goode. No doubt his singing "go, go" is meant to himself. But as underscored when a classmate congratulates George on the dance floor ("Hey, George, I heard you laid out Biff. Nice *going!*"), it is also meant for George. Early into the song, Marty turns back to Marvin with a smile, as if saying, "Didn't think I could play, did ya?" When he starts playing like T-Bone Walker, Pete Townsend and Jimi Hendrix rolled into one, Marvin's face seems to say, "Where did he come from?" He does not know that rock 'n' roll had come a long way since 1955.

"Johnny B. Goode," a rags to riches story, not only describes Marty's journey in time, it is while singing about the first mythical hero of rock 'n' roll that he becomes the hero who brings to the youngsters of Hill Valley the message and rhythm of the liberating music, freeing them from the tyranny of their parents, just as Telemachus was freed of the suitors. As in the chorus of another of Berry's songs, "School Days," Marty truly delivers his father (and mother) "from days of old." He does not know it yet, but he also delivers himself in the process. "Johnny B. Goode," after all, is his own mythic story. He too was a "slacker" in school, who wasn't good at learning but could really play the guitar.

When Marty returns Marvin his guitar, he looks at it in wonder, as if thinking, can this guitar do this? Coming from the future, Marty's playing, as they say, is ahead of its time. The audience feels about his music as he had felt coming in Hill Valley of 1955, or for that matter, the way he feels about his father in 1985. "I guess you guys aren't ready for that yet. But your kids are gonna love it," Marty not only comments about the advent of rock 'n' roll, but also about the McFly kids' response to the change in their family. Even his mother is not the square she was first cut out to be. "Marty, that was very interesting music," she comments on his electrifying performance.

As Marty informs his mother, his journey has been "educational." In one week's time he learned more than he would ever learn in twelve years of schooling. His father, too, has internalized what he has learned from his meeting with his son. "Marty, I want to thank you for all your good advice. I'll never forget it." His words recall Telemachus' words to Athena, disguised as Mentor, underscoring Marty's role as father to the man his father has become. "Friend, you have done me kindness, like a father to a son, and I shall not forget your counsel ever."[6]

Undoing the Past

Reflecting on *Back to the Future* brings to mind a line from a philosophy professor, the subject of a documentary, in Woody Allen's *Crimes and*

Misdemeanors: "Love is a return and undoing of the past."[7] This hefty line artic-ulates what is explored most wittily in Robert Zemeckis's highly entertaining *filmmyth*. What is the movie saying if not that to live more fully in the present, in order to discover the "Power of Love," the song which opens *Back to the Future*, we have to return to the past and undo the mistakes we all make? As in *The Wizard of Oz*, we have to come to terms with the shadowy parts that are mostly tied, one way or another, to our parents. We have to come to accept their imperfections and darkness. And that is precisely what Marty does in his journey in time. He sees his parents at his own age, with similar hopes and fears. He even visits both their homes (each one once). That it is Marty's seeing that is changed is reinforced by the fact that he himself remains as he is through-out the movie. The nightmare he awakes from is his own. Like the dark glasses he removes when we first see him, he ceases seeing his father through a glass darkly. Like Dorothy Gale, Marty returns home and sees it for the first time. In seeing his father (and mother) in a new light, Marty can better contend with such future tasks as becoming a father, which is precisely what Doc informs him he has become in the future. What Allen's fictionalized philosopher, Lewis Levy, says at the end of *Crimes*—"We define ourselves by the choices we have made. We are in fact the sum total of our choices."[8]—can very well sum up *Back to the Future*. The future is in our minds and in our hands. Or as the father says to his son in his last line of the movie, "Like I always told you, if you put your mind to it, you could accomplish anything."

Chapter 3

Stand by Me
Descent to the Netherworld

That summer at home I had become the invisible boy.

— Gordie Lachance

Angry Fathers, Invisible Sons

Much as in her dream journey Dorothy resolves her problem with Em, and in his journey back in time Marty comes to terms with his father, in his quest to find a dead body, Gordie Lachance deals with his angry father. Unlike *Oz* and *Back to the Future*, which are seen through their young heroine and hero, the story in *Stand by Me* is told by the grownup Gordie. His story is more personal and deals with the father-son relationship much more squarely, particularly the father's anger, which makes Gordie feel invisible, as if he is a shade in the netherworld. As Gordie remarks early in the film, when introducing his family, "That summer at home I had become the invisible boy."

Gordie's invisibility is most apparent in the one and only sequence that shows his whole family, around the dinner table, a traditional setting of family get-togethers. Gordie and Denny, who are always shown sharing the frame, are on the left. The mother (Dorothy) sits opposite them on the right. In the center, as if separating the sons from their mother, sits the unnamed father. As the camera moves in, Gordie is passing a bowl to his mother, suggesting a connection between the two. Similarly, his lack of connection with his father is emphasized by his repeatedly asking him to pass the potatoes, which go unanswered. The father is too preoccupied with his favorite son's athleticism (masculinity) to notice. In the end, while he admonishes the mother for talking to Denny "about girls," she passes the potatoes to Gordie. The father's anger turns to a smile when he addresses Denny. "Dennis, when you're out there tomorrow—" Denny cuts him short, averting the attention to Gordie, reminding their father that he has another son. "Pop, did you read the story that Gordie wrote? Gordie wrote a story. It is really good." The father throws a brief glance at Gordie, the only time he looks at him in the sequence. Only the mother responds, showing an interest in the less manly act. "What did you write, sweetheart?" But the father does not stand for this sissyness. While his angry words fade in the background, Denny and Gordie are shown together in the sequence's closing shot. "Gordie, I really liked it. It was great." Denny gives him a love tap on the back of the head, as the camera focuses on Gordie smiling happily, glad to have his brother stand by him

As shown in this brief but telling scene, Gordie feels invisible in his father's eyes because he does not measure up to his more successful brother. Gordie's stating early in the journey, "I couldn't give a shit about my own dad who hadn't laid a hand on me since I was three," seems to encapsulate their relationship from his point of view. Rejected by his father, Gordie denies his need for him. But as the scene around the table confirms, Gordie longs for some kind of "lay of hands." Like all sons, he needs to be acknowledged by his father.

Gordie's feeling invisible "that summer," the summer that separates elementary school from junior high, is also a sign of his growing up. No longer a child, but not yet an adult, this age of "betwixt and between" is a trying time for Gordie and his three cohorts, just as it is for many boys their age. "The movement from child to adult, between the dying to the old form and emergence of the new, the time of 'betwixt and between,' can be an experience of non–existence, or 'no form,' even invisibility."[1]

Though he does not say it in so many words, Chris, "the leader of our gang, and my best friend," shares Gordie's feelings of invisibility in undervaluing himself as "just one of those *low*life Chambers kids." Like Gordie, he too has an angry father. Towards the end of the movie, when he tries to console Gordie by saying that his father does not *hate* him, that he simply does not *know* him, Chris surely speaks from experience. Teddy, "the craziest guy we hung around with," is also a victim of his father's anger. The physical abuse he receives from his father parallels the emotional abuse Gordie gets from his. Like his scarred ear, physical proof of his father's "fits of rage," Teddy is *cursed* to re–enact his father's wars. In the first encounter with the train, one of the movie's embodiments of the dragon, he "shoots" the approaching adversary with his imaginary machine gun, "just like the beach in Normandy," battling the introjected enemy he projects on the train. But in the real showdown with Ace, another dragon, Teddy runs away. Unlike Gordie (and Chris), he never resolves his inner problem with his introjected father, his dragon. He never gets out of Castle Rock, remaining in the same physical (and emotional) world of his childhood.

Without father figures to see them through their coming of age, the boys turn to surrogate father figures. "You wanna be the Lone Ranger or the Cisco Kid?" Chris asks Gordie before they set out on their quest to find the body, showing him the gun he "hawked" from his father. In this symbolic attempt to be as their western heroes, Gordie assures Chris that he can see that the gun is a .45. But as his surprise at finding it loaded demonstrates, he is not the man he would like his best friend to believe.

Interestingly, in *The Six-Gun Mystique*, John G. Cawelti cites the Lone Ranger as a "supreme example" of a hero whose appeal to adolescents reflects their ambiguous relationship with the father.

> The Lone Ranger typically exposes and brings to justice those figures who exemplify the corruption of adult power: the greedy and treacherous banker who seeks to cheat the farmers out of their rightful earnings... The villain is the feared and hated father-figure while the farmer symbolizes the non–threatening aspect of the father. By exposing the corrupt villain and restoring the farmer to his rightful position, the hero expresses the forbidden wish to murder the evil father on the one hand, while protecting himself from guilt by supporting the good father on the other.[2]

When Gordie and his three cohorts cross the railroad bridge, the threshold that separates the familiar town of their childhood with the unknown terrain of adolescence, they sing about another western hero, the black knight known as Paladin. Significantly enough, all three mentioned TV heroes are not fathers. They are cow*boys*, ever ready to fight for justice and for the underdog, slaying dragons in the mythical landscape of the West.

Gordie's Katabasis

The movie's story within a story suggests two journeys. The quest for the boy's body, which takes up most of the movie, is Gordie's coming to terms with Denny's death; his *story* of that quest is his dealing with Chris's death. Likewise, as in all filmmyths, along with the outer adventure, the search for the body, is the inner journey, the searching of the hero's psyche. The inner journey is Gordie's *katabasis*, the Greek word for "descent," which refers to the hero's descent to the realm of the dead, to the netherworld, to retrieve something of great value, as when Orpheus descends to Hades to retrieve his beloved Eurydice. Considering the "invisible" *shade* he has become in his father's eyes, Gordie's quest for the body is ultimately a search for identity. "From the time of Odysseus' descent in the *Odyssey*, katabasis seems inevitably to entail at some level a search for identity. The journey is in some central, irreducible way a journey of self–discovery, a quest for a lost self."[3]

The *katabasis* is anticipated in the movie's exposition, with the grownup Gordie reading in a newspaper of Chris's death. Deep in thought in the driver's seat of his Jeep, the disturbed Gordie at first does not notice a passing pair of boys riding by on bicycles, a pair which surely reminds him of Chris and himself. Reading of his death and seeing the two bicyclers triggers the telling of the story, which begins with the subject of death. "I was twelve going on thirteen first time I saw a dead human being."

The subject of death continues as a dissolve reveals a hand picking a *True Police Cases* magazine from a magazine rack with such captions as "Gun Girl," "Secret Life" and "Kiss-of-Death." Another caption, "Mad Dog Killer," suggests the three-headed dog Cerberus that guards the gates of the underworld. "It happened in the summer of 1957," the man's voiceover continues, as the face of the twelve-year-old Gordie comes into the picture. His adding, "A long time ago, but only if you measure it in terms of years," points to the enduring significance of this event. As his voiceover informs us, it happened after his "whole world" forever changed with the death of his brother. "In April my older brother Dennis had been killed in a Jeep accident. Four months had passed but my parents still hadn't been able to put the pieces back together again."

The *katabasis* is further suggested when, like a hero descending to the netherworld to retrieve a life-enhancing object or a loved one, Gordie enters Denny's forbidden room that holds the container of the life-giving water he needs for his journey. Gordie's cautious entrance suggests that it is his first time in Denny's room since his death. The subject of death is evoked by the three pictures of Buddy Holly, who had died in a plane crash a couple of months before Denny. The wooden figure of a piggy bank on the closet door that Gordie opens to get the canteen recalls Vern's lost jar of pennies. Like Dorothy's brain, heart and courage, Gordie needs these three virtues (Pride, Integrity and Guts) that the PIG acronym spells to see him through his descent to the netherworld of his psyche and his confrontation with the dragon.

As if conjuring his brother's ghost, Gordie's bringing Denny back to life through his flashback reveals the role he played in his life. In giving Gordie his Yankees cap, Denny is the "protective figure who provides the adventurer with amulets against the dragon forces he is about to pass."[4] As he informs Gordie, "It's a good luck cap. You wear that cap, you know how many fish we're gonna catch? Bazillion. A bazillion fish." While fish is a common symbol of life, his giving him the cap brings to mind "the cap or helmet Hades wears ... [that] makes its wearer invisible."[5]

Gordie's "actual" *katabasis* is announced by the sign on the junkyard's gate, NO TRESPASSING—KEEP OUT, and by his voiceover, which alludes to Cerberus, "No Trespassing was enforced by Milo Pressman, the junkman, and his dog Chopper, the most feared and least seen dog in Castle Rock. Legend had it that Milo had trained Chopper not just to sic, but to sic specific parts of the human anatomy." The netherworld is suggested by Chris remarking that Teddy "won't live to be twenty" and his calling Gordie "a dead man." As if to retrieve life in the midst of death, the four enter the junkyard to fill up on water, just as Gordie entered his dead brother's room for his water canteen, an object which receives a close-up after Gordie scales the junkyard fence.

Instead of ghosts, in his *katabasis* Gordie encounters the two sides of the father. The good father, who represents life, is anticipated when the four decide to flip coins to see who goes to get the food, and Gordie's "Odd man goes" is countered by Teddy's "That's you, Gordie, odd as a cod." While this oddness is in keeping with Gordie's growing separation from the group, the "cod" anticipates the mounted fish above the grocer's head and his words, "In the midst of life we are in death."

Along with the provisions, the grocer Quidachiolo, recalling Tiresias giving Odysseus direction home in his descent to Hades, provides Gordie with food for thought. "Ain't you Denny Lachance's brother?" he asks Gordie without looking at him. "You look like your brother Denny. People ever tell you that?" Unlike Gordie's father, who emphasized their difference, the grocer, who also lost a brother, emphasizes their similarities. What seems to be the grocer's remembering his brother ("Quarterback he played. Boy, could he throw. Father God and Sonny Jesus!"), could also be his praising Denny's athleticism, as suggested by showing Gordie remembering his father praising Denny in the flashback around the dinner table. When the grocer asks Gordie, "What do you do?" he replies he does not know, despite the fact that he has already given himself the answer in his flashback of his family around the dinner table. As is soon revealed, Gordie has trouble accepting this creative part of himself, the part that Denny encourages and his father rejects.

In contrast to the grocer, who rouses Gordie to think of his future, of his identity, the junkman Milo Pressman, who represents death, calls him to go back. "Hey, you kid! What are you doing there?" he yells upon seeing Gordie trespassing his junkyard, echoing the grocer's question, "What do you do?" "Come back!" he continues yelling as Gordie dashes to the fence in time to escape the pursuing dog. "That's Chopper?" Gordie is surprised: Chopper's reputation as the great emasculator ("sic balls!") turns out to be an overblown myth, a paper Cerberus. "Chopper was my first lesson in the vast difference between myth and reality." Like Milo and Chopper, the castrating father is more bark than bite. It is more introjected than real.

Where Gordie and the grocer were identical in losing their brothers, in the confrontation between the junkman and Teddy, the two seem to recognize themselves in each other as if looking in a twisted mirror. Milo recognizes Teddy much as the grocer recognized Gordie. "You're Teddy Duchamp. Your dad's a loony." The junkman knows no bounds in getting back at Teddy, as if seeking to bring him down to his level of making a living from what other people discard. "He took your ear and he put it to a stove. And he burnt it off," he says to burn Teddy's pride. "He's crazier than a shithouse rat. No wonder you're acting in the way you are, with a loony for a father." That Milo represents the dark father, the obstructing figure commonly embodied by the dragon, is suggested by his repeatedly calling the four to "Come back!" and by his threat, "All your fathers are gonna get a call from me." Particularly Gordie, who is once again singled out: "I know your name. You're Lachance!"

The change in Gordie after the encounter with the two sides of the father is revealed in the way he starts to see their quest to find the body: "I'm not sure it should be a good time." At first Chris thinks Gordie is heeding the junkman's call. "You saying you wanna *go back*?" "No," Gordie replies, revealing his growing separation from the group. "Going to see a dead kid, maybe it shouldn't be a party."

Apparently, Gordie's turning to Chris with "Do you think I'm weird?" comes from his encounter with the grocer, who questioned his emerging identity. Asking Chris how he perceives him signals Gordie's searching for insight into his personality, his individuality. Not used to this type of question, Chris responds cynically. But Gordie lets him know that he really wants to know. He stops Chris, turning to face him. "Am I weird?" "Yeah," Chris answers truthfully, but softens it with, "But so what? Everybody is weird." When he reminds Gordie of the changes they are about to undergo in the coming school year, he refuses to listen. "It's not going to be like grammar school. You'll be taking your college courses, and me, Teddy and Vern will all be in the shop courses with the rest of the retards making ashtrays and birdhouses." As if under the dragon's spell, only hearing his introjected "dad talking," as Chris calls it, Gordie turns a deaf ear to his best friend, reminding him, like his brother, what he does best: "You could be a real writer someday, Gordie."

> GORDIE: Fuck writing! I don't wanna be a writer! It's stupid! It's a stupid waste of time!
>
> CHRIS: That's your dad talking. I know how your dad feels about you. He doesn't give a shit about you. Denny was the one he cared about, and don't try to tell me different. You're just a kid, Gordie.
>
> GORDIE: Oh gee, thanks, dad.
>
> CHRIS: Wish the hell I was your dad. You wouldn't be going around talking about taking these stupid shot courses if I was. It's like God gave you something, man. All those stories that you can make up. And he said, "This is what we got for you, kid. Try not to lose it." But kids lose everything unless there's someone there to look after them. And if your parents are too fucked up to do it, then maybe I should.

Gordie calling writing "stupid" is indeed his "dad talking." This is the voice of the introjected father, the dragon Gordie must slay, as must all boys his age, if they are to develop as individuals, if they are to answer their calling in the outer world.

> In mythology, the true hero fights the father to attain his own individuality, not as a mere reaction. A man follows an "inner voice" that tells him there is a new way to live... The "inner voice" a man listens to is his own urge toward individual development ... As soon as he listens to himself, as soon as he honors his individuality, he is psychologically in conflict with the father world. This is a struggle we all must go through in our personal development. To fail to separate from the father means to live a limited life as far as the development of individuality is concerned.[6]

At this point in the journey, Gordie's reluctance to "separate" is underscored by his being paired with the cowardly Vern in the crossing of the railroad bridge over the river, the threshold that separates their home and the other side where await darkness, the woods, leeches and the dead body of Ray Brower. As often happens, it is while crossing the bridge that we get a first glimpse of Gordie's "personal development." Like his brother, who stood by him, Gordie stands by Vern. He does not let him be killed like Ray Brower, or for that matter, like his brother. In being his brother's keeper by pushing Vern from behind, racing against the iron dragon, Gordie, to cite his father, is "more like Denny." This near-death experience is a crucial event in his rite of passage. For once he is not victimized by his father's voice.

Gordie's "inner voice" first emerges around the campfire, the dark night's sole source of light, when Chris, not unlike Denny before him, entreats him, "Hey, Gordie, why don't you tell us a story?" Gordie's initial response, "Oh, I don't know," echoes his reply to the grocer's question, "What do you do?" Gordie may have his doubts about his gift, but he no longer denies it. Encouraged by Chris, Gordie starts the story about Lard Ass, whose obesity makes him an outcast, an object of ridicule, though Gordie emphasizes that "it's not his fault," much as Denny's death is not *his*. Considering that the hero is a boy their age and that the other characters are male figures of authority such as the mayor, the principal and the Bossman (the famous local radio disk jockey whose broadcast accompanies the first part of their journey), the story is Gordie's projection of his feelings about his father. The story about "the greatest revenge idea a kid ever had" is his revenge. In telling the story, Gordie puts into words what has been gestating inside himself. He feels as much an outcast as his hero, David Hogan. The story is his own conscious throwing up, his catharsis, which prepares him for the terrible message of his dream. Like Lard Ass himself, who "just sat back and enjoyed what he created," Gordie sits back after finishing his story of "a complete and total barforama." His storytelling grips the others much as Orpheus charmed his audience with music and song. Each boy responds differently to the story, each according to his main problem. But there is one thing they all share. "None of us mentioned Ray Brower but we were all thinking about him."

Right after these words, the animal howling in the night, which "sounds like a woman screaming," may well be the voice of the unconscious, foreshadowing Gordie's dream. The events of the day, together with anticipating the dead body, have stirred his subconscious. The accusing words he assigns to his father, as he looks *down* at him in his dream, "It should have been you, Gordon," is the voice of the dragon, a clear case of the introjected father. Even if it is *only* an unconscious dream, Gordie allows his submerged feelings to come to the surface. At this point, Gordie can only share with Chris that he misses his brother and that he "didn't cry at Denny's funeral." It is a sign of his coming to terms with his death, but he cannot yet express how he feels in his father's eyes.

Gordie's growing individuality, his breaking away from his gang, is suggested when he is shown the following morning, sitting on the railroad track, reading a *Gang Breakers* comic book. Before the third passing of the train, he sees a deer that seems to come from nowhere, not unlike an apparition. The way the two face each other, it seems they recognize each other. Or it may be a sign that he has made a separate peace with the terrifying animal voice of the night before. Keeping this magic moment to himself dissociates Gordie from the group that has come to replace his family. "It was on the tip of my tongue to tell them about the deer. But I didn't. That was the one thing I kept to myself." His keeping it to himself is part of his becoming an individual. "One cannot become a person without first being an individual, without freeing himself from the clan, from parental domination, without becoming aware of his own individuality with a right to secrecy."[7]

The closer they get to the body, the more "the reality of Ray Brower was growing," the deeper Gordie descends to the netherworld of his submerged feelings. "For me the idea of seeing that kid's dead body was starting to become an obsession."

Return from the Dead

"Gentleman, the Royal," Chris announces when they come up to the last obstacle before their objective. After the junkyard, taking the shortcut through the unknown woods is the foursome's second straying from the charted path. It is also where they no longer listen to the radio, the collective voice of civilization. "You don't know what's in those woods!" the cowardly Vern warns, recalling *Oz*'s Cowardly Lion and the foursome's traversing the dark forest. Like the unconscious it represents, the water is deeper than they imagined. While his three cohorts fight playfully in the water, Gordie does not share their playful mood. "Hey, where do you think you're going, Lachance?" Chris calls out as the three "pile on" the reluctant Gordie, holding him in a "sleeper hold," from which "nobody gets out." The "pile on" is abruptly stopped with the discovery of leeches, life-sucking creatures from the dark water.

The baptism the four receive is a strange and terrifying one, especially the one experienced by Gordie. The blood on his penis suggests a circumcision or, worse yet, castration. No wonder he faints. Coming from the dark water, this genital mutilation conjures his unconscious fear of castration by the ogre father. The cinematography of Gordie's symbolic death by fainting and waking up, his death and rebirth, underscores his dissociation from the group. Having endured this initiation, having been wounded at the root of his budding masculinity, Gordie, who was thought to be dead (at least by Vern), is reborn a "man." The change in him is mirrored by Vern's standing up to Teddy, the "four-eyed psycho," which anticipates Gordie's standing up to Ace, a much bigger psycho. It is further revealed when he repeatedly shouts at his friends to "stop" their juvenile bickering and declares in no uncertain terms, "I'm not going back!" As in indigenous rites of passage, once his manhood is physically marked, once blood is drawn, he cannot go back to mother. ("What are you, his mother?" Teddy asks Chris when he suggests, "Maybe we should take Gordie back.") Having been initiated into manhood, Gordie heeds the *progressive* voice of the well-intentioned grocer rather than the *regressive* voice of the junkman to "come back," back to the dependence associated with the mother. "At the time I didn't know why I needed to see that body so badly. Even if no one had followed me, I would have gone on alone."

Determined as he is, Gordie does not take into account the appearance of Ace, the dragon who guards the treasure, who earlier had demonstrated his malevolence by taking the good luck Yankees cap Denny had given him. But as shown in the fourth and last time we see Ace and his gang of hoodlums, they are heading in the same direction. They too want to claim the body. As the shadowy side of the foursome, their "rite of passage" into manhood is an *outer* one, a pseudo rite of bravado and violence, revealed primarily in Ace's show-down with the anonymous truck, symbol of masculinity.

When Vern finds the body, the four are in for the shock of their young lives. "None of us could breathe," Gordie tells us, as we *see* how each boy looks at the body. The camera lingers on Gordie, focusing on him as it did when Vern first mentioned the dead body. Hearing about it is one thing; seeing it flesh and bone is another. "The kid wasn't sick. The kid wasn't sleeping. The kid was dead." This is what Denny must have looked like. "Why did *you* have to die?" Gordie turns to his dead brother. "It should have been me"—he repeats the accusing words of the introjected father, finally saying out loud what he could only say unconsciously in his dream. "Don't say that"—Chris stands by him. But this is precisely what Gordie feels. "I'm no good. My dad said it, I'm no good." Serving as both father confessor and his brother's keeper, Chris's words bring Gordie to the heart of the pain he harbors but cannot fully express. "He doesn't know you," Chris tells Gordie, as if saying, it's not *you*, it's your father. You're not invisible; he is blind! He doesn't *see* you! "He hates me." Gordie can finally say what hurts him most deeply, confronting the ogre side of his father. "He hates me. My dad hates me. He hates me, oh God." His saying it unleashes the pain buried deep inside.

"You gonna be a great writer someday, Gordie," Chris says, trying to bring him out of his mood much as Denny had changed the subject around the din-ner table by praising his writing. His adding, "You might even write about us guys if you ever get hard up for material," is precisely what Gordie does. Only, as irony would have it, it comes on the occasion of Chris's death. "Guess I'd have to be really hard up, huh?"; for once Gordie does not reject his writing. Having confronted the pain of his father's anger and hate, having allowed him-self to grieve for Denny, he can come to accept himself as a writer, the individ-ual he is destined to become

This brief moment of *at-one-ment* comes to an abrupt end with the appearance of Ace and company. In typical western fashion, what had started with Ace's taking Gordie's Yankee cap is about to become a showdown of life and death. Ace seems determined as he was in the showdown with the oncoming truck. But so are Chris and Gordie. Having "earned" it, the once "girls" are girls no more. "You're gonna have to kill me, Ace." Chris confronts the black-dressed villain like one of his western heroes. Where in their initial confrontation, before setting out on their journey, Gordie only protested halfheartedly from the sideline, now he wields the object with the power to determine the outcome of the showdown. To Ace's question, "Are you going to shoot us all?" he replies, "No Ace, just you." And Ace, who needs the gang to support his bravado, backs off. On his own, confronted with the adamant Gordie, the formerly fearless Ace backs down. As in the TV westerns, the showdown with Ace is with "the feared and hated father figure." In comparing Gordie to his brother ("You must have at least some your brother's good sense"), Ace even recalls his father. The two embody the dragon that tries to prevent Gordie from obtaining the object of his quest. As such, his archrival's acknowledging his coming of age ("This is *big* time, baby") is the next best thing to having his father's acknowledgment. What was initiated by Gordie's genital mutilation now comes into full fruition when he refers to his "fat one" as the "biggest one in four counties." As Ray Raphael points out in the aptly titled book *The Men from the Boys*, along with Gordie's genital wound, the tattooing that the boys of Ace's gang inflict on one another, or even Teddy's mutilated ear, are all attempts to separate the men from the boys.

> Genital mutilations often constitute an important part of rite of passage precisely because they produce lasting and visible results. For non–literate people they function as diplomas, marks of distinction that signify that youths have in fact gone through the required ordeals. Of course, any form of scarification — tattoos, the raising of permanent welts, the cutting of ear lobes— will likewise function as a diploma, and in fact these are frequently used. But genital operations tend to have a special force, for they mark an organ integrally linked with the sexual status that youths are about to assume.[8]

Like a true hero, Gordie does not allow his bigness, his momentary "inflation," go to his head. Having made the descent to the netherworld of his deepest feelings, having come to terms with his brother's death and his introjected father, Gordie has grown enough to understand that claiming the body does not make them heroes.

Return

"We headed home" — Gordie's voiceover announces their return. "And although many thoughts raced through our minds, we barely spoke. We walked through the night and made it back to Castle Rock a little past five o'clock on Sunday morning, the day before Labor Day." Labor Day, of course, marks the end of summer vacation and the beginning of school. Considering what the four have undergone, and the solemn mood of their return, it also marks the end of childhood and the beginning of adolescence, particularly for Gordie and Chris. Gordie's clinching line, "We'd only been gone two days, but somehow the town seemed different, smaller," recalls what Mark Twain had said about his relationship with his father: "When I was a boy of fourteen, my father was so ignorant I could hardly stand to have the old man around. But when I got to be twenty-one, I was astonished at how much he had learned in seven years."

In the reverse order of their appearance, and their personal investment (suggested by how much money each brought with him), Vern is the first to part with the group. To show what the journey means to him, what he "earned," he finds a penny. Teddy does not fare much better. "Oh guys, I better get home before my mom puts me out on the ten *most wanted* list"—for once he talks about his mother rather than about his father. Perhaps being on mom's "most wanted list" is what he really wants. Heading home to his mother, he sings what they had sung when setting out on their journey, as if he is back where he started. Gordie's words, "As time went on we saw less and less of Teddy and Vern until eventually they became just two more faces in the halls," underscore their remaining behind, their not undergoing a significant rite of passage into adulthood. As he informs us, the two never got out of Castle Rock.

In contrast to the two, Gordie and Chris do get out. Standing with their backs to the treehouse of their childhood, their thoughts are of the future. "I'm never gonna get out of this town, am I, Gordie?" Chris shares with his best friend what most troubles him, their roles now completely reversed. Having made the descent to the psychic underworld and back, Gordie has become the fatherly figure. "You can do anything you want, man," he assures Chris, much as George McFly told Marty and Glinda assured Dorothy. The two-day journey has given Chris the means to "get out." "I'll see you," Gordie says. "Not if I see you first," Chris replies before he literally disappears on the screen, before he is rendered invisible, a mere *shade* in the netherworld.

With the vanishing of Chris, we see the computer screen on which Gordie types the closing words of the story he has been telling (writing), summing up this crucial (transitional) period in his life. "Although I hadn't seen him in more than ten years, I know I'll *miss* him forever." Using the same words he used when telling Chris about his missing his dead brother sums up what *Stand by Me* is all about. Only then do we see the writer Gordie has become. And to top things off, before the very last sentence of the story and movie, when his son and friend (another pair of childhood friends) enter the room, we see the father Gordie has become. His son's telling his friend, "My *dad*'s weird. He gets like that when he's *writing*," recalls Gordie's initial question about himself ("Am I weird?") in the journey he undertook when he was his son's age. Gordie's smile on hearing his son suggests that he has accepted his "weirdness," the part that his brother and Chris encouraged and that his father rejected. From what is shown, he is open enough to allow his son to speak his mind in his presence. Looking at the screen, at us, Gordie puts the finishing touch to his story. "I never had any friends later on like the ones I had when I was twelve. Jesus, does anyone?"

Part II

⊶⊷

GO WEST, YOUNG MAN, GO WEST

Do not lounge in the cities! There is room and health in the country, away from the crowds of idlers and imbeciles. Go west, before you are fitted for no life but that of the factory.

— *Horace Greeley,* New York Tribune

Starting with Horace Greeley by way of Mae West and the Marx Brothers all the way to the Village People, Americans have been urged to go west for over a hundred years. The West presented an alternative to a life of the factory and the crowded city. It represented the Promised Land, the frontier where life began anew and dreams came true. The real West, of course, was never what it was made out to be. It was always more legendary than real.

> Certainly the West was wild, but even at its wildest, the actual events could not possibly have included the many stories of glory and suffering, heroism and savagery, love and sacrifice, that the western myth has produced. Yet somehow, the historical reality of the West provided fertile soil for the growth and development of myth. The result has been one of the richest narrative traditions of modern times.[1]

Much like the mythical nature of the West, the accepted fact that Horace Greeley coined the famous phrase "Go west, young man, go west," is closer to myth than to historical reality. In truth, another newspaperman, John Soule, was the first to pen this advice in the Indiana *Terre Haute Express*, in 1851, eight years before Greeley. However, it was Greeley, as founder of *The New York Tribune*, who gave it wide circulation. He is even said to have requested this *counsel*, which had become associated with him, on his epitaph. Like this myth, to this day both the West and the western represent a mythical world. And it is largely this mythological element that makes the western so special. It gives it a pattern of human experience easily recognized and understood. Moreover, and perhaps even more than representing the mythological landscape, the West reflects the realm of the unconscious. As Jane Tompkins notes in *West of Everything*, subtitled, *The Inner Life of Westerns*, "Westerns play, first and last, to a Wild West of the psyche."[2]

The two cinematic "westerns" that open and close this section, Howard Hawks' *Red River* and Alfred Hitchcock's *North by Northwest*, are classic cases of the "West of the psyche." Together with John Ford, the two were masters at conveying the inner (unconscious) journey through images and metaphors. Ford and Hawks downplayed these inputs in their films, but Hitchcock was quite forthcoming and articulate about his intentions (particularly in Truffaut's extended interview, *Hitchcock/Truffaut*). Perhaps what best typifies these three filmmakers is their remarkable ability to convey two simultaneous stories in an unobtrusive style — the outer adventure and the psychological journey. For Hitchcock the psychological journey is invariably a symbolic account of the hero dealing with his dark side, the side known as the *double* or the *shadow*. This shadow was not unfamiliar to Ford and Hawks. In two of Hollywood's best westerns, Ford's *The Searchers* and Hawks' *Red River*, both starring John Wayne, the two filmmakers use the backdrop of the West to portray the hero's dealing with his double with no less craftsmanship. For Ethan Edwards in Ford's western the double is the Indian chief Scar; for Tom Dunson in *Red River*, his other side is his adopted son, Matt Garth. Though both westerns are about the father-son relationship, *The Searchers*, which focuses on Ethan Edwards' journey to fatherhood, is covered in the book's last section, "Becoming a Father."

North by Northwest is not a western, but the hero does go west. Besides, who could resist a Hitchcock movie in which the hero comes to grips with the father? And doubly because most of his movies, particularly the later ones of the '50s and '60s, are about the protagonist dealing with the mother. As in all of his masterpieces of those years, *Northwest's* suspense plot is mostly what Hitchcock called the *MacGuffin*, the diversionary object that superficially drives the plot but ultimately has little to do with what really interested Hitchcock — the hero's psychological transformation. Leave it to Hitchcock to make a movie about the hero's dealing with the father without one reference to his father.

Sandwiched between *Red River* and *North by Northwest*, *City Slickers* is no less about the father-son relationship. The movie may be tagged *light entertainment* (which was also what some critics called *Northwest* when it first came out), but it is not without its depth and subtlety, not without its psychological authenticity. Likewise, the father-son relationship may not be as obvious as in Hawks' western, but it accompanies the movie from start to finish. The movie, obviously, is a retelling of *Red River*, like and unlike the original. As this clever and entertaining movie shows, times may have changed, but the mythical West and the pattern of the mythic journey have remained intact. Using them to convey the hero's psychological transformation, *City Slickers* is just as much about the "West of the psyche" as *Red River* and *North by Northwest*.

While in *Red River* and *City Slickers* the heroes drive cattle, in *North by Northwest*, given the director's famous saying that actors should be treated like cattle, Hitchcock is doing the driving. In venturing out West, all three heroes undergo a psychological transformation. They all leave their mothers behind and enter the realm of the father, where they encounter and come to terms with the introjected father, the dragon wanted dead or alive, invariably personified by a savage Indian or the villain with the black hat. As these very different filmmyths demonstrate, dealing with the dragon is what going West is all about.

Chapter 4

Red River
Holdfast and Drawfast

For the mythological hero is the champion not of things become but of things becoming; the dragon to be slain by him is precisely the monster of the status quo: Holdfast, the keeper of the past.

— Joseph Campbell, *The Hero with a Thousand Faces*

Masculine Inflation

Typical of Howard Hawks' better movies, there is much more to *Red River* than a well-told story of a cattle drive "that's never been done before." If anything, Hawks' first western (1948) is a story of a cattle drive that's never been *told* before. It tells the story of Tom Dunson, a self-centered man who leaves the woman he loves to raise "more cattle than a man could gather elsewhere in two lifetimes." But in achieving his dream, Dunson bites off more than he can chew. With all these cattle and no market to sell them to, he is broke. His only feasible option is to drive the herd a thousand miles to market. In the course of this trek, which takes up most of the movie, Dunson is "driven" to confront and work out his strained relationship with his adopted son, Matthew Garth. This father-son relationship is the driving force behind the movie. Using the mythical landscape of the West, Hawks explores this relationship by retelling several mythic tales that reveal how the father becomes a dragon and how the son a dragon slayer.

The myth that the movie about "a man with a bull and a boy with a cow" first brings to mind is the myth of Theseus and the Minotaur. Like Minos, struggling with his brothers for the throne of Crete, who promises Poseidon to sacrifice the white bull he brought forth but sacrifices another one instead, Dunson promises to call for Fen, his other half, but ends up sacrificing her for his dream of glory. Just as keeping the bull begets the Minotaur, in denying the feminine element that Fen represents, Dunson becomes more and more of a monster, half-man, half-bull. He even refers to himself as a bull when he says, "I'm not going to take it haunch-backed like the rest around here." Dunson's sidekick and voice of reason, Groot Nadine, all but calls him "bullheaded" when he says, "He's a mighty set man when his mind's made up. Mind he don't stomp on you on the way out." And if Dunson is the movie's Minos turned Minotaur, it stands to reason that Matt is its Theseus, the slayer of the monster. Tess, whose yarn of words leads the two out of their labyrinthine relationship, is Ariadne.

Like Theseus arriving in his father's Athens as a young man and hearing about the Minotaur, Matt, after being away for some time (in the army), returns home to find Dunson broke. The seven graves Groot mentions, the seven lives sacrificed for Dunson's inflated ambition, may even allude to the seven Athenian youths who had to be sacrificed to the Minotaur. Dunson's recognizing the bracelet and the gun he gave Matt when he lights his cigarette ("That's a pretty nice gun you're scratching those matches on"), recalls King Aegeus recognizing the sword he left Theseus when he appears before him in Athens. Somewhat like Minos not letting go of the white bull, Dunson wants all the cattle rounded up and branded, disregarding Matt's reminder that some of them belong to other ranchers. Matt's remark to Dunson, "You're gonna wind up branding every rump in the state of Texas except mine," and Dunson's threat to carry it out, however in jest, gives evidence to the monster he has become over the years.

Dunson's masculine expansion also brings to mind the myth of Priapus — as presented in James Wyly's *The Phallic Quest*, a book which draws on the myth of a man whose claim to fame was his uncommonly large sex organ. Describing Dunson to a T, particularly the despotism that results from his big-headedness, Wyly maintains that men generally do not do anything to change their masculine inflation "while able to maintain it. Rather, they seem to break down when the maintenance of a previous inflated state has become impossible for one reason or another."[1] Of course, the western's counterpart to the size of the phallus is the quickness by which one draws the gun.

That the gun in *Red River* is a phallic extension, a sex-shooter more than a six-shooter, is suggested by the sexual overtones in the first exchange between Dunson and the grown Matt. "How's your gun arm?" Dunson asks, and Matt replies, "I've been using it a lot in the last few years." The gun's sexual significance is further suggested by the exchange between Matt and Cherry Valance. "It's a good-looking gun you were about to use back there. Can I see it?" Cherry turns to Matt. "Maybe you'd like to see mine." He offers Matt his black-handled gun after Matt gives him his white-handled. As the color of the handles suggest, Cherry is Matt's darker voice, his alter ego, who drives him to challenge Dunson by his ability to draw the gun.

The phallus is also suggested by Groot when he throws a knife at the sugar-stealing Bunk, warning him, "I could take the end of your nose off just as easy." As this sugar stealing ultimately initiates the stampede and Matt's first real confrontation with Dunson, his words can be taken as a warning what can happen to a son when he takes what belongs to the father, as in the myth of Oedipus.

All considered, perhaps the myth that best depicts *Red River*'s rivalry between Dunson and Matt is the myth of Holdfast, "representative of the set-fast," and the young hero, "the carrier of the changing,"[2] which Joseph Campbell refers to several times in *The Hero with a Thousand Faces*. Dunson is not only like the mythological Holdfast, "the monster of the status quo," Matt is the monster slayer, or, if you will, Drawfast. Strangely enough, the movie opens with the wagonmaster saying to one of the men, "What's wrong, Campbell? We got three hours yet before we stop." Moreover, it is Campbell, in his sole appearance and with his one and only line in the movie ("Dunson here says he's leaving the train"), who introduces Dunson in both his name and his Hold-fastness. This is not to suggest that Hawks had Campbell's Holdfast in mind, but rather that his western has a mythical dimension that allows for many interpretations, that the movie is a filmmyth.

Nevertheless, the rivalry between the mythical *Holdfast* and the metaphoric *Drawfast* seems to best encapsulate the movie's father-son rivalry, a rivalry decided by the draw of the gun. It is not for nothing that Dunson is first introduced in connection with his ability to use the gun when, following Campbell's announcing that "he's leaving the train," the wagonmaster turns to him. "You're too good a gun for me to let you leave the train now," to which Dunson replies in typical arrogance, "I'm too good a gun for you to argue with." The gun is also prominent in the father and son's first encounter, when the young Matt Garth, after being slapped to his senses by Dunson, draws on him his small gun. "I wouldn't do that again," the boy Matt warns Dunson. But Dunson does it again, slapping Matt once more and taking away his gun. It is Dunson's way of grooming Matt to become Drawfast.

In Dunson's second lesson to the young Matt, which demonstrates how a man uses a gun to get what he wants, the father gives the son the dead man's gun, replacing the small one he drew on him in the previous scene. "How'd you know when he was gonna draw?" the young Matt asks Dunson, showing his desire to learn how to become Drawfast. "By watchin' his eyes. Remember that," Dunson instructs him. "I will," Matt assures him. From this point on, the only good thing the grown Matt says about Dunson in the whole movie is his telling Cherry that he is a "handful by himself" and is good with a gun. "He taught me," Matt adds, his words coming right after he outdraws Dunson in a simulated drawing contest. "You're faster about a lot of things," Dunson inadvertently acknowledges Matt's Drawfastness when he asks him to draw a map of the drive and Matt beats him to the draw by already drawing one.

Heading South

Before Dunson leaves the community of the wagon train, heading south, the wagonmaster sounds a warning: "You know this is Indian country. You might walk into trouble." This is the voice of reason, the Logos, warning the hero about the unknown realm of the unconscious. Dunson may be an honorable man, who would stay on had he signed on, but he is also self-centered and single-minded. In parting from the wagon train, Dunson also parts ways with Fen, the feminine element missing in his masculine-inflated life. His unyielding masculinity, his *Holdfastness,* is demonstrated by his turning a deaf ear to her pleading, even when she tells him that it is more for his sake than hers: "You'll need a woman. You need what a woman can give you to do what you have to do. Oh, listen to me, Tom. Listen with your head and your heart too. The sun only shines half the time, Tom. The other half is night." As her words bear out, "Oh, change your mind, Tom," Dunson's *Holdfastness* does not let the love of a woman *change* his "made up" mind. Her last attempt to change his single-mindedness, "Just once in your life change your mind," only comes at the behest of another woman, Fen's replacement. Until then, Dunson becomes more and more of a "Holdfast, the keeper of the past."

Before parting from Fen, Dunson's symbolic act of giving her his mother's two-headed snake bracelet, a gesture made on the spur of the moment, turns out to be a failed attempt at transferring his allegiance (love) from his mother to another woman. It returns at night, "the other half," worn by an Indian brave who jumps Dunson with a raised knife, recalling Fen's last words, "My knees feel like, like they have knives in them." The fact that the nocturnal fight is fought in water, in the Red River, suggests that it is a clash of two primeval (unconscious) forces, the two halves. Finding the bracelet on the Indian's wrist assures Dunson of Fen's death, but it also reminds him of the hollowness of his gesture in giving it. As suggested by the bracelet's "return to sender," Dunson is not ready to let go of his mother and have her replaced by another woman. By his own words, where he is heading is "too much for a woman." Or else, considering the implied Oedipal tie to his mother, sharing his life with another woman is too much for Dunson. As Jane Tompkins points out in her book, *West of Everything,* denying the feminine and the domestic has its roots in the hero's past.

> Historically, I've argued, the western is a reaction against a female-dominated tradition of popular culture; it buries its origins by excluding everything domestic from its worldview. This phenomenon has a psychological parallel. The form heroism takes in the western can best be understood by seeing it as a reaction to something else: the hero's invisible past, the time in his life when he was an infant in his mother's arms.[3]

Before Dunson comes to accept the feminine other half, two more people wear his mother's two-headed bracelet. The first one to wear it is Matt, who appears the morning after Dunson finds the bracelet on the Indian. Matt's towing a cow, which replaces the two cows Dunson lost in the Indians' attack, suggests that he is the return of the rejected (denied) feminine. Dunson himself points it out by deriding Matt as "soft." The fact that there is never any mention of Matt's parents adds to his being a mythical (unconscious) force that emerges from nowhere into Holdfast's life. "Where did he come from?" Dunson asks. And Joseph Campbell answers, "From obscurity the hero emerges, but the enemy is great and conspicuous in the seat of power; he is enemy, dragon, tyrant, because he turns to his own advantage the authority of his position."[4]

Unlike Fen, who Matt comes to replace, Dunson has no choice but to take him along. "He'll do," he tells Groot, as the two are shown sharing the frame, smiling like proud parents. Traveling "ever southward," the new family soon comes to another river, the Rio Grande, where Dunson speaks as if they have reached the Promised Land. "This is where we start growing good beef. Everything a man could want. Good water and grass. And plenty of it." But as is soon revealed, there is trouble in the land of milk and money. When Dunson, after branding his bull with a "D," wants to brand Matt's cow, we get a glimpse of the son's future rebellion, anticipating the eventual showdown between the two. "I don't see any M on that brand," Matt shoots back. "I'll put an M when you earned it," Dunson assures Matt, neither of them knowing what it entails.

The Drive Up North

Fourteen years go by, but Dunson, shown the same way he was last shown, does not change. The only change is his wearing a black hat, suggesting that over the years he has become a darker Holdfast. Though circumstances have changed, he and Matt still have conflicting views about branding the cows. Matt wanting to "let 'em go" while Dunson orders him to "*hold* it!" sums up the conflict between Holdfast and Drawfast. Because Marty acquiesces to Dunson's authority, at the start of the drive up north the two are still allies, as underscored by their sharing the frame while smoking together. When Dunson comments as the two watch the herd start out, "Fourteen years of hard work. And they say we can't make the drive." Matt, the obedient son, tells him the *others* could be wrong, echoing Fen's warning that he is "wrong" about not taking her with him. Later in the drive, Matt tells Dunson that *he* is wrong, even though he already feels that Dunson is wrong by sticking to his plan to take the drive "to Missouri." But just as he did not listen to Fen, Dunson does not listen to Matt's "long way," where there is life-renewing "good water" all the way.

Much as Fen pleaded with Dunson to listen to his other half, the first one to goad Matt into asserting himself against Dunson is his other half, the fast-drawing Cherry. His saying he heard there is a railroad in Abilene starts Matt thinking of another route than Dunson's. But only after three weeks on the trail, as "the days became longer, sleep was at a premium, hard work became harder and Dunson became a tyrant," does Matt start going against him by suggesting that they stop at a waterhole, where the worn-out men may be refreshed and rejuvenated. "I'll do the thinking," Dunson says, rejecting Marty's suggestion. But while Matt and the other men do not do anything about Dunson's growing tyranny, the cattle are quick to show their discontent by breaking out in a rampant stampede. As Jane Tompkins notes about *Red River*, "The cattle are the film's unconscious."[5] As such, this outbreak of the unconscious, which transpires at night, initiates the first critical incident of revolt against Dunson. The drive that starts in the South and heads up North, after all, is the unconscious coming to the surface, becoming increasingly conscious.

Push comes to shove when Dunson is about to shoot the man-boy who started the stampede, who would rather die by the gun than allow Dunson to whip him (as a father would a child). What was merely acted out in the drawing contest between Matt and Dunson now becomes reality, as Matt outdraws Dunson to wound the sugar-stealing Bunk so that Dunson won't shoot him dead. Bunk's words to the whip-wielding Dunson, "Don't do it, don't do it," must surely remind Marty of his own words at their first encounter ("I wouldn't do it"). Dunson's calling Bunk a "kid" reinforces this point. "You'd have shot him right between the eyes," Matt tells Dunson afterwards. Following the confrontation, the two are no longer shown sharing a cigarette.

The interchanging of day and night scenes, which becomes more obvious as the drive moves on, adds to the movie's growing tension between Holdfast and Drawfast. The tension is finally released when a lone "messenger" brings bad news of what lies ahead beyond the threshold of the Red River. "Everything went fine till we crossed the big Red." Having experienced the Indians' massacre first hand, not unlike the young Matt, the "messenger" suggests that they take an alternate route to Abilene, Kansas, where he heard there is a railroad, the same railroad mentioned by Cherry. "We should never have come that way," the "messenger" warns, recalling the wagonmaster. "We should have turned north at the big Red."

Once again, despite the warning, Dunson holds fast to his original route. Growing more obstinate, he aims to finish what he started, no matter what. The messenger turning down Dunson's invitation to join the drive ("No, I've had enough") spurs on three men, all wearing black hats, who had "enough" of Dunson's bullheadedness. One of the three men's "I'm heading south" recalls Dunson's words to the wagonmaster; when the other two speak their mind, suddenly Dunson finds himself in the place of the wagonmaster. "You agreed to finish this drive. I'm gonna *hold* you to it."

As always, the gun settles this second act of rebellion. Cherry, Matt and Dunson outshoot the three "quitters," whose only crime is deciding to quit "a drive we'll never finish," to go against the tyrant Holdfast. The violent crushing of the insurrection only increases the already growing discontent among the men. Dunson, who is repeatedly shown with a liquor bottle, his last source of comfort, is shown isolated from the men. Even his two last allies, Groot and Matt, are growing uneasy with his leadership. Matt, taking a cue from the *quitters'* expressed disgruntlement, is the first to express his displeasure. Standing above a (sitting) wounded Dunson, seeming to overpower him physically and morally, he speaks his mind as never before. "I'll take your orders about work, but not about what to think." As he leaves, Matt sends another message of defiance when he kicks Dunson's liquor bottle. Groot, too, uses the liquor bottle to make his point, taking pleasure in pouring the stinging "cleanser" on Dunson's wounded leg.

The closer they get to the Red River, where they first came together, the further Dunson and Matt drift apart. More than not wanting to be reminded that Dunson is "getting worse every day," Matt does not want to be reminded that he is the only one who could stand up to him. He is ambivalent about his feelings for Dunson as about his role as the "emerging hero."

The Son's Rebellion

Right before Matt emerges as hero, before the son's rebellion, the three family members are shown together by themselves one last time. In this symbolic family portrait, Dunson (hatless) is sitting between Matt and Groot, holding a familiar liquor bottle. While Groot kneels, still attending to his master's needs, Matt is shown standing above the sitting Dunson, anticipating his standing up to the father who taught him all he knows. The fact that Dunson holds his liquor bottle while Matt holds a cigarette in his mouth underscores their drifting apart from their former days of sharing cigarettes. What Matt thinks but is unwilling to carry out is expressed by what Teeler and Laredo say to Dunson, who is holding court for the defectors (brought back by Cherry). "You're crazy. You've been drinkin' and you ain't been sleepin'. If you ain't crazy, you're a skin close to it.... You wanna get this herd to market. Well, so do all of us. There's a good way to Abilene, but you won't listen to that. No. You want to drive to Missouri when you got the high, low, and jack against ya."

Distancing himself from Teeler's harsh words, Matt is shown walking away from the confrontation. But he cannot ignore Teeler's incisive words: "This herd don't belong to you. It belongs to every poor hopin' and prayin' cattleman in the whole wide state. I shouldn't have run away. I should've stayed and put a bullet in ya. I signed a pledge, sure, but you ain't the man I signed with."

No longer able to hold back his growing discontent, Matt returns to the argument. Dunson's announcing his intention to hang the quitters is the last straw. "No," Matt is heard saying off-screen. "No, you're not." When Dunson wants to know who is going to stop him, Matt announces in no uncertain terms, "I will!" echoing Dunson's opening words ("I am"). Matt's decision to stop Dunson is a big release of much pent-up (held fast) frustration and anger.

Considering Dunson's state, his assuming leadership is what the men of the drive have hoped for and expected for quite some time. As the men move away from Matt to make room for the showdown, he stands alone in the frame. When Dunson's hand seems to go for his gun, it is Cherry, Matt's brash alter ego, who carries out what he cannot. Dunson tries to draw but is too wounded to do so, his days of having his way with the draw of the gun having come back to haunt him.

As the new leader, Matt's response to Teeler's question (regarding who is leading the drive to Abilene) is "I am!"—Dunson's opening words of the movie. But more than that, the drive northwards retraces Dunson's journey south. It is his return and undoing of the past, the same past that he holds fast to so desperately. Matt's parting words, "If there's any chance at all, we'll get your herd to Abilene," recall Dunson's parting from Fen; Dunson warns Matt as Fen had warned him. "Cherry was right. You're soft. You should've let him kill me, 'cause I'll turn around and I'll be thee. I'll kill you, Matt. I'm gonna kill you. I'll catch up with you! I don't know when, but I'll catch up. Every time you turn around, expect to see me. 'Cause one time you'll turn around and I'll be there. I'll kill you, Matt."

More than fearing Dunson's promised revenge, Matt feels guilty for going against him, for deposing the father. These feelings come to the surface at night, when he is not busy with the practical matters of leading the drive. Matt is jumpy, expecting Dunson with each sound or motion, not unlike the Indian who attacked Dunson at night. Advising "Get yourself some sleep, Matt," Groot repeats what he told Dunson when he was in charge. "I'd like to," Matt replies. As he does so many times in the course of the movie, Groot sums up the situation, this time echoing Fen's words to Dunson. "Funny what the night does to a man. You're all right during the day." Or, to paraphrase Fen's linking the night with the feminine, Funny what a woman does to a man. You're all right with men. After all, only on the northern part of the Red River are there women.

The Other Half

The feminine, the other half that Dunson left behind, returns under Matt's leadership when Buster, sent to scout ahead with Cherry, is shown galloping excitedly on his horse, yelling, "Women! Women and coffee!" His good news is a stark change from what the men have encountered so far. In complete contrast to Dunson, Matt, seeing that the men do not want to stay behind with the herd, decides, "We're going together and taking the herd with us. Two days, we'll all have a cup of coffee." Significantly, where Buster opens with "women," Matt only talks about coffee. Apparently, he has not known a woman. But he is beginning to want to, as suggested by his brief exchange with Buster, who has become his closest ally. That he is to Matt what Groot was to Dunson is suggested by his "Why do they always yell for?" which echoes Groot's question about the first Indian attack, "Why do Indians always want to be burning up good wagons?" In fact, the two attacks mirror one another. Where Dunson, after leaving the wagon train to start a herd, could not save the only woman he loved, Matt is willing to risk losing the herd in order to save the women; where Dunson lost a woman in the first attack, Matt finds a woman in the present one. What's more, this woman, Tess, does what Dunson could not accept in Fen — fighting off Indians.

The arrow that hits Tess seems to come from the bow of Cupid more than that of an Indian. She is not so much wounded as smitten. Matt's initial contact with Tess is his pulling out the poisonous arrow and sucking out the poison with his mouth, redeeming the fallen woman whose profession is never called by name. She falls for Matt as Fen had surely fallen for Dunson. Only this time Matt is much softer than the tough Dunson. This softer side of Matt is most apparent in the two's nocturnal meeting, the same "other half" that Fen pointed out to Dunson. "You can talk to me. I'm right here. It would help. Oh please, you can tell me to mind my own business if you'd like." Matt's reply, "I'd like it better than talking to a mirror," suggest that his exchange with Tess mirrors Dunson's attempt with Fen. But where the harder Dunson failed, the softer Matt succeeds. This nocturnal rendezvous with the woman, with the other half, is a necessary stage in the hero's journey, for both father and son.

> Woman, in the picture language of mythology, represents the totality of what can be known. The hero is the one who comes to know. As he progresses in the slow initiation which is life, the form of the goddess undergoes for him a series of transfigurations: she can never be greater than himself, though she can always promise more than he is yet capable of comprehending.... Woman is the guide to the sublime acme of sensuous adventure.[6]

Somewhat like a therapist, a "guide to the sublime," Tess brings Matt to talk about his feelings towards Dunson. In fact, just as Matt sucked the poison from her injured shoulder, she helps him and (mostly) Dunson to talk out the hard feelings that have poisoned their relationship. "You love him, don't you? He must love you. That wouldn't be hard," she says, kissing Matt on the lips.

A sudden rainstorm forces Matt and his men to continue their drive without delay, thus compelling him to leave Tess behind much as Dunson had left Fen. Only this time his decision is determined by outer circumstances. Unlike Dunson, Matt confers with Groot about the possibility of taking Tess with them.

Soon after Matt's departure, the other half of the father-son relationship arrives at the wagon train with his men. Unbeknownst to Dunson, in going north after Matt, he is retracing his journey down south. "I'll take care of Mr. Dunson," Tess says, offering her personal help when he and his men are invited to eat. She has much more in mind than merely feeding him. Continuing her role as a therapist, she truly takes care of Dunson, who is a much harder case than Matt. In the feminine chamber of her tent, Tess brings to the light of day the hidden (repressed) dark desires that have turned Dunson into a vengeful monster. "I believe it's your beef we are eating," she goads him. "Who told you that?" Dunson asks. "The man you promised to kill," Tess gets right to the point. But when Dunson wants to know if Matt also told her that, she soothes him, as if putting him under a spell. "You're tired, aren't you? Tired, hungry and just a little bit irritable. You'll feel better after you eat. We'll talk then."

As with Matt before him, Tess gets Dunson to talk — and probably as he has never talked before in his life. Jane Tompkins writes about this kind of talking in *West of Everything*, quoting from Peter Schwenger's "Phallic Critiques": "It is by talking that one opens up to another person and becomes vulnerable. It is by putting words to an emotion that it becomes feminized."[7] This "feminizing" recalls the "other half" that Fen told Dunson about when reminding him, "You need what a woman can give you to do what you have to do." The first woman Dunson is coupled with since Fen tried to "feminize" him, Tess guides him to become a bit more like the "soft" Matt. Like a skilled therapist, who knows that "the psyche abhors the hubris of an exclusively masculine adaptation,"[8] she guides Dunson to the feelings he is holding inside. Using the silver bracelet given to her by Matt, an object laden with meaning, the dark and black-dressed Tess gets him in touch with the other half, the feminine "night" he suppresses and projects on Matt, by reviving his tormented past with Fen. "I wanted to go with him, but he had work to do. He had to get your cattle to market. Said I wasn't strong enough to go and nothing I could do or say to make him change his mind. But I wanted to go with him. I wanted him so much that...." "That you felt like you had knives stickin' in you," Dunson completes her sentence. "I suppose other people have felt that way before," Tess says, leading Dunson to admit, "They have."

Tess's power of persuasion is emphasized by her always being photographed above Dunson, whether she is standing or sitting. Her role as mediator is built into her name, Tess Millay — the two initials of Tom and Matt. "Why do you want to kill him?" she asks, forcing Dunson to take stock of his feelings towards Matt. When Dunson orders her to "stand up!" so that he can have a look at her as if she is a prized cow, she snaps back, "Don't tell me what to do," echoing Matt's words about not telling him what to think. Liking what he sees in the woman who wears his mother's bracelet, Dunson offers her *half* of everything he owns if she bears him a son, which underscores her being Fen's replacement. And even though Tess agrees to his unrealistic proposal, providing he gives up his vow to get even with Matt, an even more unrealistic proposal, she is the one who gets him in touch with his other half, forcing him to recognize, to remember, that her situation with Matt is identical to his with Fen. Tess catches Dunson off guard with "When did you fall in love with her? The girl you told me about. The one you left, walked out on.... You knew how I felt when he left me. She must have felt the same way when you left her. That's right, isn't it? Or can't you remember?" Her *telling* Dunson that she "wants to go with him" recalls Fen *asking* him to "take me with you," pointing to their likeness but also underscoring the difference between the two women. Whereas the light-dressed Fen was passive and compliant, accepting Dunson's made-up mind that results in her death, the dark-dressed Tess is an active initiator, "loosening" (*softening*) Holdfast, bringing Dunson to change his mind, and not only about her going with him.

The Showdown

Significantly enough, once Dunson accepts the feminine element, Matt and his men see the railroad. Having brought the cattle to market, the only remaining problem is Dunson's compulsion for revenge. Millville, the cattle trader and benevolent father, who is willing to buy all their cattle at "top price," asks Matt if his bringing the herd to market will change Dunson's mind. Apparently he not only refers to the *drive* when talking about a time "in man's life when he has a right to yell at the moon ... when he finishes a job he had to be crazy to start." But before Matt and his woman can live happily ever after, he must face the tyrannical father in the inevitable showdown. He must slay the dragon.

> The motif of the difficult task as prerequisite to the bridal bed has spun the hero-deeds of all time and all the world. In stories of this pattern the parent is in the role of Holdfast; the hero's artful solution of the task amounts to a slaying of the dragon. The tests imposed are difficult beyond measure. They seem to represent an absolute refusal, on the part of the parent ogre, to permit life to its way; nevertheless, when a fit candidate appears, no task in the world is beyond his skill.[9]

The obligatory showdown comes up again when Matt enters his hotel room and finds Tess waiting. Seeing it is her, he puts his drawn gun back in his holster. As he goes to her he inadvertently bumps into the hanging kerosene lamp, causing its shadow to sway on the wall as if it has come to life, a reminder of Dunson's relentless pursuit.

> He hasn't changed his mind, Matthew. We saw the railroad and I thought, I thought it might make a difference, but it didn't. Nothing would. He's like something you can't move. Even I've gotten to believe it's got to happen — your meeting. I was gonna ask you to run but, no I'm not, I'm not. It wouldn't do any good. You're too much like him.

The lamp's shadow stops swaying only when Matt quiets Tess's incessant talking by putting a hand to her mouth. From all that was shown up to now, Matt does not lack the skill to outdraw Dunson. As Millville says to Cherry just before the showdown, "You know that young man isn't gonna use his gun, don't you?" It is going against the father that is *holding* Matt back.

But nothing seems to hold back Dunson, who is shown walking through the cattle herd towards Matt, the camera emphasizes his striding forward. Having twice taunted Matt about using the gun, Cherry finally puts his money where his mouth is by challenging Dunson, who draws first. He wounds Cherry, who is fast enough to wound Dunson in return. But Cherry is hardly an obstacle in Dunson's path. Despite his wounded side, the determined Dunson continues walking towards Matt like a raging bull charging towards a relaxed and confident "*Matt-ador*." Matt knows Dunson will never shoot someone he knows does not intend to shoot first. As Dunson had taught him, he can see it by looking in his eyes.

Frustrated by Matt's self-assured calmness and refusal to draw, and by his own sense of honor, which does not allow him to shoot a man in cold blood, let alone his son, Dunson throws his gun to the ground. This is one face-off that will not, and cannot, be settled by the gun. "You're soft! Won't anything make a man out of you?" He seizes Matt's gun from his holster and throws it away. "You once told me never to take your gun away," he says, recalling their first meeting, and slapping him as he did then.

After taking few more blows and insults, Matt starts fighting back, what he could not do in their first meeting, if only because of his size. Dunson is surprised but relieved by Matt's retaliation. Without the guns that settle conflicts from a shooting distance, the two are forced to physically grapple, the only way they can get close to each other. All Dunson and Matt need to take the final step of reconciliation is the help of a woman, the other half. Although some critics see the scene with Tess as a weak point in the movie, her appearance is in keeping with the Holdfast myth.

> The hegemony wrested from the enemy, the freedom won from the malice of the monster, the life energy released from the toils of the tyrant Holdfast — is symbolized as a woman. She is the maiden of the innumerable dragon slayings, the bride abducted from the jealous father.... She is the "other portion" of the hero himself.[10]

As the father and son brawl like two children, giving expression to the pent-up (held fast) emotions, a gunshot is heard off camera, recalling Matt's initial off-camera "No" to Dunson's plan to hang Teeler and Laredo. "Stop it! Stop it!" Tess puts an end to their exchange of blows, putting into words what they each feel for one another but cannot say. "You, Dunson, pretending you're gonna kill him. Why, it's the last thing in the world you"—(Dunson's moving stops her in mid-sentence). "And you, Matthew Garth, getting your face all beat up and all bloody. You oughta see how, you oughta see how silly you look.... What a fool I've been, expectin' trouble for days when, when anybody with half a mind would know you two love each other." Then, Tess turns to Dunson again, putting into words what was in the air for quite some time. "It took somebody else to shoot you. He wouldn't do it."

Tess now takes another approach to bring the two together: "Go ahead. I *changed my mind*. Go ahead. Beat each other crazy. Maybe it will put the sense in both of you." Tess points the gun in their direction, but then shoves it into a man's stomach, the same man who remarked earlier in the drive, "I don't like to see things go good or bad. I like 'em in between." By using a six-shooter with the same hand that wears the significant two-headed snake bracelet Dunson had given

Fen at the beginning of the movie, Tess combines the masculine gun and the feminine bracelet. She integrates the two *halves* that were first mentioned by Fen.

Significantly, the father and son's reconciliation is achieved without the traditional western icons of masculinity — the hat and the gun. "You'd better marry that girl, Matt," is Dunson's way of acknowledging Matt. In advising Matt that he'd "better marry" the woman who wears his mother's double-headed bracelet, Dunson successfully transfers his allegiance to his mother to another woman, what he failed to do with Fen, if only because he was not ready to do so. "Yeah, I think I"— Matt agrees, but then catches himself. "Hey, when are you gonna stop telling people what to do?" "Right now," says Dunson, smiling for the first time since they crossed back the Red River. Adopting a serious tone, he continues: "When we get back to the ranch, I want you to *change* the brand. It'll be like this," Dunson draws the Red River D in the sand, just as he had done 14 years before, adding the letter M on the other side. "Red River D ... and we'll add an M to it. You don't mind that, do you?"

"No," says Matt, all smiles.

"You've earned it," says Dunson, at peace with himself at last.

With these words the father, smiling back, finally accepts the son as an equal, acknowledging him as a man. He fulfills his original promise to *change* the brand rather than the other promise to kill Matt. The new brand he draws in the earth completes the original one-sided drawing, the *Holdfast* logo. Ironically, just as Matt has earned his father's respect by going against him, by standing up for what he believes is right, he shows his love by not using his gun against him. But then, Matt was never out to kill Dunson. He was out to slay the dragon, the inflated masculinity that turned Dunson into *Holdfast* and kept him from changing his mind and opening his heart.

Bearing in mind Dunson's opening and closing words in the movie, he has truly made a long and arduous journey. He has changed from the self-centered "I am" (and later "I am the law!") to the affirmation of the other half in "You've earned it." Like Matt, he too has "earned it." He has earned his readiness to accept the feminine element and balance the two halves that were missing in his one-sided life. Only then can the father and son attain at-one-ment. And if Dunson, in Campbell's words, is "Holdfast not because he keeps the past but because he keeps," then there is no better symbol for his letting go than the two-headed snake bracelet. The two heads in one bracelet suggest "at-one-ment," but the snake's habit of shedding its skin points to Dunson's shedding his Holdfast armor and to Matt shedding his Drawfast outfit. Having shed the masculine egos that kept them apart all these years, the hatless (and gunless) father and son come together as one, as symbolized by the closing picture of the "finished" double-lettered Red River brand, which replaces the double-headed bracelet that Dunson failed to give to Fen, now worn by her replacement. What started with Dunson's bull and Matt's cow is now replaced by the at-one-ment of father and son.

Chapter 5

City Slickers
Ride of Passage

You came out here city slickers! You're gonna go home cowboys!
— Clay Stone to the City Slickers (Father to Sons)

Red River *Revisited*

Of the seven men who signed for the cattle drive in *City Slickers,* it is the father of the group who brings up the drive in *Red River.* Considering he is there with his son suggests that the movie's cattle drive, as in the classic western it parodies and pays homage to, is the working-out of the father-son relationship. In bringing in the herd, like Matt before him, Mitch and his two buddies deal with both their real and introjected fathers. The movie is not only a '90s revisit to the western, and to *Red River* in particular, out West is where the city slickers become cowboys, where the sons of "absent fathers" become men. What the West comes to represent for *City Slickers'* three heroes is precisely how Jane Tompkins describes it in *West of Everything,* subtitled "The Inner Life of Westerns." It is "a place where those who had remained boys for reasons beyond their control could become men. Above all, it was a place for self-transformation, for a second chance."[1]

Though not in the same league with *Red River, City Slickers* nonetheless shares many things with Hawks' classic western. Mitch Robbins "loses" his wife much as Tom Dunson loses Fen. He adopts Norman just as Dunson adopts Matt. In contrast to Dunson envisaging a great future ("This is it. This is where we start growing good beef.... Everything a man could want"), Mitch describes a dismal future to his son's classmates. Where Dunson is broke economically, Mitch is broken in spirit; where in *Red River* fourteen years pass between the prologue and the main story, in *City Slickers* it is one year. And where Matt represents the softness Dunson rejects, Curly, "the toughest man" Mitch has ever seen, represents the toughness he so lacks. For Dunson and Mitch the drive is a do-or-die undertaking; for Matt and Mitch it is a rite of passage. As Mitch puts it to his two friends when they decide to drive the herd by themselves, "And you think that bringing in this herd will bring all the broken pieces of your life back together?"

In the best tradition of the western, and as in *Red River*, their "finishing what they had begun," which recalls Dunson's very words, does bring the broken pieces of their lives together. Just as Dunson reaches at-one-ment with Matt by the end of the drive, Mitch (a name that recalls Matt) starts as a son but ends as a father, and not only to Norman.

El Dragon

The ceremony of Pamplona's running of the bulls is much more than just another of Ed's crazy attempts to prove his manhood. It is a fitting exposition for the bigger rite of the cattle drive. In fact, the two rites function as mirrored images of one another. While in the Spanish ceremony the heroes are chased by male bulls, in the American West they drive the female cattle, the horde of men becoming a herd of cattle. The running of the bulls is a test of manhood; the cattle drive out West is a rite of passage to adulthood. As suggested by the opening, at this point in their lives the three city slickers are each running away from something. And as further suggested throughout the movie, especially after we hear each one tell about the best day of his life, the bull is associated with the father. It represents the Mino*taur*, the introjected father in the labyrinth of their psyche, the dragon that holds them captive in juvenility.

After a reveille of Spanish horns announces the commencing of the ceremony, the opening shots show a mass of people in red and white, hailing the embodiment of the dragon: "Toro, Toro, Toro." A human hand opens the solid wooden doors, setting the bulls free. This outbreak of brute force, not unlike the eruption of the unconscious, initiates the running of the bulls. But more so, it unleashes the dragon that the three city slickers, shown running for their lives (with Mitch in the middle), must slay. Even in this brief exposition, the three's individual reactions to the pursuing bulls are right in character. Mitch is disgusted, Ed is delighted, and Phil is terrified.

Mitch's "Whose idea was this anyway?" conveys his general "out of it" feeling. While almost everyone is dressed in the traditional white and red, Mitch wears red, white and blue, a shirt that reads New York and a Mets (metropolitan) baseball cap — the getup of a city slicker. Phil's "They're gaining on us" fits right in with his feeling of being pursued by his wife and her father, Mr. Levine, who embodies a Jewish dragon. He feels emasculated. "I'm telling you, they got me by the balls. She's got one, he's got the other," he remarks while watching the ranchers castrate a horse on the ranch in New Mexico. In this state, it is not surprising that he is hatless. Only Ed, who initiated the ordeal, feels at home. With his white and red attire, and a significant red beret, he is the only one of the three who enjoys what to him is an exhilarating moment. Unlike Mitch, who makes a habit of seeing the empty half of everything, Ed looks at the positive side of things. But that is because he does not look at the other half. His masculinity seems to be intact, but it needs an overhaul. As with all three, his problem is tied to his father.

Each of the three city slickers reacts differently to what is behind them and gaining fast. Phil's "He's after me!" continues his basic feeling of being pursued. Nevertheless, he manages to get out of the bull's way by latching on to an iron bar and hanging on for dear life. Ed, on the other hand, gets out of the bulls' way by jumping into a crowd of bystanders, laughing and savoring the moment. Only Mitch fails to escape the bull's wrath. "Stop following me!" he shouts to a pursuing bull, who has singled him out just as Curly does on the drive, as if he has a personal score to settle with him. In the spirit of the movie, the stab from behind is a reminder to catch the bull by the horns.

In the second part of the exposition, which reveals the trio's dynamics, once again Mitch is singled out. While the "el doctor" sewing up the bull's goring anticipates his standing behind the cow as midwife to Norman, Mitch rails at Ed, "You're a macho lunatic," then at Phil and himself for being "sheep." The "I told you so" he expects from his wife Barbara takes us to the third and last part of the exposition on the plane going home. Ed's encouraging words, "Maybe she won't notice" the bandaged behind, which are right in line with his always seeing the full half, prove wishful thinking. Barbara, not unlike a mother looking disapprovingly at what remains of his test of manhood, notices much more than Mitch's bulging behind. "Come on, it's not so bad," Mitch says, trying to downplay his condition. "I look like your mother."

At this point in his life, to Mitch, Barbara is more a mother than a wife. But this is nothing compared to Phil's butchy (if not bitchy) wife, from whom Phil runs away by "pretending to be asleep so he doesn't have to talk to her." Only Ed, still sporting the red handkerchief and beret, seems to be happy with his partner. But he is not without his problems. "You know, maybe it's just me, but I think our little adventures lately are becoming ... stupid," Mitch informs Ed. "What did you call them?" he asks Barbara, who is only too happy to help: "Desperate attempt to cling to your youth?" But Ed refuses to see it that way: "That's bullshit." As he says to his girlfriend, "Here comes Mr. Bull," Ed sees himself as a masculine creature of sexual virility who will not be fenced in by fatherhood. "Ed, have you noticed, the older you get, the younger your girlfriends get?" Mitch points to Ed's empty half, his fear of growing up. "It's never enough for you, Ed. When is it ever going to be enough?" Mitch's question, meant for all three, is ultimately answered in the course of the movie, after each city slicker slays his own dragon.

Dead or Alive

The transitional New York segment, one year later, opens and ends with *bridges*, two bookends that bridge the running of the bulls in the East and the cattle drive of the West. With the passing of time, Mitch's life has only gotten worse. Where Ed clings to his youth, Mitch cannot shake the certainty that he is growing old, getting ever closer to death. The three digits on the alarm clock on his side of the bed, 5:15, both recall the three friends, with number one (Mitch) in the center, and introduce the birthday boy sandwiched between his wife (to his left in bed) and the mother (to his right on the phone). Mitch is corralled between his two friends and trapped between the two women of his life. With the minutes changing, another annual ceremony starts right on time, one that Mitch knows by heart. Although the occasion is his thirty-ninth birthday, to his mother he is still a baby. It reminds the mother of her baby's birth day and Mitch that he is one year older. Aside from saying "I'm losing feeling in my left leg," the father is barely present in this annual ceremony.

The mother's question, "What are you going to do now, birthday boy?" is the big question Mitch has been evading. Coming on his birthday, it anticipates the *rebirth* he undergoes out West. The mother's turning to Barbara ("Give my boy a kiss") suggests that she is the mother's surrogate. In not seeing the mother, in only hearing her voice, we can only imagine what she is like. And by the look of things, she is a Jewish Medusa. Just as the mythical Medusa turned those who looked at her into stone, Mitch's mother tries to petrify her son as an eternal baby. As always, to break away from the mother, to break her spell, Mitch needs a father who can initiate him into manhood. But as we see, especially when he is shown walking to work like a zombie in a crowd of people, Mitch is losing his feeling like his father. "What is my job? Basically, I sell air.... At least my father was an *up*holsterer. He made a sofa, a couch you can sit on. Something tangible." The role the father plays in his son's life becomes clear after Mitch recounts his best day. But where on that day he sees the Yankees with his father, in Spain and throughout the first part of the drive Mitch wears the Mets cap, as if denying his father. That it is a sign of his rebelling against his father is underscored by Mitch replacing it with the surrogate father's cowboy hat when he joins his partners to bring in the herd.

The birthday ceremony over, Mitch says goodbye to his mother, switching her off by the press of a button. He is perfectly aware of his mother's hold on him, but cutting himself from her is not as convenient as pressing a button. "Well, at least she said my age in years," he tells Barbara. "Usually she uses months, like I'm still an infant." But if to his mother Mitch is still a baby, to his wife he is Mr. Death. Somewhat like a mother to a little boy, Barbara threatens to cancel his birthday party unless he stops acting "as if he is in a Bergman film." "I don't need you any worse that you've been," she tells him. That this is the low point in Mitch's life is amplified by the rest of the segment.

On the way to work, the place where modern man fulfills the traditional masculine role of breadwinner, Mitch is portrayed as trapped, insignificant and lifeless, more dead than alive. "You used to go out and get advertising. You hustled, you were creative," the boss reminds him. Like Barbara, he too senses the change in Mitch. "What's going on with you?" he asks. "Ever reach a point in your life where you say to yourself 'This is the best I'm ever gonna look, the best I'm ever gonna feel, the best I'm ever gonna do,' and it ain't that great?" Mitch confesses. "Happy birthday," the boss wishes him, but clips his wings that barely fly as it is.

At his son's classroom, in the role of father, Mitch comes off even worse (especially coming after the crude but vigorous father who appears before him, a father the kids truly enjoy). Mitch's son is so ashamed of his father's work that he makes him out to be a commander of men. The scenario Mitch gives the kids of what the future holds, a death in life, is right in line with what we have seen so far. As he says to Barbara, after sharing with her the events of his birthday, "I'm trapped."

At Mitch's birthday party we get an updated picture of the three buddies. Ed is the only one who has made any headway in his life. He is still reluctant to have kids, still unwilling to become a father, but he has taken the first step in that direction by getting married. "Admit it," his wife Kim tells Mitch, "you didn't think Edward would ever get married." Phil, on the other hand, has reached the end of his rope. "This is quite a life you carved out for yourself," Mitch says to him. "Do you ever think about quitting?" he asks Phil, but in effect is asking himself, if to go by Barbara's question, "What are you saying, that you wanna quit?" Phil's answer also reflects Mitch's situation. "Start over with two kids to take care of. At this age, where you are you are." But despite his fear of having to start over, Phil starts over by breaking off his emasculating (castrating) relationship. When Phil and Ed present Mitch their birthday gift to drive a herd of cattle (Ed reminding him, "Remember Mitchy the Kid?"), he refuses, declining to be "what you always wanted to be." In keeping with his paralysis, he replies, "I can't do it."

Just as Medea helped Jason yoke the *bulls* of Hephaestus and get the Golden Fleece from the deceiving *dragon*, and just as Ariadne helped Theseus slay the Mino*taur*, Barbara helps Mitch overcome his fear of retrieving his smile, reclaiming the life he once had. "Go away with Ed. Take Phil. I'm giving you these two weeks. It's my gift. Go and find your smile." She virtually sends him out West to retrieve the Golden Fleece, guarded by a mythical dragon, who "sleeps with his eyes open." "What if I can't?" Mitch finally owns up to what frightens him and keeps him trapped. "Jump off that bridge when you come to it," Barbara confronts Mr. Death with his biggest fear: becoming alive.

Ride of Passage

Two exhilarating aerial shots transport us to the great wide-open space of the West, a clear contrast to the claustrophobic streets of Pamplona and New

York. Where the movie opened with an *old* Spanish ritual, now we are in *New* Mexico for a life-renewing adventure. After a high panoramic view of the ranch and its activities, the camera comes to rest on the three protagonists, standing *outside* a corral, watching a cowboy wrestle down a bull, as if showing them the dragon they must slay. Once again, Mitch is in the middle, still complaining: "My ass hurts just watching." For Ed, ever the optimist, this couldn't be better. "Are you kidding? This is fantastic!" Phil, still pursued by the beast, seeks revenge. "I wonder if I can do this to Arlene?"

Launching right into the subject matter of the drive, the father-son pair is the first of several pairs to be introduced in this gathering of men. Like the three heroes, the father and son are city slickers (Baltimore). "We're *black* and we're dentists," the son introduces the duo. "Let's not make an issue out of it." "They're not making an issue," the father straightens him out, "you're making an issue." But the point has been made. The father and son *are* the issue. Their presence is a reminder of what the three's drive is all about. It is not for nothing that the pair leaves the drive once the three heroes reveal what was their best day, which in each case is connected to the father.

The introduction of the two brothers of the group further emphasizes the familial pairing, the close familial bond the three lack. Another pair is the professional cowboys, T.R. and Jeff, two virtually indistinguishable cowhands, a Western edition of Rosenkrantz and Guildenstern. Like the other pairs, they function as foils, as minor characters who are there mostly to magnify the major characters. Having finished their role, they are dispensed with just as was the pair in *Hamlet*.

The introduction of the last member of the party, Bonnie Rayburn, underscores the fairy-tale character of the drive. Together with Jimmy Durante's singing on the soundtrack that fairy tales can come true, the song that accompanies the start of the cattle drive, the one woman with seven men more than suggests "Snow White and the Seven Dwarfs," particularly by the manner in which the encounter is presented. Abandoned by her boyfriend at the last moment, just as Snow White was left in the forest to fend for herself, Bonnie feels like an intruder. She has doubt about her place among the seven men who, like the dwarfs, are more than happy to have her around. In this brief exchange, the seven are staged in an upturned "V" formation, as if opening to receive her, each one of the pairs on either side, with Mitch at the apex.

A gunshot abruptly ends this brief fantasy. The ranch owner brings the fairytale family back to reality. "This is not pretending," he says, giving them a fair warning of what is in store, and recalling Dunson's speech to his men before the drive in *Red River*. While the rancher describes what they are all going to do for the next two weeks, Mitch and Phil look at each other as if saying, what did we get ourselves into this time? "We're going to go to work in the morning. And I mean work. You came out here city slickers. You're gonna go home cowboys!"

In the trying-out of cowboy outfits for the work in the morning, once again nothing has changed. Ed picks a hat in one try, drawing against himself (in the mirror) like a little kid with a pair of imaginary six-shooters. Having replaced the father in his family, he is his own worst enemy. As Mitch tells him during the drive, "It is a game. It's your regular game, Ed. Don't you see it? 'Am I better than my father?'" Phil, too, finds a hat with no problem — on his second try — just as for him the whole drive becomes a second try, a do-over. Only Mitch cannot find a new hat no matter how many he tries. He holds on to the Mets cap as if he is still back home. But as he finds out when he tries to save a damsel in distress from the two drunken cowhands, he is no longer in New York City. He is in the Old West, where his comical approach, his "'90s behavior," does not work.

Just when all hell is about to break loose, out of nowhere comes the trail boss, putting a stop to all the shenanigans. From high above, a silhouette in the setting sun, he is the ultimate picture of the mythical western hero. Portrayed as a threatening patriarch, everything about him means business. Significantly, when he demands that Jeff apologize to Bonnie, Mitch is the first to volunteer. Apparently he feels he has done something that calls for apology. But what? As it were, the fairy tale of Snow White provides an answer. Being bigger than the dwarfs not only points to Bonnie's role as mother, it explains Curly's rescuing her and his threat of castration to those who may exceed the boundary in wanting her for themselves. In juxtaposing the upturned V formed by the seven men to receive Bonnie (with Mitch at the apex) with the V formed by the cowhand's spread legs (with the phallus at the apex), Curly's hurling of the knife inches away from the man's manhood suggests that his threat of castration is meant for Mitch. And to drive the point home, the father of the drive brandishes the knife inches away from Mitch's "phallic" nose, recalling Groot's threatening the sugar-stealing Bunk to take off "the end of your nose." As such, Curly is both the hunter who saves Snow White, tipping his hat to her with his knife, and the threatening Father who warns the boys not to get any bright ideas. "Don't let it happen again," he says with authority. That Curly's warning is meant for Mitch is underscored by his response, "That is the toughest man I've ever seen in my life." His job done, this toughest of men rides off into the sunset, not unlike the mythical Shane before him. (In that 1953 movie, Jack Palance's Curly played the black-dressed arch villain, the dragon.)

The "myth of Curly," who is reputed to have "killed a man in a knife fight," captures the seven dwarfs' imagination. "He slit him from neck to nuts," says, the father of the bunch, reminding the "sons" of Curly the castrating Father. Ed, as usual, sees the bright side of it all. "This guy is a cowboy. One of the last real men. He's untamed, a mustang." Where Mitch sees the patriarchal Curly as "hanging the help," Ed sees him as "helping us." Still in search of the absent father, Ed believes "it'll do us good to be in his world for a while." That for Mitch Curly is the dragon, much like the bull in Spain, is suggested by his "He's behind me," when he comes over to call it a day, his boots and spurs receiving an extreme close-up. "Time to turn in," he reminds the tenderfoots as a father to his boys. Mitch's last words before the drive, "He's gonna kill me!" sum up his status in the Oedipal drama.

Whereas in the first sequence of the ranch, the seven "dwarfs" were lined up in an upside-down V formation, just before the start of the drive the eight tenderfeet are lined up in two diagonal lines. On the left side are the three heroes and Bonnie. Mitch is singled out by his wearing his Mets cap while the other three are wearing cowboy hats. On the right side are the two pairs—the father and son and the two brothers. Like Mitch, the son is hatless and wears sunglasses, while the other three wear light cowboy hats and glasses. This pairing underscores the son in each group.

The part when the father brings up the start of the drive in *Red River* is also organized in a series of *pairs*. The father dominates this sequence, receiving most of the screen time and doing most of the talking. Mitch and the son (Steve) are paired again when they are the only two who have trouble "yeehawing" like men. But unlike Steve, who does not finish the drive, Mitch is shown trying again, this time much more successfully. It is a first sign of the "second chance," of "self-transformation," that Jane Tompkins associates with the West.

At the beginning of the drive, the three New Yorkers horse around, thinking the drive is another packaged adventure, play rather than work. The two brothers are also pictured calling back East, unable to distance themselves from their business or the New York Mets. Right in character, Ed tries to sidetrack Mitch with his sexual conquests. But Curly (for the second time) gets them back on track: "Pay attention, girls, we've got strays." Once again Mitch expresses his fear of the threatening father. "Kill anyone today?" he asks Curly. "The day ain't over yet," the father warns the son. Come night, cooling down the boys with a pail of water, Curly warns them for the third and final time. "You're spookin' the cattle!"

The turning point in Mitch's dealing with the father, which opens with a majestic shot of Curly at sunup, begins when he does exactly what he was warned not to do. His spooking the cattle and starting the stampede by grinding the coffee is right out of *Red River*, where Bunk starts the stampede by making noise while stealing sugar "like a little kid." In the mayhem that ensues, Curly remains unaffected and almost unmovable, observing the whole ordeal from up on high, like an amused god who lets the boys play before him. His legendary authority is demonstrated in his stopping the stampede with a single shot from his six-shooter. Again, just as in *Red River*, where Dunson wants to whip the culprit after the cattle have been rounded up, Curly comes after Mitch. "You're coming with me," he announces. "Just the two of us?" Mitch asks; his worst nightmare is coming true. Things turn from bad to worse when Curly decides to camp for the night. "God, it's *Deliverance*," is Mitch's initial reaction. Of course, this recalls another movie about men's rite of passage into manhood, but it also anticipates Mitch's "delivery" of Norman, symbol of his new life.

Watching Curly sharpen his big knife, Mitch deals with his fear the only way he knows, by cracking another one of his cynical jokes. "Getting ready to shave?" "You make a lot of smart remarks at my expense, don't you?" Curly calls attention to Mitch's defense mechanism, to what keeps him from taking a serious stand. But after Curly warns him repeatedly to put away his harmonica, Mitch finally stands up to the threatening patriarch. "If you're gonna kill me, get on with it. If not, shut the hell up! I'm on vacation!" These are the kind of manly words Curly understands. What is more, the tune Mitch is playing, "Tumblin' Tumbleweeds," is a song that Curly can easily take to. Sitting next to the surprised Mitch, Curly starts singing the words, harmonizing to Mitch's hesitant harmonica playing. This unexpected at-one-ment is underscored by their sharing the frame throughout the song.

That Mitch's fear of Curly, the castrating father, is more in his head than in reality is underscored the next day, when Curly changes from a threatening "ogre" to a paternal mentor and guide, an initiator into life. The two's man-to-man talk about women and love recalls, by both subject matter and the cinematography, Mitch's earlier talks with Ed. Only whereas the two friends were shot from identical angles, underlining their equality, Curly is once again shot from (slightly) below and Mitch from (slightly) above, emphasizing their father-son relationship. The two may have made peace with one another, but they are far from equal. Curly's story about the love of his life, and his riding away because "I figured it wasn't gonna get any better than that," echoes Mitch's words to his boss about how his best years are behind him, "and they were not that great." But unlike Mitch, Curly assumes responsibility for his choice, without misgivings or regrets. He has a code of conduct, the code of the Wild West. "A cowboy lives a different kind of life — when there were cowboys. We're a dying breed. It still means something to me, though." What Curly is talking about recalls Mitch talking about his own father "at least being an upholsterer." He had that one thing he was good at. But from what we have heard so far, Mitch's father was not much of a mentor for his son.

"You know, that's great. Your life makes sense to you," Mitch says with great admiration. But what Curly says next catches him completely off guard. "You city folk, you worry about a lotta shit, don't you? Spend about fifty weeks of the year gettin' knots in your rope, and then — then you think two weeks up here will untie 'em for you. None of you get it." Curly stops his horse, as if to emphasize the import of his words. "You know what the secret of life is?" He turns to Mitch, who does not have a clue. "Just one thing. You stick to that and everything else don't mean shit." With the initiate wanting to know the secret, the western guru replies, "That's what *you* gotta figure out." By the look on Mitch's face, Curly's words scare him almost as much as his knife. Once passed on from father to son, Curly's legacy weighs heavy on Mitch's conscience. He has been initiated into "the secret of life." With the cow ready to give birth, he literally has to reach inside and pull it out. With the Father (literally) at the head of the initiating ceremony, Mitch is transformed from city slicker to cowboy, from a son to a father.

Coming right after the experienced Curly informs the novice Mitch about the meaning of life, the whole rite-of-passage sequence is presented as a classical case of the father initiating the son into manhood. Curly orders the hesitating Mitch three times to "reach in and pull out the calf," to reach into that maternal womb, what is often represented in myths by the cave that holds the treasure, which in many cases is guarded by a dragon. Before "going in," Mitch takes off his Mets cap, which has come to represent his city-slicker self. Upon his entry, he loses his watch, the keeper of time which so troubled him back home, emphasizing his fear of growing old without ever having lived. As in many rites of passage, before he gains something new he has to lose (sacrifice) something old.

When he pulls the calf out from inside the cow, Mitch is more surprised by what he has done than in what comes out. "Look what I did! I made a cow!" Joking "He looks like you," Curly all but calls Mitch a father. Once the newborn is out of the womb, Curly shoots the suffering mother. Considering what transpired so far, and what comes next, with this act Curly cuts Mitch from the mother's umbilical cord once and for all, setting him free to become a man, to find his smile, to figure out what that one thing is in his life. "Good job, cowboy," says Curly, putting a fatherly arm around Mitch's shoulder.

Having been initiated by Curly, Mitch seems to be slightly apart from Phil and Ed. While the two argue about the greatness of their baseball heroes, Mitch has his own hero in Curly. When the trio tries to show Bonnie why baseball is so important in a man's life, Phil introduces the father stage of the journey. "When I was about 18 and my dad and I couldn't communicate about anything at all, we could still talk about baseball. That was real."

The communicating of father and son reminds Mitch of his communicating with Curly. "You know what the secret of life is?" Mitch awakens the others' curiosity. "One thing. Just one thing." "And what's that?" Ed asks. "I have no idea. But ask Curly, because he seems to know." But having done his job, having "brought the herd in," the father departs from the journey. Standing around Curly's makeshift grave, once again Mitch is at the apex of the upside-down "V," flanked by the two brothers as he delivers his eulogy, perhaps a further sign of his separateness from his two buddies. "What can I say about Curly? I didn't know you well, but I'll never forget you. You lived life on your terms. Simple, honest, brave." These three qualities, like Dorothy's three companions, are Curly's legacy, what Mitch is summoned to incorporate in his life.

Just as the maternal cow was sacrificed in giving birth to Norman, Curly's death signals Mitch, formerly Mr. Death, moving into the realm of life. Like a true father, Curly's spirit (and words) is a *driving* force in Mitch's *ride of passage.* He has given the grownup Mitch what his father gave him once upon a time as a boy. After the burial of the journey's patriarch, the trio's account of their best days turns out to be each one's most significant moment with his father. As each one's introjected father, it is the dragon they have to deal with before they can "bring in the herd."

Appropriately enough, Mitch's recounting his best day with his father sounds like a birth of some kind. "I'm seven years old and my dad takes me to Yankee Stadium. First game. Coming in this long dark tunnel underneath the stands, I'm holding his hand and we go out of the tunnel into light. It was huge. How green the grass was. The brown dirt, and that great green copper roof. Remember? Now, we had black-and-white TV so this was the first game in color. I sat through the whole game next to my dad. Taught me how to keep score. Mickey [Mantle] hit one out. I still have that program."

Phil's account is also connected to his father, who, on his wedding day, "gives me a little wink. You know? I mean, he's not the warmest of men. But he winked. You know, I was the first to get married and have a real job. And I remember thinking, I'm grown up. I'm not a goofball anymore. I've made it. Felt like a man. Best day of my life."

Perhaps because of the pain that this day represents for Ed, perhaps because it reveals how much he takes after his father, he is reluctant to take part. But never backing down from anything or anyone, Ed comes through. "I'm fourteen and my mother and father are fighting again. You know, because she caught him again. Caught him? This time the girl drove by the house to pick him up. I finally realized he wasn't cheating on my mother, he was cheating on us. So I told him. I said, 'You're bad for us. We don't love you. I'll take care of my mother and my sister. We don't need you anymore.' And he made like he was gonna hit me, but I didn't budge. Then he turned around and left. Never bothered us again. But I took care of my mother and my sister from that day on. That's my best day."

This pivotal sequence not only reveals each one's relationship with his father, it serves as a catharsis for all three. In sharing the event that characterizes each one's relationship with his father, the three free themselves from the shadowy figure that trails them like the bulls at Pamplona. It frees them to tackle the trials that are just around the next turn. For without Curly to keep the helpers in rein, without the father to keep the boys in line, things start coming apart. First Cookie gets drunk and drives the food wagon and horses over a ravine, obliging the father and son to leave the drive in order to accompany him to where he can receive medical help for his broken legs. The son protests, but the father gets him to go along by the kind of words that the other three probably never heard. "*Ride* with me. It will still be fun."

Come night, the two cowhands get drunk once again, this time challenging Mitch by harassing Norman. As a symbol of his new life, Mitch has to stand up for Norman. He tries to talk to the cowhands as he had talked back to Curly.

Only this time it does not work. And without Curly, Mitch has to face the avenging cowhands by himself. In the fight that breaks out, it is Phil, of all people, who saves the day. Like a true hero, he knocks the threatening gun out of Jeff's hand with one swift kick. Just as he was pushed to stand up to his wife at Mitch's birthday party, now he is pushed to confront the person who represents for him his bullying father-in-law. "I'm not gonna let you bully us anymore. My father-in-law is a bully. I hate bullies. Because the bully doesn't just beat you up, he takes away your dignity."

Having released much of his pent-up rage, Phil is ready to look squarely at his present situation, thus freeing himself from his past. "Oh God, I'm at a dead end. I'm almost forty years old. I wasted my life." For the first time in the movie, Mitch, holding Phil, tries to get him to see the "full half." "Now you have a chance to start over. Remember when we were kids. And we'd be playing ball and the ball would get stuck in a tree or something. We'd yell, 'Do over!' Your life is a do-over. You got a clean slate."

In the debate about what to do after the cowhands skip out in the middle of the night, recalling *Red River*'s quitters, Ed announces that he will drive the herd by himself. Unlike his reluctance to tell his story, he is the first to take action. Now it is Mitch who refuses. In this moment of truth, he chickens out. And when Ed thinks "I can bring in the herd," Mitch reminds him. "No you can't.... You couldn't even manage your stores. You had to *bring in* your cousin." He even reminds him of his need to constantly outdo his father. But as Ed confesses, "I need to do it." Much to Mitch's dismay, Phil joins Ed. "I'll do it with you." And when Mitch tries to talk him out of it, Phil replies, "Why don't you accept that maybe you don't know what we're going through?"

From the expression on his face, Mitch is torn between riding with his best friends and taking the easy way out, even if it means not finishing what he had started. Next day, as they ride out, Phil seems more surprised at Mitch's decision not to go along with them than Mitch was about Phil's decision to join Ed in driving the cattle. On the one hand, it is the first time he does not let Ed talk him into doing what he does no want to do. On the other, having been initiated by Curly, having crossed the bridge of not return, this time is the first time he knows this is what he must do.

Bringing in the Herd

Out on their own, without the mediating Mitch, Phil and Ed do not get along with one other or with the cattle. "They're not cooperating," Phil comments in frustration. But when the herd seems to come apart, Mitch appears over a hilltop like a reincarnated Curly. "It's Mitch!" Phil hollers. "Mitchy the Kid!" And indeed this is a new Mitch. He is wearing Curly's black cowboy hat and reciting his words. "Curly said, 'There's nothing like bringing in the herd!'" Ed responds approvingly, "Nice hat, partner."

With the coming of the storm, and with their coming to the threshold of the river they must cross, the stage is set for their biggest trial. "We're lost, but we're making good time," Mitch says, describing their situation. Phil wants to call it a day, but Ed buckles down. "No! A cowboy doesn't leave his herd." "You're a sporting goods salesman!" Phil reminds him. "Not today," Ed pronounces. Once again, Mitch and Phil follow Ed. Only this time it is their decision. As Ed says to himself going down the slope to the river, echoing Tom Dunson's words to his men, "I started this, and I'm gonna finish it." But however hard, the real trial is not getting the herd across their own Red River. Rather, it is the life-threatening experience of saving Norman, the symbol of Mitch's new life. Coming close to losing his life, Mitch regains it, but not without the help of his two best friends, who form a human chain to rescue him. As their laughter illustrates, their scrape with death, their heroic act, releases them from the clutches of the dragon, that shadowy figure first depicted by the running of the bulls. To paraphrase Clay Stone, they came out adolescents, they're going back grownups.

The pastoral scene that follows reflects the trio's new state of mind. "Let's bring them in," Mitch (once again in the middle) calls out, just as Curly had started the drive with "Move 'em out." In their singing the *Bonanza* theme song, and with the father and son and the Shalowitz brothers looking on, the three ride together as if they are the Cartwright brothers. Like Ben and Steve, the father and son of the drive, they are the sons of *Ben* Cartwright; like the Shalowitz brothers, they are the three Cartwright brothers. Furthermore, if to go by Steve's "good yahoo," and his suggesting that he and his father drive the cattle back to New Mexico, the "shadowy" father's and son's new relationship mirrors the three brothers/sons' new relationship with their own fathers.

The three's jubilation is dampened for a minute by Clay Stone's announcement that he is selling the herd for "top dollar," another reminder of *Red River*. It brings them back to the real world. But what stays with them is the *ride of passage* they have undertaken. "Two weeks ago you boys were worthless as skin shit on a pump handle, and look at you now," says the benevolent father, making good on his promise. They are "going home cowboys." "You've done real good, cowboys"—Clay Stone's words to the three echo Curly's words to Mitch. The lesson each has learned about himself wraps up the drive in reverse order to their opening comments about a cowboy wrestling down a bull, the western version of the dragon. Phil is first: "I've gotta stop being a schmuck. You know, you were right, Mitch. My life is a do-over. It's time to get started." Ed finally overcomes his fear of becoming a father, a father like his father: "I'm going home, and I'm gonna get Kim pregnant." And Mitch, holding up his index finger, finally gets what Curly meant. "I know what this means.... It's whatever is most important to you. For me, when I was in the river, I was only thinking about one thing. All that other stuff just went away. Only one thing really mattered to me."

The next picture, which transports us back to New York, shows what is the "one thing" for Mitch. Whereas in the opening of the movie, they were "going home," now they have "arrived." Mitch has returned as a new father and husband. His daughter welcomes him back, echoing Dorothy of *Oz* upon her return to Kansas, "Dad, you're home!"

The brief exchange between Ed and Mitch reveals the change in Ed. When he suggests that next year they go to the North Pole, and Mitch counters with "Next Tuesday, coffee and cake," Ed's response, "Better," shows that the journey out West had been *enough*. He finally got what he really wanted. Completing the trio's coming back with the boon, Phil has gotten Snow White, a complete contrast to Irene, the fairy tale's castrating (devouring) mother. If to go by the women's initials, in *Bonnie Rayburn* Phil has his own *Barbara Robbins*, which also mirrors back on Mitch, whom we see meeting with his own "Snow White," dressed in red. He has come back with his newfound smile and new attitude. Just as ultimately he did not quit the drive, now he is not quitting his job. "I'm just gonna do it better. I'm gonna do everything better." As he says to Barbara, his "best day," long associated with his father, is now with his wife and children. The arrival of Norman, with the porter calling him *Mr. Robbins*, is the icing on the cake. Mitch has brought his new life back to New York. In something that recalls Ethan Edwards' last words in *The Searchers*, "Let's go home," Mitch takes charge of the driving in the family van, with the symbol of his new self in the back.

The closing shot tracks the van crossing the bridge, the threshold to the ordinary world that is promised to be *better*. What started out with the "running from the bulls," and continued with the driving of the cattle, ends with the hero assuming the driver seat, *driving* the family back home.

Chapter 6

North by Northwest
O for Oedipus

EVE KENDALL: *What does the "O" stand for?*
ROGER THORNHILL: *Nothing.*
— *North by Northwest*

The Letter "O"

More than any other Alfred Hitchcock movie, *North by Northwest* tackles the hero's problem with the father. Hitchcock underscores this point by having the hero, Roger Thornhill, falsely accused of slaying the father. But as always in Hitchcock's movies, this is only the tip of the iceberg. The slaying is mostly in Thornhill's unconscious, which does not differentiate between what is real and what is fantasy. He may be falsely accused in the real world, but in the unconscious, where slaying the father is part of every son's Oedipal fantasy, he is no less guilty. That the movie deals with fantasy, with the unconscious, is suggested by Hitchcock himself. "The whole film is epitomized in the title — there is no such thing as north-by-northwest on the compass. The area in which we get near to the free abstract in movie making is the free use of fantasy, which is what I deal in."[1]

Thornhill's problem with the father is subtly presented in the scene immediately following the father's "slaying," as the crime is called by the shown newspaper headline. The father's presence is evoked by the opening shot of the shiny (United States Intelligence Agency) rectangular plaque reflecting the Capitol Building, shrine of patriarchy, which anticipates the four presidents of the Mount Rushmore monument near the movie's ending. The father is further evoked by a series of three symmetric (conical) shots. In the first, as head of the family, the Professor, who "fathered" George Kaplan (whose identity Thornhill has assumed), sits at the apex of the conical configuration, holding a phallic pipe; in the second he is replaced by a statue of (what appears to be) George Washington, Father of our Nation (just as *George* Kaplan's name is mentioned); in the third the Professor is out of the picture, just like Thornhill's father.

Complementing the Professor, the woman of the group, Mrs. Finley, is the mother. The two are singled out in that they are the only ones called by name. Moreover, his calling her "my dear woman," together with the three identically dressed men, brings to mind the classic fairy tale family of mother, father and three sons. They are the positive to the negative "Mr. and Mrs. Townsend" and their three errand boys. Mrs. Finley's "Goodbye Mr. Thornhill, wherever you are," both echoes "Mrs. Townsend's" parting words and foreshadows Thornhill's saying his last "goodbye" to his mother (shown in the opening of the subsequent scene). But it also insinuates that he is to be the third son assassinated by Vandamm. As the Professor replies to Mrs. Finley's question regarding Thornhill's chances of staying alive, his escaping the father's retribution, which brings to mind the Oedipus myth, "That's his problem." But as in fairy tales, one of our more ingenious expressions of the unconscious, the third son succeeds where the first two failed. Where Oedipus marries the mother by slaying the father, Thornhill gets the fair princess by slaying the dragon, which perhaps explains the George in his assumed name.

Oedipus is further suggested by Thornhill's introducing himself to the woman who replaces his mother as "Jack *Phillips*," the name of the father she sleeps with (*Phillip* Vandamm), and as from "*Kingby* Electronics," perhaps a reference to *King* Oedipus, particularly as it comes as he is running away for "slaying the father." Taken together, the two names suggest that the "O" in Thornhill's monogrammed matchbook stands for Oedipus. In his book, *Find the Director*, Thomas M. Leitch suggests the same. "Thornhill's middle initial, which stands for nothing, might just as well stand for Oedipus."[2] In claiming that it stands for "nothing," in denying what the "O" stands for, Thornhill relegates it to the unconscious. But in a movie that deals with the hero's Oedipal fantasy from start to finish, and where the absent father is everywhere, the "O" is everything. To paraphrase Hitchcock, the whole film is epitomized in the letter "O."

Another Man's Place

As in fairy tales, as in dreams, every detail in *North by Northwest* is packed with meaning. Even the opening intersecting lines, moving in the four directions of the compass, filling the screen with countless rectangles against a green background, anticipate the spy *net*work that Thornhill is soon entangled in, forcing him to resolve his problem by disentangling himself and his woman from the father figures. The first sign of impending danger comes up just before Thornhill emerges from a crowded elevator, when a blonde woman dressed in red (among all the men and women in gray suits) passes on the screen, from right to left (east to west), foreshadowing the blonde Eve wearing red (twice) in the second half of the film. Thornhill, dressed in a gray suit, which he wears throughout most of the film, is introduced as a man clever with words in a casual (childish) manner, as if he is not accountable for what comes out of his mouth. The seemingly "wasted" exchange with the elevator boy ("Good night, Eddie. Say hello to the missus." And Eddie's reply, "We're not talking!") introduces Thornhill's problem with the missus. On the one hand, he "talks" to the mentioned woman through his secretary and gifts; on the other, he cannot get a message to his mother. What is more, in a movie where names are most significant, the name *Eddie* may very well be short for *Oedi*pus, thus naming Thornhill's problem right from the start.

Thornhill's "insignificant" taking the waiting man's place in the taxicab, significantly sandwiched between his *two* attempts to send witty yarns of words to Gretchen Sabinson and his *twice* reminding his secretary to get in touch with his mother, serves as an exposition to his fundamental problem. In view of his obvious attachment to his domineering mother, who tries to keep her little boy in line, sniffing his breath for alcohol "like a bloodhound," the man whose place Thornhill has taken is his absent father, who is never mentioned in the entire movie, as if repressed from existence (unconsciously slain). Why else does he ask his secretary, "Say, do I look heavy-ish to you?" It is surely because, having taken the father's place, Thornhill "feel(s) *heavy-ish*" with guilt. This guilt, however unconscious, is what is behind his failing to tell his secretary where to contact his mother only seconds after he twice reminded her to do so. And being unconscious, no verbal acrobatics, twisted logic or "expedient exaggeration" can make it go away. As Thornhill is about to discover, it is going to take much more than "*think* thin" to remedy his situation, to resolve his Oedipal problem.

Thornhill's attachment to his mother is more pronounced in the subsequent scene, when he drinks with the three identically dressed businessmen at the Plaza's bar. Speaking of drinks, a favorite oral gratification for overgrown boys, one man apologizes for getting a head start. "That won't last long," Thornhill assures him, looking at his watch (thinking of mother). "You may be slow in starting, but there is nobody faster coming down the homestretch," his friend, Herman, the one who knows Thornhill, attests. Considering what has been suggested up to now, these words point to Thornhill's overtaking another man (the father) and his reluctance to renounce the bottle, common substitute for the mother's breast. Like his friend's name, Thornhill is *her man*. His two unsuccessful attempts to replace her in marriage are proof enough. Significantly, it is when Thornhill tells the boys about his mother that his new identity is heard in the background and Vandamm's henchmen come into view. The juxtaposition of the two is another suggestion that he is punished for taking another man's identity (place) in his relationship with his mother.

Because he is replacing another man, both literally and metaphorically, Thornhill is taken to be judged and sentenced by the avenging father. As suggested by the theater metaphors through which the two communicate, Thornhill's theater date with his mother is now replaced by another drama, in which the father and son, who circle one another like two adversaries, are play acting. Both have taken another man's place. While Vandamm knows he is playing a role and believes Thornhill is Kaplan, Thornhill knows he is not Kaplan but believes Vandamm is Townsend. This surreal situation is more emblematic of the unconscious than real everyday. As it were, Thornhill is the only one who actually calls Vandamm by his borrowed name. His question "Who is Townsend?" never gets answered. Much like Oedipus, Thornhill has to discover the father's identity, and his own, by himself.

The theater metaphor continues with Vandamm drawing the curtains, shutting out the reality outside but also turning them into a prop for the two "performers" who appear to stand before a stage curtain. In place of the natural light he has shut out, Vandamm turns on the artificial (stage) light of the two lamps, momentarily standing in the shadow. Actually, each one stands before a similarly shaped lamp, but only the one behind Vandamm is lit, suggesting that he is enlightened about Thornhill's abduction, while Thornhill remains in the dark. Unaware (unconscious) of being mis*taken* for another man (of having *taken* his place), Thornhill's refusal to play along suggests his denying (repressing) taking another man's place in the Oedipal drama. The lamp's backlighting also highlights Vandamm's shadowy and menacing role in the drama. Like these shots, and others, the two's dialogue is full of double meanings. Vandamm's "games" and "play-acting" allude to both Thornhill as Kaplan and to his artificial lifestyle, but also to his crime, which, in the father's words of warning, "is not going to lead to a very happy conclusion." Thornhill's line to Vandamm, delivered while he stands before the "stage" curtain, "I have tickets for the theater this evening, to a show I was looking forward to," refers to both his theater date with his mother and the theater of the unconscious. The play, of course, is the Oedipal drama, and as suggested by Vandamm's haughty review, "With such expert play-acting, you make this very room a theatre," Thornhill's theater date is with the father rather than with the mother.

Like Oedipus, who was disposed of by his father before he deposed him, Thornhill, as the mythical Kaplan, is sent to his death by the paternal Vandamm. "A pleasant journey, sir," he says as he exits the stage, leaving the dirty work for his three henchmen, his sons, who give Thornhill "a libation" before he is set on his "journey" to death by driving. Though under the influence, Thornhill musters enough will power to push his executioner out of the car, the first of three vehicles he *drives* in the movie, all of them stolen and used to escape death.

Having escaped one paternal threat, Thornhill has a run-in with the law and is hauled into a police station, hall of paternal authority. Once again, his mother is present, this time on the other end of the telephone line. Thornhill finally succeeds getting through to her, though under unfavorable circumstances. In calling his mother ("Mother, this is your son, Roger Thornhill"), despite the police officer's advice to call his lawyer, Thornhill does what he recommended to elevator boy Eddie (talk to the missus), as if he is *Oedi* as in Oedipus. The telephone conversation, shown through the doorframe, is rendered in one symmetrical shot, with Thornhill in the left half of the frame and the policeman in the right, the two sharing the frame as father and son on opposite sides. When Thornhill's mother wants to know the arresting policeman's name, the two share a private amusement that is never explained. They share a laugh at the expense of the figure of authority's name, as if in cahoots against the un-named father.

The symmetrical shot is repeated in the very next exchange between Thornhill and the interrogating doctor, another figure of authority. The two sit opposite each other on either side of the frame divided in the middle by books and the American flag. The police station scene (and the first segment of the movie) ends with Thornhill crawling into a fetal position, a fitting image for someone so attached to his mother.

Where in the first New York segment another man's name was foisted on Thornhill, in the second one he actively assumes this man's name. And where the first segment was dominated by the father, the second, a retracing of the first, is dominated by the mother, just as she dominates Thornhill's life. In the retracing, as if reflected in a mirror, things are turned around. Fact becomes fiction and vice versa. Where the night before there was talk about Thornhill's kidnappers not giving him "a chaser," now there is talk of their giving him "a chase." Where the day before Thornhill's *identity* was in question, now his *character* is on trial. When his lawyer answers the judge that he knows him "to be a reasonable man," it is contradicted by his mother's cynical remark. The judge wanting to "determine if his story has any basis in fact" surprises the incredulous Thornhill. "After all, Your Honor, would I make up such a story?" "That is precisely what we're intending to find out, Mr. Thornhill," says the court's patriarch, ending the proceedings. Of course, one source which could "make up such a story" is the ever-resourceful and spontaneous unconscious.

Thornhill's return to the Townsend mansion is shot in practically the same way as his first arrival, and the same woman answers the door (in the same dress, only this time with an added apron). As fits this maternal segment, "Mrs. Townsend" replaces "Mr. Townsend." Once again, the library becomes a theater, this time for the performance of "Mrs. Townsend." The setting, too, has been changed. Thornhill tries to show the bourbon stains of yesterday's abduction, but the father's crime has been covered up. There are no stains just as there are no liquor bottles in the cabinet "where they keep the liquor," which have been replaced by books. Thornhill's biggest doubter, perhaps because she knows him best, is his mother. "I remember when it [bourbon] used to come in bottles," she says, continuing her lack of support in the courtroom.

Where the day before Vandamm insisted that Thornhill, despite his protesting otherwise, was Kaplan, now the acting "Mrs. Townsend" (who also never refers to herself by her borrowed name) insists on calling him Roger, talking to him as a mother to a mischievous boy. "You haven't gotten into trouble, Roger?" Her words are echoed by Roger's real mother, "Has he gotten into trouble!" This "echo" and the identical earrings the two wear underscore the two mothers' likeness. As such, this is Thornhill's encounter with his real and symbolic mother, another suggestion that "Mr. Townsend" represents the father in this Oedipal drama. "What a performance!" Thornhill says, complimenting the actress who, by mentioning that Mr. Townsend is addressing the U.N. Assembly, convinces the investigating party that her play-acting is real and that Roger is making up the whole story, that the drama is all in his head. The last picture of this scene shows one of Vandamm's henchmen in the role of a gardener, pruning the bushes with a huge pair of shears, a clear suggestion of castration. This is the same man, the "son" of the acting Mr. Townsend, who kills the real Mr. Townsend with the phallic knife, intended for Thornhill.

In keeping with the retracing nature of this segment, Thornhill's second arrival at the Plaza, this time to seek out George Kaplan, is shot much like his first arrival. Only now he is accompanied by his mother. "I don't see why you want me along," she asks him with little protest, calling attention to his attachment to her. On the way to Kaplan's room, as Thornhill's partner in the crime of obtaining the room's key under false pretense, the mother recounts her son's list of crimes, as if to make him feel guilty. "Car theft, drunk driving, assaulting an officer, lying to a judge, and now housebreaking." This list of crimes is nothing compared to his next crime of slaying the father.

Instead of finding George Kaplan in his hotel room, Thornhill is constantly mistaken for him. His brief exchange with the cleaning woman about his identity ("Do you know who I am?") defines his Looking Glass situation. He takes another step in assuming Kaplan's identity when he tries his suit for size. Still another step in that direction is his answering the ringing telephone, despite his mother's advice not to. To his protestation that he is not Mr. Kaplan, one of Vandamm's henchmen replies, "Of course not. You answer his telephone, you live in his hotel room, and yet you are not Mr. Kaplan." In his very next phone call, to the hotel operator, to find out where the call came from, Thornhill identifies himself as "Mr. Thorn — Kaplan," all but fully assuming his name.

In his escape from the henchmen in the elevator, Thornhill once again takes another couple's place in the taxicab outside the hotel. As it were, his escape is both from Vandamm's henchmen and from his mother, who calls out to him, not unlike a wife to her husband, "Will you be home for dinner?"

Having broken off with his mother, Thornhill starts his dealings with the father in the U.N. building, which replaces the C.I.T. Building where he was first introduced, thus completing his retracing. Identifying himself as "George Kaplan," Thornhill's taking another man's place is complete. What started when he was mistaken for George Kaplan by the acting "Townsend," now ends as he identifies himself as George Kaplan in his meeting with the real Townsend. But this is not the only twist of events. Where the acting "Townsend" sent(enced) Thornhill to his death, before he can answer Thornhill's question about the identity of the man in the picture who has taken his place, the real father is killed in place of the son. Once again, this bizarre situation, the acting George Kaplan blamed for the acting son's slaying the father, seems like something only the unconscious would "make up."

The shot that closes the first part of the movie, of Thornhill running for a taxi and for his life, taken from high above the U.N. Building, is a mirrored image of the movie's opening shots of the office building reflecting the New York traffic. The many-windowed U.N. Building, occupying the right half of the frame, like Thornhill taking another man's place, replaces the many-windowed skyscraper that formerly occupied the left half of the frame. Similarly, where in the beginning Thornhill seemed in full control of his familiar surroundings, now he is victimized by circumstances beyond his control.

Just before he starts his north-by-northwest journey, from Grand Central Station, the father is once again represented by two pairs of plainclothesmen and policemen, a double dose of patriarchal law, who come together at the center of the frame, looking for the "slayer" of the father. As they walk opposite directions in pairs, the camera pans to the right to show Thornhill in a phone booth. His first words, "Yes dear, I know," give the impression that he is talking to his woman friend, when in fact, as made clear in the very next sentence, he is talking to his mother. Just as his mother recounted his crimes on their way to Kaplan's hotel room, now Thornhill recounts them to his mother. "I'm a car thief, a drunk driver and a murderer." In saying "goodbye" to Mrs. Thornhill over the telephone, echoing the CIA woman's goodbye to *Mr.* Thornhill, the accused murderer "disconnects" from his mother once and for all. As he exits the phone booth, a waiting man looks at him accusingly, as if reprimanding him for breaking off with his mother — or for slaying the father.

Another Woman's Place

Running into Eve Kendall, whose last name sounds much like his last name, both real and borrowed, Thornhill starts the first leg of his journey in reclaiming his identity. If to go by Eve's introduction ("I'm twenty-six and unmarried. Now you know everything") and Thornhill's attachment to his mother, *Northwest* is the coming together of her plans and his problems. While Eve's original plan to have Thornhill killed does not work out, it gets him to the point where her proposition is replaced by his proposal. Her "belonging" to the two father figures suggests that their relationship is a dramatization of

Thornhill's Oedipal problem. On the one hand, Eve replaces his mother by virtue of her dining with Thornhill on the very same evening his mother expected him to be "home for dinner." On the other, Thornhill replaces the bad father she sleeps with and the good father she works for — the two paternal figures who play prominent roles in the undercover (unconscious) production in which he is called to make several life-saving performances.

In one of Hitchcock's "notorious" links of sex with murder, Eve both lures Thornhill to her sleeper and to his doom. Sex and murder, after all, are what the Oedipal drama is all about. When Thornhill lights Eve's cigarette with a match from his monogrammed matchbook, her caressing the hand that holds the lighted match is all the invitation Thornhill needs. But like the train's horn sounding a warning in the night right after she blows out the match, Eve means to put out his lights. As Thornhill confesses to her, even on the train he is pursued, not unlike a little child playing hide-and-seek, hiding from the pursuing agents of paternal authority out to get him for slaying the father. The title of the book Eve is reading, *The Agreeable Age*, the one she has started but does not "particularly like," may very well point to Twenty One, the restaurant where he was to dine with his mother. It is another suggestion that Eve replaces his mother. After all, the sleeping compartment is as much a chamber for an amorous night as it is a womb, especially the upper berth in which Thornhill hides from the detectives, as if he found the womb he wanted to crawl into at the police station. The breaking of his (identity-hiding) sunglasses, while hiding, is another sign of his progress in reclaiming his true identity, a rebirth of sorts. He does not wear another pair for the remainder of the movie.

Not unlike a little boy who imagines his mother belongs to him, Thornhill believes that Eve is all his. He is unaware (unconscious) that she belongs to someone else, that once more he is taking another man's place. This is underscored when the porter's interrupting their verbal fore*play* sends Thornhill to hide in the washroom, where he studies Eve's small shaving brush and razor like a little boy who discovers his mother's feminine paraphernalia while she betrays him with a note to Vandamm (she knows what to do with him at night but not what to do the morning after). Thornhill's simultaneous studying of the diminutive (but phallic) shaving brush and razor (which receives a close-up, while rotating in his hand) suggests the father's threat of castration, especially when we witness the content of Eve's note and its receiver.

The next morning, after spending the night with Eve, Thornhill once again takes another man's place. This time it is as a phallic Red Cap, as if wearing his guilt on his head (in his unconscious). Similarly, while hiding her treachery, Eve cannot help wear her heart on her sleeve; at least enough for Thornhill to notice that she is no longer the cool *femme fatale* she was on the train. She has been smitten by him no less than he has been smitten by her. When he asks, "Where will I find you?" "Eve does not answer, but the movie eventually does, and just as one would expect of a fairy tale: in the dragon's lair, needing to be rescued."[3]

Soon enough, over a dissolve of Eve's face, which marks another chapter in Thornhill's pursuing the man whose place he has taken, he gets a demonstration of the father's retribution in the famous prairie stop scene. The utter desolation of the landscape, revealed by the long aerial shot that opens the scene, and the bizarre attempt on Thornhill's life, evoke the uncanny setting of a dream. The unlikely displacement of the airplane from crop duster to shooter of bullets, and the way it is shot, constantly cutting back and forth between the spectacle and Thornhill's vision, reinforces the feeling that the attempt on his life is his own psychic production to alleviate his guilt for usurping the father, for having taken his place with his woman. The bullet-firing airplane suggests a fire-spitting dragon, projection of the introjected father.

Like the crashing of the plane into the truck, the converging of two intersecting objects, the entire scene is a "crossroad" in Thornhill's journey. Starting with the approaching bus, with Thornhill as a passenger, and ending with the stolen pickup disappearing on the horizon, where he is behind the wheel, it signals his change from a passive passenger running *from* to an initiating hero heading *towards*. Where in the first driving of "Laura's Mercedes" he was forced to do so in a drunken (semi-conscious) state, now he is fully conscious and sober, though still unaware (unconscious) of the undercover plot. In pursuing a man who does not exist, and whose identity he has assumed, Thornhill is pursuing himself.

While in Thornhill's first appearance there was a woman in red, at his next station, the hotel where he believes Kaplan is staying, the color red, associated with danger and the devil, is the dominant color. The hotel's name is written in white letters on a red background, the doorman wears a red coat, and Thornhill himself, brushing his dusty suit, stands against a background of a red-bricked wall. Inside, too, there is a big red carpet, a red curtain and a woman with a red coat. Informed by the desk clerk that Kaplan had checked out before Eve claimed to have talked to him, Thornhill realizes something is amiss. Just then, as if to emphasize her deceit, he spots Eve in a flowery red dress, crossing the lobby on the big red carpet.

Assuming that Thornhill is dead, from having read the newspaper headline of the airplane crash, Eve is both surprised and relieved to see him at her door. Her twofold "surprise" is underscored by the double meaning in Thornhill's "No getting rid of me, is there?" The two's double-edged words serve opposite functions. For Eve it is to hide the truth, for Thornhill to find it — another game of hide-and-seek. With her back to Thornhill as she mixes the drink he "can use," which emphasizes her deviousness and discomfort, he spies the headline in the newspaper, recalling the first headline about his slaying Townsend. The juxtaposition of Thornhill seeing the headline and Eve asking, "How did it go today?" magnifies her deviousness. The whole scene, a sort of verbal charade where each one says one thing but means another, is a re-enactment of the one in Kaplan's room at the Plaza, another case of Eve replacing his mother.

Seeing this scene as another performance in Thornhill's Oedipal drama, where the son is told by his "mother" (who belongs to the father) that they are "not going to get involved," the clever dialogue takes on a whole new meaning. Surely what Eve, who plans to meet Vandamm shortly, feels for Thornhill is part of the reason she has her back to him throughout most of the scene. But despite her refusal to "get involved," it is in Eve's room that her plans and his problems start getting "connected." As the two face one another, sharing the frame, Thornhill raises a toast. "To us. To a long and lasting friendship." But Eve has her obligation to the father. "I do have plans of my own, you know, and you do have problems." Just when he proposes a (re)solution, "wouldn't it be nice if my problems and your plans were somehow connected," the phone rings, echoing the ringing of Vandamm's men in the earlier scene at the Plaza. Where the earlier call started Thornhill's rushing out of Kaplan's room, this call initiates Eve's departure. As she tells him, he is too "big" to continue what was once permissible, when he "was a little boy." Informing him that he is "a big boy now," Eve nevertheless leaves him, however unconsciously, a clue to where he may find her, which recalls his forgetting to tell his secretary where she can reach his mother, yet another suggestion that Eve has replaced his mother.

With Eve's unconscious "help," Thornhill arrives at the auction gallery, another setting for the unconscious drama, where desirable objects are acquired by new possessors. For the first time in the movie he is not after George Kaplan, whom he assumes is in South Dakota. Now Thornhill is after Eve. But as revealed by the auction gallery's opening shot, of a possessive hand around the back of Eve's neck, not unlike a dragon's claw holding the princess captive, she belongs to the father.

With the auctioneer's introducing the next item up for bidding ("This magnificent *pair* of Louis Seize Fauteuils. *Original gilt* finish"), which calls attention to the son's (original) guilt at seeing the pair, the camera draws back to reveal that the hand around Eve's neck is Vandamm's and that Leonard, the son, is by his side. The three are sitting by themselves, as if in a theater's boxed seats. Continuing to draw back, the camera comes to rest on Thornhill standing at the back of the gallery, connecting him to the trio. This connection is underscored by the juxtaposition of the auctioneer announcing the next object to be auctioned, "And now Low Number 103," and the showing of Thornhill (*one*), with the O of his middle initial, spying on the *three*. The family triad is further suggested by Thornhill's opening line, "The three of you together," especially the way Eve, whose reaction is shown in close-up, looks first at Thornhill then at Vandamm and Leonard. While she is shown, Thornhill adds, "Now, that's a picture only Charles Addams could draw," a reference to the *New Yorker* cartoonist known for his macabre cartoons (who *fathered* the Addams Family), but perhaps also referring to "Van Adam" and Eve, the *pair* who brought about mankind's *original guilt*. For Thornhill this shock of recognition is not unlike a boy's original discovery that mom belongs to dad.

The Oedipal triads are highlighted by the shooting scheme of "the-three-of-you-together." The four pairs of mirrored shots, like the number of players in the drama, form two triangles—Eve, Vandamm and Leonard (mother and father with the dark son), and Eve, Vandamm and Thornhill (mother and father with the light son), which are subtly set apart by the shooting angle. Moreover, as the mirrored shots show, Leonard, with his dark skin, black hair and black suit and tie, is Thornhill's shadow. The two face each as two sons on opposite sides of the father.

The Oedipal conflict between father and son comes to a head with the display of the "piece of sculpture," the third object to be auctioned and the one that Vandamm is there to acquire. "I'll bet you paid plenty for this little piece of sculpture," says Thornhill, the spurned son, giving expression to his feeling of betrayal. "She's worth every dollar of it, take it from me. She puts her heart into her work. In fact, her whole body." With the auctioneer's announcement, "Sold to Mr. Vandamm," Thornhill discovers Vandamm's real name — who the object of desire belongs to.

Once again the talk turns to the theater, reverting to the Oedipal drama that the movie keeps alluding to. Like his mother before him, the paternal Vandamm recaps Thornhill's journey by recounting the "various roles" he has assumed, concluding with, "It seems to me you fellows could stand a little less training from the FBI and a little more from the Actor's Studio." "Apparently, the only performance that will satisfy you is when I play dead," says Thornhill, playing along. Having recounted the past, Vandamm now foretells the future much more than he realizes. "Your very next role. You'll be quite convincing, I assure you." It is another allusion to the father sending his son, Oedipus, to his death.

Facing each other, with Eve sitting between them, Thornhill enlightens Vandamm of what is really between them. "Are you going to ask this female to kiss me again and poison me to death?" When Eve rises suddenly to slap Thornhill for his offensive remarks, he stops her with his hands but more so with his incisive words, "Who are you kidding? You have no feelings to hurt." Considering his initial introduction as a self-centered advertising man in a gray suit, Thornhill knows what he is talking about. If to go by the tears in Eve's eyes that are emphasized by the close-up her face receives, Thornhill's words cut much deeper than he realizes. Despite herself, Eve is not impervious to what transpired between them. All this is observed by the "all-seeing" Professor, who is shown after the camera moves in closer on Vandamm, singling him out as he realizes that Eve is more attached to Thornhill than he first realized.

With the escape routes blocked by Vandamm's boys, and with Eve leaving with the father, the theatrical setting of the auction, with stage and audience, suggests that Thornhill has finally made it to the "show he was looking forward to." Only now, as in a dream, it is his own production in which he plays the lead role. His outrageous improvisation, one of the comical highlights of the movie, gets him out of dire straits once again. It gets the police to rescue him from his latest brush with death. But in typical fashion, it only gets him into another performance, truly "his very next role" of playing dead. The arresting police-men, agent of the benevolent father, are instructed to take him west to Chicago's *Midway* Airport, the mid-way of his westward journey, though not before the driver reprimands the mischievous son, "You ought to be ashamed of your-self." Considering all that has been suggested, his words refer to much more than Thornhill's outlandish performance.

Under the Fathers' Gaze

Thornhill first meets the paternal Professor, the "father" of George Kaplan, at the "Northwest Airlines" terminal because "it has come necessary" for him to "interfere." The Professor uses Thornhill to advance his cause. But as a benevolent father figure, he also advances him on his journey by taking him to the monumental Fathers and the dwelling place of the dragon, "a rather formi-dable gentleman." At first Thornhill refuses to play "a *red* herring," reverting to his familiar habits that include "a mother, two ex-wives and several bar-tenders dependent upon me." Only when the Professor reveals Eve's true iden-tity and her precarious situation does Thornhill overcome his reluctance, for once thinking of someone other than himself. Like the names of the airport and the airline, m*idway* in his journey n*orthwest,* Thornhill starts transcending his infantile egocentricity.

Just as the Professor enlightens Thornhill about Eve's situation, a plane's light illuminates his face, which receives a close-up. This close-up, dissolving to the faces of the Fathers of the Mount Rushmore Monument, signals yet another chapter in Thornhill's journey — where the son comes face to face with the fathers. As suggested by his "spying" on the four faces of American presi-dents (the four of them together), what is "at stake" is Thornhill's resolving his Oedipal problem by confronting the fathers. Like a naïve boy in the Oedipal drama, up to now he was unaware, unconscious, of the role he was playing. Looking at the monumental fathers through the phallic telescope, he *feels* they are looking at him, especially the president with his initials (reversed). The fact that this whole last section takes place, as it were, under the Fathers' gaze, points to Thornhill's feeling guilty for usurping the father.

The Professor, whose name is never "pitched," just as Thornhill's father is never mentioned, is one of the fathers who remind Thornhill that he is "the cause of our present troubles." The allusion to the son's guilt for going against the father is reinforced by the brief exchange between the two. "I don't like the way Teddy Roosevelt is looking at me," complains Thornhill, feeling the father's accusing gaze. "Perhaps he's trying to give you one last word of caution, Mr. Kaplan: 'Speak softly, and carry a big stick.'" Bearing in mind that the two share their names' initials could very well suggest that Thornhill is looking at

himself. Actually, the president that "looks" at Thornhill is *George* Washington, famous for chopping down a cherry tree and confessing to his father, "I
cannot tell a lie. I cut the tree." It is yet another allusion to the son's feeling
guilty in the father's eyes and his fear of castration, especially as Thornhill,
brainchild of the Professor, assumes another George's identity "for the next 24
hours."

In Thornhill's meeting with Vandamm and his "family" in the cafeteria,
a re-enactment of the auction scene, the talk soon turns to the theater and his
acting ability in the role of Kaplan, which he now plays fully conscious. But
that does not preclude the unconscious not coming into play, as when Thornhill declares to Vandamm, "I want the girl." He is supposed to "restore her" to
the father, but in the Oedipal drama he wants her for himself. Vandamm's
observation, "She really did get under your skin," alludes to what lies underneath his words and echoes the "skin-deep" former life that Thornhill led in
Manhattan before he got involved in this production. Ever the improviser,
Thornhill grabs Eve before she exits the stage and out of his life. After repeatedly telling him to "let go of me" and "stay away from me," like his double identity, Eve shoots Thornhill-Kaplan twice, her horrified face seemingly more real
than acting. Eve's firing blank bullets, which correspond to her "phony tears,"
at a man who does not exist, is the staged killing of the fictitious George Kaplan.
It frees Thornhill from the dramatic role he was obliged to play.

With his symbolic death, Thornhill's new relationship with Eve is highlighted by the symmetrical *mise-en-scène* of their subsequent tryst in the woods.
Their two cars, on either side of the frame, are parked in such a way that it
appears as if, were they to continue straight ahead, they would converge at the
monument, the very place where her plans and his problem get "connected."
Eve's *Lincoln* Continental not only connects her to the Fathers, the paternal
monument is positioned between the two, as if keeping them apart, a subtle
image of the Oedipal triad. The "conical" shot, with the four Fathers at the
apex, recalls the three shots in which the good father was first introduced in
Washington, D.C. When Thornhill starts walking towards Eve, who responds
by walking towards him, meeting halfway, the overshadowing monument disappears from the frame as the camera tracks in closer to complement their
closeness. It does not appear again for the remainder of the scene.

No longer under the Fathers' gaze, Eve and Thornhill are completely honest and open with one another for the first time in the movie. Eve's confessing
to seeing "only" Vandamm's charm, suggests that her taking up with this paternal figure is more unconscious than conscious. Despite her obvious sophisti-
cation, she got involved with Vandamm as a substitute for a marriageable man,
or a father. Her relationship with the bad father, after all, mirrors Thornhill's
relationship with his mother. Pointing out that Thornhill's "problem" in not
believing in marriage, Eve, back to business before pleasure, begs him not to
"undermine my resolve, just when I need it most." Thornhill is willing to play

his part in the drama as long as he thinks he will have her "after this night." Where he is "off to the hospital," she is "back to danger."

In their walk towards the Professor's car, Thornhill promises to get together with Eve ("After your malevolent friend Vandamm takes off tonight, you and I are going to get together and do a lot of apologizing to each other, in private"). This talk of their getting together is done in a single shot, which constantly shows the couple together at the center of the frame. But as Eve's response ("You know this can't be") and the cinematography demonstrate (the single shot of the two is broken by a shot of the Professor, who enters and remains in the frame), this is not to be. They each have their obligations to the father. Only when he learns that the Professor intends for Eve to go off with the bad father, that she still belongs to him, does Thornhill confront the good father head on.

No longer play-acting, no longer a pawn in the Fathers' "games," Thornhill's reply to the Professor signals the start of his breaking free from the fathers' hold. "If you fellas can't beat the Vandamms of this world without asking girls like her to bed down with them and fly away with them and probably never come back, perhaps you should start losing a few cold wars." As the Professor admits, the fathers are no longer as "formidable" as in the past. Primarily because Thornhill is no longer a little boy. He is "supposed to be critically wounded," but as he confesses to Eve, "I've never felt more alive."

Just as the "fathers' gaze" opens every scene of the movie's third and final segment, the Mount Rushmore Monument is mentioned in the radio news report about Kaplan's "shooting" that Thornhill is listening to in his hospital room. The announcement, which describes Kaplan as "tentatively identified," is another sign of Thornhill's reclaiming his true identity. Locked in his hospital room, barred from saving the captive princess, he is shown pacing back and forth like a caged animal, nervously playing with his (phallic) comb. The Professor providing him with new clothing underscores his role in Thornhill's renewal. Not only has Thornhill risen from the dead, he has awakened from a state of unconscious. He is a new man, resolved to save Eve from Vandamm. But to achieve this he must overcome the Professor and Vandamm, the benevolent and the malevolent fathers, two obstacles who obstruct him from attaining the object of his desire. Thornhill easily overcomes the Professor, by fooling him into thinking he is "a cooperator." Overcoming Vandamm, the formidable dragon that holds the princess captive, requires much more improvisation and heroism.

The Dragon's Lair

Thornhill's approach to the dragon's lair, by cab, is once again under the gaze of the formidable Mount Rushmore monument. This time, however, by the way it is positioned in the upper left frame, it is indeed Theodore Roosevelt who is "looking" at him. But Thornhill, no longer under his spell, is impervious to his "look." The first thing he sees of the castle is the drawing of the curtain, which recalls Vandamm's drawing the curtains in the Townsend library, thus continuing the theater metaphor but also pointing to its being a re-enactment of Thornhill's first encounter with Vandamm at the Townsend home. Only now it is Vandamm's own home, the dragon having come home to roost. Moving to the other side of the house, Thornhill has a backstage view, a privileged observer rather than a reluctant participant.

Inside, while reviewing Eve's shooting Kaplan, which seems to have attained the desired results, Vandamm once again has his hand around her neck. And just as in the auction gallery, the camera follows the two to the right, revealing Leonard's presence. Once again, Thornhill observes his projection of the family triad in the Oedipal drama. Vandamm's vow to Eve, "Soon we'll be off together and I shall dedicate myself to your happiness," echoes Thornhill's "Yours, always darling," in response to Eve's "Whose side are you on?" in the forest. It is another reminder of the two's rivalry — for Eve. Moreover, Leonard asking Vandamm to "have a few words of parting," adding "in private," recalls Thornhill's very words to Eve in the forest.

Left alone, Vandamm turns to Leonard. "Well, Leonard, how does one say goodbye to one's right arm?" "In your case, sir, I'm afraid you are gonna wish you had cut it off sooner," Leonard's reply suggests castration, complemented by the "right arm" with his left hand in his pants pocket. The next time we see him, after Thornhill fails to get Eve's attention by throwing coins at her bedroom window, Leonard has his right hand in his *coat* pocket. When he sits down to face the standing Vandamm, we (and Thornhill) see the gun he furtively takes out of his coat pocket and hides behind his back. Failing to persuade Vandamm of Eve's deception, Leonard shoots at him right after he comments about his place in the family triad ("I think you're jealous"). By shooting Vandamm with the same gun that Eve shot blank cartridges at Thornhill, Leonard both proves Eve's deceit and acts out an unconscious desire. Where up to this point the father and son were shown sharing the frame, the shooting and Vandamm's knocking down Leonard are shot identically, with a lighted lamp on the left side of each one, emphasizing the two as mirrored images of one another and recalling similar shots of Thornhill and Vandamm in the Townsend library.

Whereas the first shooting of blanks was designed to restore Eve to Vandamm, this second shooting (there is a third) puts her at his mercy. The two "are on" to Eve but not to Thornhill's presence. With the information gained from his privileged observation point, Thornhill is in a position to save Eve from her doom. But beyond that, his observing a performance of the son's firing a gun at the father is another of his unconscious projections. This is suggested by the shot of Leonard receiving Vandamm's fist, which matches the shot of Thornhill receiving the fist of the Professor's driver. Just as the Professor has his driver do the punching, Thornhill has Leonard, his shadowy double, do the shooting. As if receiving their deserved punishment for patricide, one real (knifing Townsend) and one performance (shooting blanks at Vandamm), Valerian and Leonard are killed at the movie's end.

In an act of reclaiming his name, Thornhill scribbles a message to Eve on his monogrammed matchbook, "They're on to you. I'm in your room." The written message, which corresponds to Eve's message to Vandamm on the train, has the opposite intent. Whereas Eve was part of the plan to send Thornhill to his doom, now it is her own doom that he wants to prevent; whereas she sent him to be killed *by* an airplane, he saves her from being killed *from* an airplane. As Thornhill is shown trying to find the right moment to throw the matchbook so that Eve will see it, Vandamm is overheard chastising Leonard, not unlike a father to a son. "You always were the spoilsport, weren't you?" Addressing Leonard but showing Thornhill is yet another suggestion that it is his unconscious projection. Unknowingly (unconsciously), Leonard helps Eve escape by putting Thornhill's matchbook on the table right under her nose.

Thornhill's message recalls the message he was trying to send to his mother. But where he failed with his mother, he succeeds with her replacement, whom he warns about the father. As Eve discovers Thornhill's message, Leonard is heard describing the plane's approach to landing, which can be taken as his describing what Thornhill, shown three times during Leonard's account, must do to save Eve. Going up to her room, she sees him for the first time since he was knocked unconscious. As his monogram indicates, he is back to being Roger Thornhill, and a rejuvenated (conscious) one at that. "What are you doing here, Roger?" she asks, calling him by his name for the first time in the movie. In complete contrast to her sending him to Prairie Point, Thornhill warns Eve, "Whatever you do, don't get on that plane." The camera stays with Thornhill inside the house as Eve, Vandamm and Leonard, the three of them together, leave the house and walk towards the nearby airfield.

The end of the theater metaphor and the start of the real "performance" is signaled by the housekeeper's catching sight of Thornhill's reflection in the TV screen. While the dramatic role of George Kaplan gets him in touch with his unconscious, with his repressed Oedipal problem, it is in being (the conscious) Roger Thornhill that he resolves his problem. Representing the last maternal obstacle in reclaiming his identity, the house*keeper* holds Thornhill at gunpoint, ordering him to "Stay where you are." At the very last moment, as Vandamm is shown parting from his "son," and just before Eve boards the plane from which she will "fall" to her death, two shots are heard from Vandamm's house, where Thornhill has just realized that the housekeeper's gun holds blanks, much like the "blank" identity of George Kaplan. Completely free from the mother, Thornhill, like a prince on a white horse, comes to the princess' rescue driving the father's car, this time consciously replacing the father.

Complementing Thornhill's resurrected identity, Eve also undergoes a transformation. When her shawl gets caught in a tree branch, after she and Thornhill are forced to abandon the car and flee by foot, rather than waste time in untangling it, Eve leaves it behind, signaling her parting with her undercover role of pretense and deceit and her freeing herself once and for all from the father. Running hand in hand, the two come to the top of the Mount Rushmore monument, an apt setting for resolving an Oedipal problem.

The change in Thornhill becomes apparent when, "face to face" with the Fathers, he corrects Eve, who mistakes his proposal for proposition. Unlike their first meeting, when Eve propositioned Thornhill and called the shots, now she is the damsel in distress, her life depending on his heroics. Eve's biggest threat of death comes when Thornhill holds her with one hand while he clings to a ledge with his other. The way this event is shot, Leonard's black shoe on the upper half of the frame squashing Thornhill's lighter hand on the lower half of the frame, it is another indication of their being two sides. More than the movie's final intersection of the horizontal with the vertical (the ledge being the horizontal and Leonard's foot and Thornhill's arm the vertical), this shot (shown twice) shows the meeting of the two halves, the two sons— of the malevolent and benevolent fathers. This is reinforced by Leonard holding the desired statue and Thornhill holding the woman.

Only with Leonard's death (and Vandamm's arrest) is Thornhill completely free from his shadow and from the ogre father who embody the dragon. As Lesley Brill notes in his book *The Hitchcock Romance*, Hitchcock's explanation is recorded in François Truffaut's *Hitchcock*: "An odor of dragon-killing lingers in the deaths of Vandamm's knife-throwing gardener and Leonard.... Leonard's death is of particular interest, in part because Hitchcock has spoken with satisfaction of dividing the villain's role among Vandamm and his associates."[4]

As shown next, Thornhill saves Eve and makes good on his proposal. Having made the descent to the dark *under*cover world, the unconscious, he is finally free to pursue his feelings on a higher plain of consciousness, without guilt or deceit. What starts as Thornhill's pulling Eve up from her likely fall in Mount Rushmore is completed by his pulling her up to the *upper* berth of the sleeping compartment on the train going home. In contrast to the many intersecting lines that run throughout the movie, particularly the movie's opening, the "Southern" train going through the tunnel is the masculine penetrating the feminine, in a happy north-north*east* direction. As Hitchcock himself has remarked about this final shot, "There are no symbols in *North by Northwest*. Oh, yes. One. The last shot, the train entering the tunnel.... It's a phallic symbol. But don't tell anyone." Of course, coming from Hitchcock, it is much more than mere tongue-in-cheek. *Northwest*, after all, is replete with symbols from start to finish. The final act of marriage, Thornhill giving his father's name to the new "Mrs. Thornhill" (the first time the two are linked together in the movie) is the "connection," the coming together, of Eve's plans to get married and Thornhill resolving his Oedipal problem. It is best symbolized by the dark hole of the tunnel that the train enters, an image which brings to mind the "O" of Thornhill's monogram but also the ring of matrimony.

Part III

ABSENT FATHERS

You'll never be fainthearted or a fool, Telemakhos, if you have your father's spirit.

> —Athena, disguised as Mentor, assuring
> Telemachus in Book II of *The Odyssey*

Absent fathers are nothing new. Many fairy tales and myths tell of father-less boys who fend for themselves, or find surrogate fathers, on their way to manhood. One of the better-known absent fathers, and perhaps its prototype, is Odysseus. He is even referred to as "the absent one." As the name of Homer's epic indicates, *The Odyssey* is his story, recounting his drawn-out return home after many years of absence. Nevertheless, the son's longing for his absent father's return does not go unnoticed. After all, part of what makes Odysseus the hero that he is, what makes him the complete man, is his fatherhood. In fact, *The Odyssey* begins with the son and the father's absence and ends with their joining forces in regaining their home, with Odysseus becoming the father Telemachus never had.

When we first meet Telemachus, he is "sitting there, unhappy among the suitors, a boy, daydreaming. What if his great father came from the unknown world and drove these men like dead leaves through the place, recovering honor and lordship of his domain?"[1] He dreams of his absent father and what he would do on his return. As suits a young hero, however, Telemachus does not remain "sitting there" forever. He embarks on his own mini–Odyssey in the *Telemachia*, a prototype for the father quest just as *The Odyssey* is a synonym for the hero's journey. In his journey by sea, just like his father, Telemachus sails "to ask for news about his father, gone for years."[2] And since the tale opens with the *Telemachia*, which underscores Telemachus' need for his absent father, we are apt to have him in the back of our minds as we follow Odysseus' adventures. We want Odysseus to rescue Penelope from the suitors just as much as to return so that Telemachus will have the father he so longs for. As he reveals to the goddess Athena, disguised as Mentor, "He's gone, no sign, no word of him; and I inherit trouble and tears." Athena replies: "Ah, bitterly you need Odysseus, then!"[3]

In his father's absence, Athena becomes, as it were, Telemachus' *mentor*. Knowing that Odysseus is alive, she serves as the initiator of his rite of passage. Her encouraging words rouse him from his daydreaming, putting "new spirit in him, a new dream of his father."[4] As Athena-Mentor imparts to Telemachus, "The son is rare who measures with his father, and one in a thousand is a better man, but you will have the sap and wit and prudence—for you get that from Odysseus—to give you a fair chance of winning through."[5]

With Athena's assurance, Telemachus embarks on a quest for his father, which marks his separation from his home and mother. Rather than accept his mother's account of his father, he must find out for himself. "My mother says I am his son; I know not surely."[6] Telemachus' search, which parallels Odysseus' own odyssey back home, teaches him much about his legendary father. He visits two of his father's old friends, Nestor and Menelaus, who cannot give him the information he seeks, whether his father is dead or alive, but they encourage him and tell him about his father's heroics in the Trojan War. In the words of Nestor, which anticipate Odysseus' out-smarting the suitors, "He had no rivals, your father, at the tricks of war."[7]

In his quest, Telemachus finally gets a picture of his father as experienced by other men, thus assuring him of his manliness. They serve as surrogate fathers who initiate Telemachus into the world of men, a world where his father has no rivals. And yet, Telemachus still needs his father's return to put all this into action. Without a father to initiate him into manhood, he is in a bind, just as many sons of today's absent fathers. "If father is not there to provide a confident, rich model of manhood, then the boy is left in a vulnerable position: having to distance himself from mother without a clear and understandable model of male gender upon which to base his emerging identity."[8]

In contrast to some of today's absent fathers, many of whom are absent even when present, upon his return Odysseus provides what his son sorely needs. He initiates him into adulthood by engaging him in the fight to regain their home from the suitors. Interestingly, despite knowing only his mother while growing up, there is no mention of Telemachus resenting his father for repossessing his woman. Not that he ever lost her. Telemachus is no Oedipus. He is truly glad to have his father back. The way the two connect is precisely how every son wants to connect with his father — through love and collaboration rather than rivalry and guilt. As Samuel Osherson points out in his book, *Finding Our Fathers*, "We have grown up thinking of Oedipus rivalry between father and son, the guilty wish to surpass the father, but we need also attend to the Odysseus theme, the wish to be like father, to find a father, a sturdy man we can rely on."[9] Of course, as sturdy and reliable fathers go, Odysseus has "no rivals."

Odysseus' "unrivaled" fatherhood is revealed early in *The Odyssey* when his ability to fight is tested by King Agamemnon's messenger, who has come to summon him to war. The wise Odysseus, who foresees the disaster in going to fight the Trojans, tries to evade the summons by playing insane, harnessing an ox and an ass to the same plow and sowing salt instead of seeds into the soil. Putting his sanity to the test, the messenger places Telemachus in front of the plow. Odysseus's plowing around him proves his saneness but also his love for his son. Unlike Abraham, who was willing to sacrifice his son, Odysseus has a different set of priorities. His son comes first.

Unfortunately, nowadays many sons feel like sons of Abraham, sons who feel sacrificed for their fathers' personal priorities. Odysseus' love for his son and his joining forces with him are largely absent in today's father-son relationships. Unlike Telemachus, many sons no longer seek out their fathers, thus relegating their need for a father to the unconscious, where it becomes a dragon, the introjected father. Regrettable as this situation may seem, one way to still experience *The Odyssey*'s type of father-son relationship is through the movies, which provide the next best thing. Just witness the huge following of George Lucas' *Star Wars* trilogy, which is probably the most prominent (popular) movies that deals with the absent father and the son's father quest. Much as he is unlike Odysseus, Darth Vader's startling words to Luke Skywalker, in *The Empire Strikes Back*, "I am your father," perhaps the key line in the trilogy, echo Odysseus' words to Telemachus, "I am that father whom your boyhood lacked and suffered pain for lack of."[10] Surely the father-son theme and the presence of Darth Vader, Dark Father, the dragon of the filmmyths, is part of *Star Wars*' enormous success. What son does not long for his absent father?

The three movies covered in this section, *E.T.*, *Field of Dreams* and *Lone Star*, may not follow Odysseus' adventure, but they are no less expressions of the son's longing and need for his father. Unlike most of *The Odyssey*, these movies focus on the son. Each story is told from his point of view. In each film something extraordinary takes the hero out of his ordinary world, prompting a journey where he deals with his absent father. In *E.T.* it is the extra-terrestrial; in *Field of Dreams* it is Shoeless Joe Jackson; in *Lone Star* it is skeletons from the closet and ghosts from the past. And as in *The Odyssey*, in each movie there is some semblance of the absent father's return; each of the three cinematic heroes shares something with Telemachus. Elliot is visited by E.T. as Telemachus by Athena. In *Field of Dreams*, the hero joins forces with his father in playing catch in the field of dreams just as Telemachus joins forces with Odysseus in killing the suitors. In *Lone Star*, while investigating an historical crime, the hero's learning about his legendary father recalls Telemachus finding out about his mythological father.

Beyond what they share with *The Odyssey*, all three movies reflect and address a problem shared by half of all American families, a problem that only lately has started to be dealt with in the media and in a growing number of publications. One of the recent books on the subject, David Blankenhorn's *Fatherless America*, opens with a grim exposé of the absent father:

> The United States is becoming an increasingly fatherless society.... Fatherlessness is now approaching a rough parity with fatherhood as a defining feature of American Childhood.... Never before have so many children grown up without knowing what it means to have a father.[11]

Together with the findings that today's parents spent 40 percent less time with their children than the previous generation, and that fatherless children are more prone to end up on the bad side of the law, the future is far from promising, to say the least. Sad and distressing as this may seem, *absent fathers* has become an accepted fact of our lives. According to Blankenhorn, "the most important absence our society must confront is not the absence of fathers but the absence of our belief in fathers."[12]

In this section's three movies, each of the fatherless heroes comes to *believe* in his father after undertaking an inner journey. While Elliot of *E.T.* undergoes the journey as a child of ten, Ray Kinsella of *Field of Dreams* and Sam Deeds of *Lone Star* deal with their fathers, their dragons, as men in their midlife. Like many contemporary father-son stories, the father's absence takes its toll on all three sons. Unlike many of these stories, however, and much like *The Odyssey*, all three movies have a happy end. In each one the unfinished business with the absent father is resolved. In each case, what changes is the way the son perceives his father, how he deals with his introjected father, his dragon. Elliot overcomes the painful experience of abandonment, slaying the dragon that keeps him apart from his family and other kids. Ray Kinsella slays the dragon that bars his way to home plate by playing catch with his father in a field of dreams he had built for his coming. In his investigation, Sam Deeds slays the dragon that obstructs his view of his legendary father, whom he holds culpable for killing Charlie Wade and breaking up his relationship with Pilar.

All three movies resemble *The Odyssey* in that they are *cathartic* in the classical sense of the word. The moving endings of *E.T.* and *Field of Dreams* bring many of us to tears. Watching these movies dissipates, however momentarily, our demons. For a short while the dragon disappears. We may even come to feel we are our fathers' sons.

Chapter 7

E.T.: The Extra-Terrestrial
Advent of the Absent Father

I really always thought E.T. was a story about divorce. And it was sort of my story about my parents who got divorced when I was a teenager ... and the effect it had on me. And I really felt that picture was about looking for a surrogate father, looking for someone to fill the void of the missing parent.
— Steven Spielberg, *AFI's 100 Years ... 100 Movies*, television program

A Tale of Two Stories

Perhaps more than any other contemporary filmmaker, Steven Spielberg is a direct descendant of such cinematic storytellers as Ford, Hawks and Hitchcock. He uses the American landscape much as Hawks and Ford used the mythic West, and like Hitchcock, he knows how to build and sustain suspense. "Hitchcock was probably my best teacher,"[1] Spielberg has acknowledged. That he learned his craft well was demonstrated by the enormous success of such movies as *Jaws* and *Close Encounters of the Third Kind*. But it was not until his seventh film, the 1982 *E.T.*, that Spielberg came into his own as a cinematic storyteller.

> I think the responsibility of an artist is to just get to know themselves really well, and to put as much of yourself in your work. And not pretend to be somebody else. Don't try to be somebody you admire. I did that for a lot in the early part of my career. I wanted to be John Ford. I wanted to be Alfred Hitchcock. I wanted to be everybody but me. It took me a whole number of films before I was comfortable with allowing myself to be seen through my films.[2]

No doubt *E.T.*'s unprecedented success is partly due to Spielberg (finally) telling his own story — about his "missing father." Through Elliot's parting from E.T., which is a re-enactment of his father's abandonment, Spielberg re-enacts his own parting from *his* father. "I really have always thought *E.T.*

was about the divorce of my mom and dad. Ever since my parents' divorce (I think I was 16 or 17 years old) I had a lot of stories in my mind about how to tell it, and I had this story kicking around about a boy who finds an imaginary friend (in this case would be an extraterrestrial friend), and that was going to fill his many, many needs for the missing father."[3]

Spielberg's earlier movies had touched the subject of the absent father, particularly *Close Encounters of the Third Kind*, but it was never such a personal and heartfelt story as *E.T.* In his first movie about a boy, Spielberg shows what he felt as a boy without a father, sharing with us an intimate and crucial time in his life. With E.T., whose hiding place is the walk-in closet, Spielberg came out of his emotional closet. Tellingly, the "game master" with "absolute power" (in the Dungeons and Dragons game) is named Steve, and, with the advent of E.T., that power is transferred to Elliot. "I made my most personal film in 1982 with *E.T.* And to this day I think it remains my most personal film.... All the kids in the movie are combinations of myself and my own family growing up."[4]

Together with Spielberg telling his story, *E.T.* is also a mirrored *Wizard of Oz*: three humans helping the extra-terrestrial return home. It is a retelling of Dorothy's adventure in the Land of Oz. Outer space replaces Kansas and the California suburb the Land of Oz. And just as Dorothy's adventure in Oz is her dream, and thus unconscious, the movie repeatedly suggests that E.T. is a projection of Elliot's unconscious.

> Although separated by more than forty years, *The Wizard of Oz* and *E.T.* have in common the fact that they are two of the most popular films of all time.... Probably the explanation for the success of these films lies with the fact that they dramatize some unconscious fantasies that children feel to be primordial; these films speak to the deepest part of themselves.[5]

The fact that the extra-terrestrial is a kind of creature many children dream about and wish for is another suggestion that E.T. is a product of Elliot's unconscious, a dream come true. Like his first spoken words, "Be good," E.T. is all good. There is not an ounce of meanness or cynicism in him. He is innocent, though not without a healthy sense of humor. He is a mixture of such cinematic figures as Peter Pan, Mary Poppins and Shane — archetypal figures from another world (the unconscious) that change the life of the children they encounter. In earlier movies, such as *Lassie Come Home* (which sounds much like "E.T. phone home") and *Old Yeller*, this figure was often portrayed by a friendly dog. And as if hailing back to those movies, Elliot also has a dog, whose name is presumably borrowed from the movie *Harvey*, where the hero (James Stewart) sees and talks to a six-foot-tall white rabbit he calls Harvey that no one else can see. But the extra-terrestrial easily outdoes both Harveys. He is everything a boy could wish for.

Surprising as it may seem, considering his kinship with children, this friendship between a boy and a benevolent creature is a first for Spielberg. In two of his first three features, *Duel* ('71) and *Jaws* ('75), America's "premier filmmaker" dealt with the dark and malevolent (unconscious) forces, forces commonly depicted in myths and fairytales as dragons. While in *Duel* it came in the shape of a monstrous, revenge-seeking truck, driven by a faceless and anonymous driver, in *Jaws,* Spielberg's first blockbuster, it was embodied by a gruesome shark. In fact, Spielberg sees *Jaws* as another *Duel,* as "something which is a truck, only the truck is a Leviathan under water."[6]

After dealing with the dark and malevolent forces that came from *behind* and *below,* Spielberg counterbalanced it with two "light" (versus dark) movies about benevolent creatures from *above, Close Encounters of the Third Kind* ('77) and *E.T.* In both movies the benevolent creatures come from outer space, but *E.T.* is much more about inner space and inner feelings, represented by the extra-terrestrial's red heart-light. Through his emotional relationship and painful parting from E.T., who is all feelings, Elliot deals with his feelings of abandonment before they become a menacing dragon, like the dragons represented by the hostile aliens of many science fiction films of the fifties that the young Spielberg saw while growing up. In the process of telling both Elliot's and his own story, Spielberg, who "uses film rather like a psychiatrist tackling a phobia — not just for his patients, the audience, but for himself,"[7] deals with the dragon in the unconscious dungeon we all share. In the best tradition of Hawks, Ford and Hitchcock, his brilliant storytelling and subtle depiction of the unconscious "speaks to the deepest part of" ourselves.

A Dream Come True

Conveyed with only pictures and sounds, *E.T.*'s exposition sets the mood of the movie by its "fantasized, perfect, oceanic bliss of reunion with the pre-verbal mother, a reunion where there are no words or thoughts, but purely empathic, intuitive communication."[8] This harmonious ambiance, this "oceanic bliss," comes to an abrupt end with the arrival of shadowy figures, much as Elliot's feeling of home comes to a sudden end when he is abandoned by his father.

E.T.'s opening shot shows a starry night sky, the place from which the spaceship comes to earth. With a variation on E.T.'s musical theme on the soundtrack, the camera tilts downwards, as if making a soft landing in a forest, a familiar symbol of the unconscious. The downward shot stops when the screen is equally divided between sky and earth, the two worlds of E.T. and Elliot. This image, like much of the exposition, suggests a connection between the two. Another connection is suggested in the following shot of the spaceship, where in the upper left side of the frame are the lights of Elliot's suburb. Though we do not know it, our first glimpse of E.T. is the shadowy pair of thin elongated fingers reaching for a branch in the foreground (an image repeated several times in the course of the movie), which serves as another reminder of the movie's *twin* motif. We next see the extra-terrestrial walking towards "twin" monolithic trees, an image suggesting the symbiotic relationship between E.T. and Elliot, especially as they are also shown *twice*. As the extra-terrestrial comes up to the starry landscape of the lighted suburbia down below, in two shots/ reverse shots, we see (for the first time) his point of view, looking at the lighted homes below, as if drawn to Elliot. The second shot of his looking in Elliot's direction is abruptly disturbed by the appearance of a lone car with sets of twin headlights, disrupting the idyllic night, with more cars arriving right behind. Among shots of the men's lower parts, the camera follows a jangling set of keys hanging from one figure's belt. As the repeated shots of the keys suggest, this man is the key to the movie. The cars' fuming exhaust pipes and the muddy puddles signal the "poisoning" of the innocent, the expulsion from the *Garden of Eden,* both E.T.'s and Elliot's.

After showing the mother ship's entrance, where a lone extra-terrestrial stands, as if waiting for the tardy E.T., much as Elliot's mother waits for him in Halloween, the camera cuts to E.T. hiding in the bushes, radiating an inner red light and emitting a sound of fear that gives him away. On the verge of being discovered by the shadowy figures' searchlights, a complete contrast to the extra-terrestrials' inner light, E.T. rushes towards the mothership, which takes off without him. Left behind, he is shown following the mothership fly away in the night sky, the same sky that the dark figures are beaming their flashlights at. He is last seen walking towards another source of light — Elliot's suburb. The exposition's closing shot of the well-lighted suburb below repeats its opening shot of the starry night sky up above, making one last connection between E.T. and Elliot.

Being that the father's abandonment is mostly left to our imagination, E.T.'s abandonment "imagines" what Elliot must have experienced, particularly as his introduction parallels the exposition. As Elliot's mirror image, E.T. reflects what he must have *felt.* Both are left behind — E.T. by his mother ship, Elliot by his father. Much as the dark, flashlight-wielding figures disrupt the idyllic scene of extra-terrestrials visit, causing E.T. to be left behind, the father's leaving with his girlfriend disrupts Elliot's family.

The Advent of E.T.

Just as the suburb lights in the exposition double for the starry night sky that opened the movie, the opening shot of Elliot's home doubles for E.T.'s mother ship. Likewise, where the exposition's second shot showed the lamp-like spaceship, now the second shot, inside the house, shows a flowery, bell-like lamp above the family dining room table around which four boys are playing *Dungeons and Dragons.* Elliot, in the center of the frame, is left out of the game as E.T. was left behind by his own people. The sequence's first audible sentence, "You got an arrow right in your chest," part of the *Dungeons and*

Dragons game, may very well describe what E.T. must have felt, especially considering his glowing chest. It may also allude to what happened to Elliot, who has been wounded by his father's abandonment.

Dungeons and Dragons, a popular fantasy game in the '80s, is one way to deal with their introjected fathers, embodied in the unconscious dungeon by the dragon. This is reinforced by one boy phoning the local radio station, requesting the song "*Papa*-Oom-Mow-Mow," which is repeated several times, as if to emphasize its significance. Taken together, Elliot's "I'm ready to play" intimates that he is ready to deal with his introjected papa, the dragon that came alive with his father's leaving.

Before he is allowed to join the game, Elliot is sent outside by Steve, the game master, to wait for the ordered pizza, another sign of his separateness. As if for protection, he takes along a baseball and a glove (which, as we learn later, he associates with his father), the same baseball through which he initiates his connection with E.T. While a dog is heard barking outside, from inside the house "Papa-Oom-Mow-Mow" comes from the radio, the words anticipating the papa's "coming around" and showing his face. The fact that it is heard while Elliot hears E.T.'s noise, coming from the tool shed, a place commonly associated with the father, alludes to the *coming around* of both E.T. and the father, the "papa" who shows his covered face only after entering Elliot's house in his search for the extra-terrestrial.

Elliot's thinking the noise comes from his dog Harvey is another suggestion that E.T. is for Elliot what the white rabbit named Harvey was for Elwood P. Dowd (James Stewart) in the movie by the same name. Both uncanny friends are more imagined than real — Harvey by "fact," E.T. by suggestion. Elliot tosses his baseball into the tool shed, only to have it tossed right back, a sign that there is some form of intelligence inside, and a *playful* one at that. Bearing in mind that his father is no longer around to take him to ball games, or play ping-pong (on the table shown on the back porch), a game for two *players*, Elliot's connection with E.T. takes up where the father left off. Because of the appearance of E.T., Elliot never gets to play D & D. But with his advent he gets his wish to play, and much more. More than a playmate, he gets a soul mate. He gets to play E & E, a real live fantasy, his own way of dealing with the dragon in his unconscious dungeon.

Running parallel to the absent father, the mother's absence is of a different kind. She is present, but hardly as a mother. "How do you win this game, anyway?" she asks, as if, like Elliot, she wants to join the game as one of the boys. She is provocative in her red kimono and not very successful at keeping order. She fails to keep the boys from going outside to see what Elliot claims is out there. She can't even get them to put away the kitchen knives. The only sign of authority is her holding the flashlight, her scepter, the same tool used by the male agents in the exposition. As this brief scene shows, the mother could use a man around the house. Once she realizes that there are strange footprints in their yard, however, she shoos the boys like a hen with her chicks, anticipating her "coming around" to her motherhood in the course of the movie.

After a privileged view of what is in the tool shed, of E.T.'s two fingers wrapping around the shed's door, the camera cuts to a picture of Harvey, the dog that Elliot thought was making the noise. The juxtaposition of the two is another suggestion that E.T. replaces Elliot's best friend, much as Keys replaces his father. This pair motif is underscored by the picture of Harvey and the clock (that reads two) sharing the frame and by the bunk bed that Harvey and Elliot share, not to mention their sensing that something is out there. As it soon becomes apparent, E.T. can sense Elliot too. That is why he comes around in the first place — he feels what Elliot feels: abandoned. The two's twin-ness is highlighted when, in their first encounter, they are equally frightened. Even though we mostly see the response of Elliot, with whom we have come to identify by now (after first identifying with E.T.), the rapid crosscutting emphasizes the mutual response, thus neutralizing the two's fear of one another. Significantly, Elliot drops the flashlight, the instrument that previously searched for E.T. in a most threatening manner. The sequence's closing shot shows Elliot looking up at the night sky with a slight smile, as if thanking a benevolent being (the Father) for making his wish for a friend come true.

That for Elliot E.T. fills the space left empty by the father is suggested during the first family sequence at the dining room table. The four family members are around the triangular table, with Elliot in the middle, sitting, as it were, at the base of the isosceles triangle. The rest of the family sits on the lateral sides. Apparently the father's place, now empty, was next to Gertie, opposite Michael (who is sitting next to his mother and shares the frame with her in the first part of the sequence, as if now he is the acting father).

From the talk around the table, it is clear that no one believes Elliot's story about the extra-terrestrial. "All we're trying to say is, maybe you just probably imagined it," says his mother, intimating that E.T. is Elliot's "imaginary friend." Saying "Dad would believe me," Elliot reminds her of the change their family has undergone, of her husband's abandonment, and that she cannot fill his empty place. The fact that the first time the father is mentioned is tied with E.T. underscores the connection between his absence and the advent of the extra-terrestrial. Elliot's reply to the mother's "Why don't you call him," "I can't. He's in Mexico with Sally," seems to express both his pain of abandonment and his anger at his mother who could not hold on to her husband. It upsets her enough so that she leaves the table, emphasizing her unavailability to her children. Like a father, Michael upbraids Elliot: "Dammit, why don't you grow up, think how other people feel for a change?" which is exactly what Elliot does from the moment he meets E.T. He both feels what another being feels and grows up by reliving the pain of his father's abandonment. This is intimated by the last shot of the sequence, which shows Elliot rinsing his dishes under hot water at the sink. Shot from outside, where E.T. is (and also the father), Elliot wistfully looks skywards through the hot water's steam, as if he feels E.T.'s presence or thinks of his father's absence. From what is shown so far, it is probably both.

This look heavenward is continued in the opening shot of the next scene when Elliot, having fallen asleep on a patio chair, aims the beam of his flashlight upwards, as if signaling the creature he saw the night before. Hearing sounds from the tool shed, he wakes up to see E.T., the camera slowly closing in on his face to show his reaction. Now that he meets the creature that he sought, it's much more frightening than he first believed. As E.T. slowly approaches him, the terrified Elliot tries to call out to his mother and Michael. Much like their initial meeting, when Elliot first tossed a baseball and E.T. tossed it right back, the extra-terrestrial reaches with his two elongated fingers to return some of the Reese's Pieces that Elliot left in the forest. Now, in their third meeting, after a sign of good will from the extra-terrestrial, the two finally meet face to face and do not flee from one another. Despite E.T.'s initial "unattractiveness," it is clear that he is a friendly and benevolent creature. With the extra-terrestrial in his room, and assured that he is gentle and friendly, Elliot can finally fall asleep after two sleepless nights in which he waited for his return, just as he surely waits for his father's return.

That Elliot is waiting for the father is suggested by the brief scene sandwiched between his first night with E.T. and the next day, which singles out the man with the keys among the faceless men searching for E.T. at the spot where he was last seen before heading towards Elliot's home. The man's finding the Reese's Pieces left by Elliot implies that, however unconsciously, he left it for him just as much as for E.T. Particularly as the advent of E.T. initiates the advent of Keys, and the closer Elliot and E.T. become, the closer Keys comes to finding them. And to remind us that the movie is about Elliot's psychological growth, the candy also serves as a transition to the first of the three stages of psychological development that make up the next part of the movie. Only after outgrowing these three stages does he abandon the wish to keep E.T. for himself and starts helping him return home.

Growing Up Together

Oral Stage

The opening shot of the morning after E.T.'s arrival, showing Elliot with a thermometer in his mouth, and all the talk of food, introduces what may be called the "oral stage," the first psychosexual stage where the mouth is the principal erogenous zone. As the organ by which the baby intakes food, it "expresses the drive toward taking into oneself, absorbing, contracting, grasping (in the sense of understanding) — as well as grabbing into one's possession."[9] This is underscored by Elliot showing E.T., among other foodstuff, a Coke can ("Coke. You see, we drink it. It's a, it's a drink. You know, food") and the fish in his small aquarium: "And look. Fish. The fish eats the fish food, and the shark eats the fish, but nobody eats the shark." Of course, the shark recalls another, much hungrier creature, Jaws, who is mostly mouth. A clear reference to oral greed is *Greedo*, the first of the small toy figures that Elliot introduces to E.T. But the clincher is Elliot's rather long explanation to E.T. about his world. "See, this is Pez candy. See, you eat it.... You want some? This is a peanut [a piggy bank shaped as a giant peanut]. You eat it, but you can't eat this one, 'cause this is fake." When E.T. starts eating the plastic toy car that Elliot explains "is what we get around in," he asks, "Are you hungry? I'm hungry."

This mutual hunger is the first sign of the two's symbiotic relationship. Elliot's parting words to get some food, "I'll be right here," anticipate E.T.'s parting words prior to his return home. The *two in one* motif is further highlighted by the first crosscutting between the two—Elliot downstairs getting food from the refrigerator, E.T. upstairs playing with Elliot's earthly objects. The two are startled simultaneously when E.T. unexpectedly opens the easy-open umbrella. His dropping the umbrella rhymes with Elliot's dropping the milk carton, clutching his chest. The shot of the spilled carton of milk reinforces the two's first significant communication through food, and (mother's) milk at that. When Elliot returns to his room with *two* plates of food, he finds E.T. in the closet, hiding behind stuffed animals, trembling in fear. "Want a Coke?" He tries to calm E.T. down as a mother would a baby.

At this stage of their relationship, Elliot plays the mother to the new arrival, who depends on him for his survival. Providing E.T. with his needs builds the trust that characterizes the oral stage and their developing relationship. But where a child passes through the three stages during his early years, with his extraordinary intelligence and powers, E.T. passes through them in a couple of days, until he starts to talk. And by virtue of their symbiotic relationship, E.T.'s growing also has a direct effect on Elliot's growing up. As Elliot puts it, they "grow up together."

Anal Stage

Michael singing (twice) about "So many people ... you can add to your *collection*," and his opening the refrigerator door with "nothing but health *shit*," starts what can be described as the anal stage, the second stage characterized by the child's pleasure in passing and withholding his feces, which "represents self-assertion, assertion of existence, power, possession, control over mother, objects and people as well as over oneself.[10] Through E.T., Elliot not only obtains absolute power, his room becomes the center of the three siblings' universe. As fits the retentive anal stage, he wants to "keep him."

The series of closing shots of the three siblings looking at E.T. conveys the new *agreement* that characterizes their relationship. Especially the closing shot of all four sharing the frame — the same *four* represented by the mandala that is visible behind the three siblings. They are united in their secret of E.T. The final image of the nuclear family is the five putty balls that E.T. brings to revolve in the air like a solar system, with E.T. having replaced the absent father as the nucleus.

As Elliot and E.T. grow closer, so do the government men get closer to their whereabouts. Their penetrating threat is suggested by the camera closing in on a window where E.T. is shown leafing through an elementary ABC picture book. Comparing the flowers in the book, as they should be, with the wilted geraniums Gertie had given him, he restores them to life. Of course, the three flowers, two larger yellow geraniums and one small pink one, that assume additional significance as the movie runs its course, represent the three siblings E.T. has brought back to a more normal semblance of family life.

The ABC picture book anticipates the next day's crosscutting sequence that is largely associated with school (Elliot) and learning (E.T.). At the school bus stop, the three boys shown at the beginning of the movie taunt Elliot. Only now, having undergone a change, Michael is on his side, and Elliot stands his ground. In the exchange of insults, Elliot gets the idea to call the extra-terrestrial "E.T." Tyler's word play, "Where's he from? Uranus? Get it. Your anus?" caps off the anal stage.

Phallic Stage

Appropriately enough, the third stage of development, the phallic stage (where "the primitive energy expression turns ... toward an outgoing phase of involvement which eventually culminates in relatedness and the union of the opposites of sexuality"[11]), starts and ends with Elliot and the blonde girl. She is the first person shown at the bus stop among the waiting boys and girls as Elliot arrives on his bicycle. If to go by the glances she gives Elliot while talking to another girl, the talk is about him. Apparently she has a crush on him.

The "relatedness and the union" starts right away, as Elliot, in biology class, draws the extra-terrestrial's picture and writes the initials of E.T.'s new name, shown just as the teacher talks of "many similarities." The two are physically separated but are connected in their hearts and minds, a connection suggested by their wearing flannel shirts of identical patterns, Elliot's red shirt matching E.T.'s blue. While the teacher talks of "fluids," back home E.T., having grown from Coke to beer, goes to the refrigerator and starts drinking one of man's favorite *fluids*. He is doing the drinking, but it is Elliot who burps. It is the first sign of their being biologically connected. The whole classroom turns to him, but it is the blonde girl who receives a close-up. Elliot sliding down in his seat to the teacher's "similarities" corresponds to E.T. falling backward to the floor. Looking back at the blonde girl, she gives him a tolerant "what a jerk!" look, underscoring their connections. The "nuisance" that E.T. inadvertently misspells on the "Speak Spell" game describes what Elliot becomes in the classroom.

The TV movie of the spaceship beaming up a flying plane, shared by a man and woman, corresponds to the next shot in the biology lab, where the teacher hands out two jars of frogs to Elliot and the blonde girl, who are now sitting next to each other. Elliot asks his frog if it can talk just as he had asked E.T. The trapped frog that he observes in the classroom gives E.T. a feeling of being trapped. As part of the phallic stage, Elliot wants to save the phallic frogs from dissection (castration). Saying "Run for your life. Back to the river. Back to the forest," he refers to the place where E.T. landed and to the unconscious. His yelling "I gotta let him go!" recalls his wanting to "keep him" in the anal stage, suggesting he has to let go of E.T., who can only be "saved" by going home, just as Elliot has to *let go* the trauma of abandonment.

In keeping with the phallic stage, the analogy between the frogs and E.T. suggests that the extra-terrestrial is what Eugene Monick calls the "phallos, the erect penis, the emblem and standard of maleness."[12] In terms of Elliot and E.T. growing up together, "Phallos opens the door to masculine depth,"[13] to the realm of the father, whose advent E.T. initiates. A sign of Elliot's entering the masculine, his becoming a "man," comes when he and the blonde girl act out the parts of John Wayne and Maureen O'Hara in John Ford's *The Quiet Man* that E.T. watches on TV. Together with O'Hara screaming at seeing her own reflection, the blonde girl, shown standing on a chair in her black shoes and white socks (an image recalling the shot of Dorothy Gale's red shoes), screams at seeing a phallic frog placed on her shoe, which recalls Elliot's initial reaction to E.T. Elliot kisses the blonde girl just as Wayne grabs and kisses O'Hara. The last shot of the kissing sequence returns to the pair of feet inside the black shoes. As in *The Wizard of Oz*, the image of the feet inside the shoes has obvious sexual connotations. It certainly makes a fitting ending for the phallic stage, which "culminates in relatedness and the union of the opposites." Where Elliot, together with E.T., initially used his mouth for the intake of food, now that he has grown up he uses it to kiss a girl. Likewise, E.T. uses his mouth to start talking, which marks a new stage of growth.

E.T. Phone Home

Like the Ford movie he watched on the television, up to now E.T. has been a "quiet man," communicating through telepathy and gestures. Now that "he can *talk*," he goes to the telephone, which he has seen enough of in his short time in Elliot's house. Paired with the blonde Gertie, like Elliot and the blonde girl, E.T. calls the "phone" by name. Like the "show and tell" TV program that Gertie watches, he shows and tells what he wants, step by step. "He wants to call somebody," Gertie intuits when E.T. walks to the window and points to the sky, saying "E.T. home phone." It is the boys, however, as the "men" of the house, who help him "phone home" by going to the garage, the father's domain, where they try to find a practical solution to a real problem in the outer world. The crosscutting sequence between the boys in the garage and the eavesdropping Keys, recalling the earlier crosscutting of E.T. at home and Elliot in school, points to the latter's growing role as a father surrogate. Just as E.T. learns to talk, Elliot, having outgrown the three stages (together with E.T.), is ready for the father to enter his life, which is suggested by three consecutive crosscuts.

1 (a) In the sequence's first shot, the camera slowly tracks in on the two brothers kneeling around a small table, with a lamp between them, which remains between them for the sequence's three shots. Michael points out that E.T. "doesn't look too good anymore." "Don't say that, we're fine," Elliot says, perhaps thinking that if you don't talk about it, it doesn't exist. "What's all the 'we' stuff?" Michael asks, anticipating the symbiotic sickness that has already begun.

1 (b) Just as with the boys, the camera cuts to a profile of Keys. It is the first time his face is shown, though it is mostly hidden by the listening device he holds next to his ear. Only his eyes are shown. On the right side of the frame are two lights (from the instrument panel) that correspond to the one light between Elliot and Michael. It represents the two brothers just as the single light between them represents the surrogate father listening in on them. Keys hears Michael pointing out again that E.T. "might be getting kind of sick" and that Elliot keeps saying "we" all the time now.

2 (a) The camera tracks in a little closer on the two boys, as Elliot finds their father's shirt. "Dad's shirt," he smiles longingly. "Remember when he used to take us out to the ball games and take us to the movies, and we had *pop*corn fights?" "The ball games" are the same game through which Elliot first connected with E.T.

2 (b) Once again, the camera tracks in on Keys just as it did on the boys. "We'll do that again," he hears Michael reassuring Elliot. "Sure," Elliot replies pessimistically. The fact that Keys is shown in the boys' talk of the father's possible return is another allusion to his advent.

3 (a) Back to the boys for the third and final shot. They smell their father's shirt, each remembering him differently, as suggested by their different identifications of his deodorant (his *ab-scents?*).

3 (b) As the father's memory comes up, the camera crosscuts to Keys for the third and final time. Once again, just as it did with the third shot of the boys, the camera tracks in closer, the closest we've seen him yet. Likewise, he is closing in on E.T.'s whereabouts. The next time we see him, he enters the boys' house.

The juxtaposition of Keys listening to the boys with the shot of Mary reading to Gertie from *Peter Pan* suggests that he is listening on the two. But as the subsequent shot reveals in this parallel sequence, it is E.T. who is listening, yet another analogy between the two. Likewise, as with the lights in the previous sequence, the three lights represent the three children, recalling the three Darling siblings in *Peter Pan*. Only where in the J. M. Barrie's story the girl was the oldest and Michael was the youngest, in *E.T.* the girl is the youngest and Michael the oldest. Moreover, as suggested by the next shot, which shows E.T precisely when Mary continues, "He leaps," he is the three siblings' Peter Pan. But where Peter Pan "rescues" the children from the pirates, E.T. saves the three children from a largely dysfunctional family. And as suggested by his healing Elliot's bleeding finger, wounded by the father's saw blade, E.T. heals the emotional wound caused by his abandonment. He heals it before it becomes an obstructing dragon in Elliot's growing psyche. The psychic wound is suggested again when the naive E.T. tries to heal what he assumes is the wound caused by the fake knife that Michael wears on his *head* for Halloween.

On Halloween, understanding that the telephone is an earthly device used to call long distance, E.T. starts his return home when he manages to "phone home." "Ready?" Elliot asks E.T., recalling his first words of being "ready to play." "Ready," E.T. answers in his last time in the closet. That he leaves one home to return to another is underscored by his taking Gertie's place beneath the cover of the costume and by the "family" picture of the three that the mother takes. Finally she can "see" E.T., though it is through a camera and in her belief that it is Gertie underneath the sheet. This picture, together with the three siblings joining forces to help E.T. communicate with his own family, reinforce the feeling of family. It is further underscored when the mother waits for her children to return home just as E.T. waits for his mother ship to come take him home. Growing concerned, finally, the mother goes out to look for them, acknowledging their father's absence in her muttering, "Their father's gonna hear about this one."

The first step in the mother's reclaiming her home is her collecting Michael and Gertie from their trick-or-treating. When Elliot is late to return, she is somewhat reluctant to answer the investigating policeman's question, "Any family problems or recent arguments?" But the question forces her to acknowledge the truth of her painful situation. "My husband and I just separated recently," she replies, adding, "and it hasn't been easy on the children." She accepts their abandonment but cannot accept that one of them would "run away," like their father. Having acknowledged her husband's *running away*, having accepted their *separation*, as she closes the refrigerator's door, Elliot is standing behind it. Considering it is the same door that earlier, when she had opened it, knocked E.T. down without noticing him, it is as if she is seeing Elliot for the first time. Her initial reaction is anger, thinking more about herself than the feverish Elliot. But then she catches herself: "Sorry I yelled at you." Her apology, her accepting his running away, coming after her acknowledging the father's running away, sets the stage for the advent of the absent father.

Advent of the Father

Coming after E.T. "phoned" his mother ship, the appearance of a man's shadow on the driveway to Elliot's house suggests that he comes at the extra-terrestrial's calling. The dramatic music reinforces the momentous event of the advent of the father, identified once again by the jangling keys. His advent parallels the mother's reclaiming her home and family. Now that she is no longer in her self-orbit, now that she has acknowledged her husband's departure, she is finally able to see E.T., lying on the bathroom floor next to Elliot. Despite the children's protests, her maternal instinct wants her children as far away from E.T. as possible. As she takes the sick Elliot in her arms, away from E.T., his protesting ("You don't know him! You don't know him! We can't leave him alone!") surely also refers to himself, especially considering the two's connection. Her motherhood is further brought out by her response to the government men invading her house. "This is my home!" she screams most firmly.

Identified one last time by his jangling keys, Keys walks through a plastic tunnel that leads from the driveway to the house. As he enters the house, at last his face is revealed. Bearing in mind that the only other shown faces we see in this sequence are those of the family, and the mother is the only adult shown so far, by virtue of showing his face among the numerous scientists who have turned the house into a laboratory, Keys is part of the family. His connection with Elliot runs parallel to Elliot's separation from E.T., the first of three separations that he undergoes. Just as the mother protested the scientists' invading her home, Elliot protests their treatment of E.T.

Among the many scientists, who communicate in a technical language, Keys is the sole human. First he looks at E.T., who returns his look, their eyes meeting in a long look before the extra-terrestrial slowly shuts his eyes, as if his work is done — the father has arrived. The notion of the father's advent is reinforced by his tapping, like E.T., with two fingers (three times) on the clear cover that quarantines Elliot, whose image is reflected on the glass cover of Keys' mask, thus visually connecting the two. "Elliot," Keys says, calling him by name. Elliot looks up to him. With one brief sentence, "I've been to the forest," Keys lets Elliot know that he is just like him. The two connect straight away. When a figure of authority tries to stop Elliot from communicating with him, Keys protects him like a father. He may not communicate like E.T., but he communicates their shared wish. "Elliot, he came to me too. I've been wishing for this since I was 10 years old." For both man and boy, father and son, the coming of E.T. is a wish come true. Like a good father, he acknowledges Elliot's actions, once again calling him by name. "Elliot, I don't think that he was left here intentionally. But his being here is a miracle, Elliot. It's a miracle. And you did the best that anybody could do. I'm glad he met you first."

Having acknowledged Elliot, Keys squeezes his hand and smiles benevolently, letting go just as his separation from E.T. commences. Like their initial meeting, it is mostly shown from Elliot's point of view, underscoring that it is his separation. He reaches out to E.T., beseeching him to stay connected. Considering that Mary uses the same word about her and her husband's parting, and that Elliot has just separated from Keys, his *separation* from E.T. is a re-enactment of his separation from his father. In feeling the pain of abandonment, what he apparently did not allow himself to experience with his father, Elliot frees himself from the dragon's claws. This is reinforced by the father not being mentioned again and by Keys assuming a more prominent role in Elliot's life.

Elliot wants to hold on to E.T., but as two doctors confirm one after the other (three times), "Boy and Creature are separating." Peeling off the stickers that connect him to the monitoring instruments, Elliot screams repeatedly, "He came to me!" Of course, what has also come to him, as his echoing Keys' words suggest, what came around and shown his face, as the song "Papa-Oom-Mow-Mow" anticipated, is the father. As Elliot observes the attempts to revive E.T., together with the rest of the family, his mother slowly approaches him, calling his name with much empathy. "Mom," Elliot calls back, as the two hug warmly for the first time in the movie, a sign that he forgives her for not holding on to his father, just as he relaxes his hold on E.T. All this is observed by Keys, who is once again part of the family's reaction to E.T.'s death. Where up to now he was only shown talking to Elliot, after E.T. is pronounced dead, the camera lingers on Keys, who removes his head gear and slowly approaches E.T., kneeling by his bedside. With Elliot shown in the background, the three (males) sharing the frame, he gently shuts E.T.'s eyes with his gloved hand. In an analogous shot, a tearful Mary is holding the crying Gertie who is clutching the doll, the three (females) sharing the frame. The two shots are another suggestion that Keys, who matches the new mother, is the new father.

"Would you like to spend some time alone with him?" Keys places a fatherly arm around Elliot's shoulder (as E.T. and Elliot had done to one another). As a benevolent father, as one who shares Elliot's feelings, Keys understands that Elliot needs to have a few moments with his friend. In their intimate sequence, Elliot (and E.T.) are shown mostly through the round window of the freezing chamber's cover, an image recalling the shot of the two riding across the full moon in happier times. "You must be dead, because I don't know how to feel. I can't feel anything anymore. You've gone someplace else now. I'll believe in you all my life, every day," Elliot says to E.T. in parting, echoing *Peter Pan*. Then he adds, "E.T., I love you."

As in fairy tales when the (three) magic words are said, E.T. comes back to life. But Elliot, gently shutting the lid of the casing, does not notice E.T.'s red heart-light coming back, the first time it glows since he was left behind. Elliot realizes that E.T. is alive when sees the three geraniums coming back to life. He rushes back to E.T., opening the lid. "E.T. phone home," E.T., now completely revived, says to a joyous Elliot, who unzips the plastic bag, revealing his head. "Does that mean they are coming?" Elliot asks. "Yes," E.T. answers, repeating "Phone home" and calling Elliot's name. With E.T.'s revival, the flowers bloom fully. And perhaps sensing this, Keys asks Elliot if he wants the revived flowers. Equally significant, the boys' including the mother in their secret of E.T.'s return to life is another sign in the change of their relationship, their revived sense of family.

In their saving E.T. by kidnapping, Michael is the one who drives the van, but Elliot is giving the orders. He is also the one who disconnects (separates) the plastic tunnel, the maternal umbilical chord, attached to the back of the van. This separation is shown right after the "union" of Mary and Keys, suggested by their identical reaction ("Oh, my God!") to E.T.'s resurrection, which echoes Elliot's very same reaction, yet another sign that Keys is becoming part of the family. Having re-enacted his separation from his father by his separation from E.T., and having been acknowledged by his mother, Elliot now separates from her and bolts for freedom.

In a complete turnaround of Elliot's first appearance around the Dungeons and Dragons game, now he is the game master who includes the other boys in saving E.T. Shown leading the chevron of bicycles with E.T. in the basket on the front of his bicycle, he has absolute power. The forest they are flying to is the same forest where we first saw E.T., and where Elliot first spotted Keys. In their escape from the countless cars, Elliot (with E.T.) briefly breaks off from the others, underscoring that it is mostly his rite, before joining up again. Just when they think they have "made it," they are suddenly surrounded by the many threatening figures of authority, the collective dragon who had the treasure stolen from under its nose. About to be caught, Elliot is shown in three consecutive shots, each one a little closer than the other, closing his eyes as if making a wish, which E.T., shown in an extreme close-up, makes come true. Suddenly, with E.T. and Elliot leading the way, the boys take flight on their bicycles. Whereas in their first flight Elliot and E.T. were shown flying across the image of the full moon, a traditional symbol of the mother, now the whole group is shown flying across the setting sun, a traditional symbol for the father.

The father motif continues when, upon making a soft landing at the bald spot in the forest, Elliot rushes to uncover the radial saw (token of the father and the wound that his leaving engendered) from under a pile of dry leaves. Then, as if the rite is complete, the light of the descending mothership appears. The mothership's return correlates with the advent of the absent father just as its leaving E.T. behind paralleled Elliot's abandonment by his father. And to underscore this point, throughout this brief soft-landing, Elliot is shown separate from the four boys, as he was at the beginning of the movie. Only then he was the "outsider"; now, with E.T. by his side, he is the "insider."

Back at the house, Gertie shows the adults (her mother and Keys) the way to the rendezvous, where the two families, E.T.'s and Elliot's, are reunited at the very place of separation. Holding the potted geraniums, Gertie joins her two brothers and E.T. The four are grouped together, apart from the other boys. Likewise, Elliot is not shown while Gertie and Michael part from E.T. His parting, his final separation, is a special one, as indicated by the extra-terrestrial's body glowing red (like Elliot's red parka) when he approaches to part from E.T.

While Elliot bids him to "stay," E.T. invites him to "come." In a very ceremonial gesture, E.T. puts a long finger to his mouth and says "ouch," with Elliot following suit. Their parting is equally painful. E.T. gives the tearful Elliot a long embrace, which is observed by the emotional mother with Keys by her side, softly placing a hand on her shoulder. The camera cuts to Elliot's face, in the arms of E.T. and in tears, then to the mother who is also in tears, and back to Elliot. By the look of the two's faces, the mother understands (feels) what Elliot feels. They share the same feelings, the same pain of separation from E.T. and from the father-husband. E.T. slowly brings his long finger forward, which lights up as it touches Elliot's forehead. For a second Elliot flinches, but then relaxes as E.T. repeats his very words in their first separation, "I'll be right here." What came from outer space is now forever lodged in Elliot's inner space. Just as E.T. healed his wounded finger, now he heals his wounded psyche. Holding back the tears, no longer a child, Elliot parts from E.T. with a simple "bye."

The shot of E.T. kneeling down for the potted flowers, representing the three siblings, while Mary is shown in the background, leaves no doubt about the reunited family. Particularly as the next shot is a close-up of the mother rising to her feet next to Keys. With the children getting back their mother (and father), E.T. picks up the flowers and heads for the ramp leading to the mothership. As the ramp is hauled up, Elliot (once again with Harvey) and E.T. (standing at the ship's entrance) are repeatedly shown looking at one another through the ramp's grating, the partition that separates them. Underscoring that the separation is Elliot's, the closing up of the entrance to the mothership, not unlike an aperture of a camera, is shown through his viewpoint. The last visible point is E.T.'s red glowing heart, symbol of the love and connection between the two.

In a shot identical to the one of the spaceship taking off without E.T., now the mothership takes off with E.T. on board, undoing the initial abandonment. With his return *home*, and with the advent of Keys, Elliot's family reunites with a changed mother and a new father, and a new feeling of *home*. By the expression of their faces, especially Mary's and Elliot's, this is a cathartic event for the whole family. Even the three boys who did not include Elliot in their game are included in the closing *family portrait*. Like the wordless exposition, this finale is conveyed solely by pictures and music. The fact that E.T.'s return home is witnessed by all the parties surrounding Elliot's family suggests that what was unconscious, a creation of his imagination, is now conscious, for all to see. Elliot's dream of a friend has become a reality. His parting from E.T., his letting go of their symbiotic relationship, suggests a resolution of his problem with his father's abandonment.

As initially anticipated by the *Dungeons and Dragons*, Elliot's recovering from the wound inflicted by his father's abandonment, his slaying the dragon, is evoked by the movie's closing shots, seven in all:

(1) It starts with a close-up of a sad but not devastated Elliot, who is looking up at the ascending spaceship.

(2) A shot of the spaceship, leaving behind a rainbow tail like a blazing comet. (These *two shots*, together with the analogous last *two shots* of the rainbow and Elliot, serve as "bookends" to the three shots between them.)

(3) Mary laughing tearfully with Keys, who is out of focus, behind her, both looking up.

(4) The three boys looking up silently.

(5) Michael holds Gertie in his arms, the two looking up.

(6) A shot of the rainbow created by the spaceship.

(7) Elliot gazing up at the rainbow left behind by E.T.'s mothership.

As this portrait of the new family suggests, Elliot is no longer alone. Though he parts with E.T., he no longer feels abandoned. Just as E.T.'s advent initiated the advent of the father, his departure makes room for the father. At the end of the movie, Elliot is a boy who got his wish — his wish for a friend and a father.

Chapter 8

Field of Dreams
Father Denied

Could you believe that? An American boy refusing to have a catch with his father?

— Ray Kinsella, talking about his relationship with his father

Pre-Game

A dog and a white rabbit named Harvey are not the only link between *E.T.* and *Field of Dreams.* Both movies' agents of change, the extra-terrestrial and the voice, come from another world, from two fantastic realms, outer space and the cornfield. Like Spielberg's movie, Phil Alden Robinson's *Field of Dreams* is a realistic fairy tale where real problems are resolved by fantastic means. As in *E. T,* and as in countless fairy tales, the many threes in *Field of Dreams* point to the family triad, to the heroes' relationships with their parents, particularly with their fathers.

Though barely suggested in *E.T.*, another link between the two movies is the game of baseball. Elliot's first connection with E.T. is through a baseball, and when he and his brother reminisce about their absent father, it is about his taking them to baseball games and to the movies, two worlds where heroes still exist. Both events, America's national pastime and its most popular means of entertainment, are readily shared by parents and children, but it is the game of baseball that holds a special place for many fathers and sons. The game is a familiar sport that most fathers and sons relate to, through which they connect. And doubly so for Ray Kinsella. In his own words, after his mother died he went to sleep with stories of his father's baseball heroes, heroes who played in his field of dreams.

The mixing of movies and baseball, and the retelling of the historical event that plays a key role in *Field of Dreams,* is recounted in *Eight Men Out,* directed by John Sayles (who also directed the third movie in this section, *Lone Star*). Where the throwing the 1919 World Series by the eight Chicago White Sox players tarnished the sacred game of baseball for John Kinsella, for Ray Kinsella, his son, it tarnished his picture of his father. In the idiom of filmmyths, this tarnished picture is the dragon that obstructs Ray from forgiving and atoning with his father. Before he comes to acknowledge his father, a father whose hold on him is much stronger than he cares to admit, Ray has to bring three men into his field of dreams, three men whose dreams are connected to baseball. He offers each one a second chance to achieve his dream. In turn, they help Ray achieve his. Each one advances him another base in his infield, in his inner journey of coming to terms with his feelings for his father. As in many fairy tales, where the hero has to complete three tasks before attaining the object of his quest, only after advancing the three men in the infield does Ray's father emerge from behind his catcher's mask, their catch bringing him to *home* plate.

Play Ball

The tension between Ray and his father is evoked right off the bat by the sustained monotonic strings over the opening credits. The sound of a majestic horn, as if from another world, from the fantastic unconscious, creates a mood that something is imminent. It anticipates the coming of the voice, the appearance of Shoeless Joe Jackson and, ultimately, of Ray's father, particularly as this melody comes on with the appearance of both men. Like the three bases that Ray has to load, the exposition is conveyed in three parts.

First, Ray Kinsella starts the story and the subject matter of the movie (as a voice) by introducing his father as the boy in the sepia-toned photograph sitting in a blooming field, with a cornfield in the background. "My father's name was John Kinsella. It's an Irish name. He was born in North Dakota in 1896 and never saw a big city until he came back from France in 1918. He settled in Chicago, where he learned to live and die with the White Sox. Died a little when they lost the 1919 World Series, died a lot the following summer when eight members of the team were accused of throwing that series." The voice continues over a picture of a young John Kinsella, in a nameless baseball uniform, holding a catcher's mask, his cap worn backwards like a catcher in the field of dreams. "He played in the minors for a year or two, but nothing ever came of it. Moved to Brooklyn in '35, married mom in '38, was already an old man working at the naval yards when I was born in 1952."

Second, having introduced his father, Ray introduces himself in relation to his father (over a colored picture of his two parents, his mother holding him as a small baby). My name's Ray Kinsella (camera closes in on the mother, who is positioned between the father and son, as if coming between them). Mom died when I was three, and I suppose Dad did the best he could. Instead of Mother Goose, I was put to bed at night to stories of Babe Ruth, Lou Gehrig and the great Shoeless Joe Jackson. Dad was a Yankees fan then, so of course I rooted for Brooklyn. But in '58 the Dodgers moved away, so we had to find other things to fight about. We did."

Third, a picture of Ray in his high school yearbook starts his introducing himself and his family. After high school he went away to college, "the farthest from home I could find," purposely driving his father "up the wall." It was there, in Berkeley, that he met Annie. They were married in the summer of '74; his father died in the fall. "A few years later Karin was born," he informs us, over a picture which "mirrors" the one with himself as a baby. Replacing his mother in the middle, Annie is the one who initiates his return to the Midwest of his father. She talks him into buying a farm where the main crop is corn, just like the cornfield that appears in the opening picture of his father as a young boy. "I'm 36 years old. I love my family. I love baseball, and I'm about to become a farmer. But until I heard the voice, I'd never done a crazy thing in my whole life."

The voice heralds each of Ray's advancements to another base in his infield of dreams, in his journey of coming to terms with his hostile feelings for his father.

First Base

If to go by what Shoeless Joe tells him, "it was you Ray," the voice that Ray Kinsella hears and adheres to ("If you build it, he will come") is his own. It is the voice of his dreams, of his unconscious. In fact, the next time he hears the voice is when he wakes up in the middle of a stormy night, as from a dream. Moreover, the following morning he comes into the kitchen and sees his daughter Karin watching James Stewart in the black-and-white movie on TV (on channel 3), talking about a similar experience with a voice. Denying the voice, Ray switches the TV off with the remote control. "Why did you do that?" Karin asks him. "It was funny." Her fascination with the cinematic fantasy anticipates the three times she brings messages from the field of dreams, from the unconscious, which Ray cannot switch off like a TV. The white rabbit in the movie, *Harvey*, brings to mind the white rabbit in *Alice in Wonderland*, especially as right next to the TV there is a bag of Wonder Bread, the word "wonder" in plain view, another allusion to the unconscious. Like the white rabbits in both *Alice* and *Harvey*, the ballplayers in the field of dreams are in white uniforms.

The third time Ray hears the voice, out in the cornfield, he also *sees* a vision: two visions of a lighted ball field with a distant figure in white baseball uniform standing at center field. In the third vision he recognizes Shoeless Joe Jackson, who turns to look in his direction. Later that evening, over dinner, Ray shares his vision with Annie while the Lovin' Spoonful's "Daydream" is playing in the background, yet another sign that the voice is from the land of dreams. Or from the '60s. "I think it means that if I build a baseball field out there, Shoeless Joe Jackson will get to come back and play ball again."

By his own admission, despite his having "smoked some grass," Ray, like his father before him, has never done anything spontaneous (crazy). He has never heeded his inner voice, the voice of his dreams. Up to now, his actions seem mostly motivated by his hostility towards his father. But the voice has already begun to work its magic, even if only getting Ray to talk about his father's baseball hero. "Did you know Babe Ruth copied his swing?" he enlightens Annie. "I'd actually like to see him play again, let him play, to right an old wrong." Of course, besides Shoeless Joe, the "old wrong" also refers to his wronging his father. In telling Ray to build the field of dreams, the voice calls him to right it, to let him play again in his field of dreams.

Ray "can't think of one good reason why" he should build the ball field, but his intuition speaks otherwise. "I'm 36 years old. I have a wife, a child and a mortgage, and I'm scared to death I'm turning into my father." When Annie asks, "What's your father got to do with all this?" Ray confesses, "I never forgave him for getting old. By the time he was as old as I am now, he was ancient. I mean, he must have had dreams, but he never did anything about them. For all I know, he may have even heard voices, too, but he sure didn't listen to them. The man never did one spontaneous thing in all the years I knew him. Annie, I'm afraid of that happening to me, and something tells me this may be my last chance to do something about it. I want to build that field. Do you think I'm crazy?" "Yes," Annie, the intuitive voice, replies. "But I also think if you really feel you should do this, then you should do it."

Significantly, it is as a father that Ray is shown building that ball field. He initiates Karin (and us) into the game as a father traditionally initiates his son by briefing her on Shoeless Joe. Ray never says it in so many words, but in view of how he talks about Shoeless Joe, the legendary ballplayer is not only a hero to his father. Ray talks about this once-tarnished hero with great admiration, a far cry from his harsh words to his father. To Karin's question, "Why'd they call him Shoeless Joe?" Ray recounts the event, adding, "In 1919, his team, the Chicago White Sox, they threw the World Series.... Except Shoeless Joe. Now, he did take their money, but nobody could ever prove he did a single thing to lose those games. I mean, if you're supposed to be throwing, how do you explain the fact that he hit .375 for the Series and didn't commit one error — eh?" Unlike his father, Ray considers Shoeless Joe innocent. But needing someone to blame, he uses his father's hero to blame him.

The field completed, Ray's hostile attitude towards his father has changed. Just as building the field allows his father's hero to return to the game from which he was unjustly exiled, it initiates the return of his father from an equally unjust exile. His first word to Shoeless Joe, "Sorry," is surely also meant for his father. Especially as at night, under the completed ball field's lights, he brings up his father in connection with his hero. When he recounts how his "father said he saw him years later playing under a made-up name in some tenth-rate league in Carolina," Annie points out, "That's the first time I've ever seen you smile when you mentioned your father."

That same night, the third night he is shown in his bedroom, Ray sits alone by the window, looking at the completed ball field, waiting for his vision to materialize. "Any sign?" Annie asks him, crawling into his arms. "Something's going to happen out there," he tells her. "I can feel it." But the unconscious has its own way of revealing itself. Come Christmas, with snow covering the field, Ray is still looking out the window. His thoughts are more with the ball field outside than the Christmas party they are giving inside. But as every baseball fan knows, spring training begins in spring.

The coming of spring is announced by the game broadcaster on the living room TV, recalling Karin watching *Harvey*. With the change of seasons, Ray too has changed. He no longer waits. He is preoccupied with their financial reality in the adjacent room. But Karin's question, "Daddy, what's a southpaw?" calls him to return to the field of dreams. "Um, it means a left-handed pitcher, honey," Ray answers somewhat distractedly, the financial reality impinging upon his baseball fantasy. When Karin, as a voice off screen, tries to get her father's attention again, Ray snaps impatiently, "In a minute, Karin." In her third attempt to get his attention, Karin is *shown* as she informs her father, "There's a man out there on your lawn."

Just as he had seen in his vision, a man in a white baseball uniform is standing in shallow left field. A smile comes across Ray's face as he recognizes Shoeless Joe Jackson, who seems to be assessing his whereabouts, as if wondering if the ball field is real. He is even more surprised when Ray switches on the lights, with three switches, something unheard of in his days of glory. As Ray walks towards him, Joe turns to look at him just as he had done in his vision, only now it is in the opposite direction, as if a mirrored image. Without a single word, Joe goes to left field and waits for Ray to hit some balls his way. After a failed first attempt at bat, suggesting he has not played for a while, has not been in touch with his dreams, Ray succeeds in his next three, which Joe catches easily, the two connecting through the ball.

With three outs, Joe comes to the infield. "Hi," Ray greets him, introducing himself by name. "Joe Jackson," the legendary player replies. "I bet it's good to be playing again, huh?" Ray remarks to Joe, who is inspecting the bat he picked out. "Getting thrown out of baseball was like having part of me amputated. I've heard that old men wake up and scratch itchy legs that have been dust for over fifty years. That was me. I'd wake up at night with the smell of the ballpark in my nose, with the cool of the grass on my feet. The thrill of the grass." Then, turning to Ray, he asks: "Can you pitch?"

"I'm pitching to Shoeless Joe Jackson," Ray tells himself, as if it is too good to be true, as if it is a dream. After a few pitches, however, he forgets who he is up against. "See if you can hit my curve," he challenges the great Shoeless

Joe, who abruptly reminds him who he is dealing with by hitting the ball right at him, knocking him off his feet. Hitting one into the cornfield, Joe recalls what the game was to him. "Man, I did love this game. I'd have played for food money. It was the game, the sounds, the smells.... It was the crowds, rising to their feet when the ball was hit deep. Shoot, I'd play for nothing." What Shoeless Joe feels about not being able to play mirrors what Ray feels about his relationship with his father. Just like Shoeless Joe, a part of him is missing. He longs to be his father's son. When Joe informs Ray that "it would really mean a lot to them" to come back and play, Ray replies, "They're all welcome here," unaware that the appearance of the "eight of us" is another step in bringing back his father.

Trotting in the direction of the cornfield, above which hovers thick dream-like fog, Shoeless Joe stops and turns towards Ray. "Hey, is this heaven?" "No. It's Iowa," Ray replies with a smile. Joe is shown for the third time, in the same profile, just as Ray had seen him in his vision. We do not know it yet, but these three pictures herald the coming of Ray's father. In fact, we have already been shown this same picture of John Kinsella at the beginning of the movie. Seeing Joe vanishing in the cornfield, appreciating the field's magic, Ray tells Annie, "We're keeping this field." Despite its financial drawback, Annie could not agree more. "You bet your ass we are."

Counterbalancing the three men who Ray helps achieve their dreams, there are three confrontations with Mark, Annie's brother, who represents hard (financial) reality. In Mark's first attempt to get his brother-in-law to see his financial situation, Ray, still under the influence of the field's magic, is light-headed and giddy. To look at hard reality seems preposterous when you have just built a field of dreams. While Mark warns Ray that the "stupid baseball field is going to bankrupt" him, Karin once again interrupts, calling her father to the field of dreams, to see the whole eight White Sox players that he had told her about while building the ball field. "Daddy, the baseball game is on."

Second Base

Sitting side by side on the bleachers, anticipating his seeing the Red Sox with Terence Mann, Ray and Karin watch the eight White Sox players enjoy their return to baseball. When Annie calls it a day by calling the two for dinner, the players head back to the cornfield. Before vanishing in the cornfield, the last of the eight players echoes the Wicked Witch from *The Wizard of Oz* (mentioned by Annie in the very next scene), "I'm melting, I'm melting," perhaps suggesting that the dragon, Ray's introjected father, is beginning to dissipate. "That's so cool," Ray mutters to himself, unaware that he has only reached first base.

Heading home, Ray hears his second calling. "What the hell does that mean, 'ease his pain'?" He talks back to the voice as if they have become more familiar. He does not get an answer in so many words, but he intuits its meaning while Annie stands up for Ray's hero at the PTA meeting they are attending that very same evening, claiming he "was a warm, gentle voice of reason during a time of great madness." In the heat of the confrontation between Annie and the woman calling for banning books while holding Terence Mann's *The Boat Rocker*, just before it becomes the opposite of "peace and understanding," Ray has his epiphany. "I know whose pain I'm supposed to ease. I figured it out. Terence Mann." But as Annie reminds him, now he has to figure out "what's Terence Mann got to do with baseball?" Or with his father?

Where the first task concerned his father's hero, the second one concerns Ray's hero, a father figure if ever he had one. The Afro-American author, who once upon a time slew dragons with his pen, is the shadowy side of his father. In his search for answers in the library, Mann's world of books, Ray comes to an article, "Where is Terence Mann now that we really need him?" The title, of course, also refers to Ray's quest. The photo negative of Mann that appears in the article, together with the story that he wrote about a character with Ray's father's name, reinforces the suggestion that he represents Ray's shadowy father. Not only does the montage of Ray's research recall the opening montage of his father, Mann resembles him in his desire to play with the Brooklyn Dodgers in Ebbets Field. Despite the ballpark having been destroyed, and the Dodgers having moved to the West Coast, Mann's dream has not gone away, much as Ray's problem with his father. The fact that today Mann helps young people, in Ray's words, to "resolve their conflicts peacefully," points to his role in Ray's journey. What convinces Ray (and Annie) that he is on to something is their joint dream, their shared messages from the unconscious, of Ray and his hero sitting on the first base side at Fenway Park. In his double role as hero and alternative father, Mann warms up Ray for his atonement with his father.

Like the three bases he has to reach before his father appears, in his quest for Mann in Boston, Ray turns to three people in the writer's neighborhood before arriving at his door. It also takes him three tries to get "the voice of the sixties" to hear him out. Only when he reminds Mann, who threatens Ray with a crowbar (a poor substitute for a baseball bat), that he is a pacifist, does he stop long enough to listen. And only when he tells him that what brought him to Boston is a good story, does Mann submit to his calling, however reluctantly. Like Ray, who wants to atone with his father but does not know how, Mann seems to want to go to a ball game but needs someone like Ray to take him. In turn, by taking his hero to a ballpark, Ray advances to second base.

At the ballpark, when Ray turns to the legendary author, asking, "So what do you want?" and Mann gives a spiel of not wanting to be the Oracle for the disenchanted youth, Ray brings him back to the here and now by pointing to the three men at the refreshment stand, attired in the American red, white and blue, arms folded, waiting to serve them, thus fulfilling the part in the dream of eating hot dogs in the bleachers. As suggested by the twin "ARCHWAY" sign behind them, they are the threshold guardians to the second stage of the two's shared quest, which sends them to find *Archie* "Moonlight" Graham.

Third Base

In the third inning, as indicated by Ray's scorecard, when the voice repeats "Go the distance," once for each man, the camera focuses on Ray, as if he is the only one who hears the voice, the only one who sees the verbal message on the scoreboard, instructing where to "go the distance." As he *writes* down the message, what Mann has not done for seventeen years, the writer turns to Ray, asking, "What's the matter?" Like Ray, Mann is slow to acknowledge the voice. He denies it just as he denies his gift for writing. Or as Ray denies his love for his father. But as suggested by another message, the neon sign reading **BOOKS** that drifts across the windshield of Ray's van in which he drives Mann back home, as if a projection of the unconscious, his return to writing has already begun. Just before they part ways, the writer turns to Ray, asking, "You got another message, didn't you?" Seeing Mann's condition, Ray lets him off the hook by denying the bait. "It said, 'The man had done enough. Leave him alone.'"

Successful and famous though Mann may be, it is not enough. And he knows it. Just as his book *The Boat Rocker* changed Ray, now Ray assumes the role as his hero's *boat rocker*. By taking him to his first game since the Dodgers left Brooklyn, a team Ray used to see play at Ebbets Field with his father (as indicated by the last picture that shows him with his father), he initiates Mann's return to writing and to baseball. At the very last minute, Mann acknowledges the field of dreams' message. He not only admits he saw the name "*Moonlight*" *Graham* and that he heard the voice telling them to "go the distance," he knows what it means. "It means we're going to Minnesota to find 'Moonlight' Graham."

In Chisholm, Minnesota, the two are greeted by an archway of sorts, a street banner proclaiming the town's centennial. "Follow me," Mann says, echoing the White Rabbit, taking the lead in this part of the quest. He points to the local newspaper, thus continuing the *writing* motif. It is another step in Mann's return to writing. Inside, the woman editor briefs the two on "Doc" Graham's brief time in the majors and his life as a doctor and a fairy godfather to many of the town's needy children. "His baseball career never amounted to much. So he went back to school. His father was a doctor." Instead of pursuing his dream of playing in the majors, he followed his father's footsteps, thus, unlike Ray, acknowledging he is his father's son. Informing them he died in 1972, the editor reads the eulogy, "The Passing of a Legend," one of three (shown) printed tributes to the deceased Doc Graham, as he was known in his hometown. The woman who deals with words recognizes Terence Mann and acknowledges his good writing. Like Annie, she is another feminine voice that advances the hero on his journey. Encouraged by her words, in the next scene Mann is jotting down (writing) what three oldtimers say about the legendary Doc Graham. Whereas to the editor Graham was a godfather to countless children, to the three oldtimers he is a romantic Dapper Dan, who always carried an umbrella, perhaps a substitute for a bat, not unlike Mann's crowbar. Becoming a doctor is perhaps his calling, but playing in the majors was his dream.

Outside their motel a lighted sign reads "Stop Searching," but in their shared room Ray and Mann try to make sense of what their search has yielded so far. A sign that their quest is related to their fathers turns up when, upon reading a *newspaper*, Ray discovers that Mann is considered "missing." "His father, who lives in Baltimore, notified the police after receiving no answer to repeated telephone calls," Mann reads out loud, adding, "I better call him." "What do I tell him?" the writer laughs with the telephone in his hand. His words foreshadow Ray's asking Annie the very same question upon seeing his father. Moreover, his "I better call him" suggest what Ray must do—call out to his father, connecting with him through ball and glove.

Leaving the motel room so that Mann may talk to his father in private, much as Annie does when he meets his father, Ray walks down a moonlit street. Unnoticed by Ray, Doc Graham passes by in the background, walking the opposite direction on the other side of the street. The two are the only ones in the otherwise deserted street. Somehow Ray has stepped into a twilight zone, the land of dreams. Three *verbal* signs tell him that he is in 1972, the same year that Doc Graham passed away: The picture of Richard Nixon, with the caption, "4 more years, re-elect the President," recalls Mann's talking about Nixon being elected twice. The "4 more years" are not unlike the four men returning to the ball field for a second chance to realize their dreams; the words on the movie marquee, aside from referring to 1972, announce another paternal figure, *The Godfather*; the year on the parked car's license plate assures Ray what he already suspects.

Only after the three signs does Ray spot Doc Graham, walking down the foggy street underneath a streetlamp, which recalls the invisible rabbit that leaned against a lamp post in the movie *Harvey*. A close-up of the umbrella brings to mind what one of the oldtimers had said about him, reassuring Ray of the man's identity. "Are you 'Moonlight' Graham?" Ray runs up to Graham, introducing himself. "No one's called me 'Moonlight' Graham in fifty years," Graham walks up to Ray. "Do you mind if I join you?" Ray asks, foreshadowing his asking his father about playing catch. "I mean, I'd like to talk to you." He gets Graham to tell him of his brief moment, his half inning, in the majors. "So what was that like?" Ray asks about his never getting to bat, surely thinking about his father. "It was like coming *this close* to your dreams," Graham holds his thumb and index finger close to each other. "Then watch them brushing past you like a stranger in a crowd. At the time you don't think much of it. You know, we just don't recognize the most significant moments of our lives while they're happening. Back then I thought, 'Well, there'll be other days.' I didn't realize that that was the only day."

Returning from his reverie, Graham turns to Ray. "What's so interesting about half an inning that would make you come all the way from Iowa, to talk to me about it, fifty years after it happened?" Playing the fairy godfather, Ray replies, "I didn't really know till just now, but I think it's to ask you, if you could do anything you wanted, if you could have a wish." Graham's only wish is to get "to bat in the major leagues." And Ray can take him to where there is "enough magic in the moonlight to make this dream come true." Graham's wishful-thinking about baseball recalls Shoeless Joe's reminiscing about the game; his dream to bat in the majors is identical to Ray's father and, as it turns out, to Terence Mann's.

Thinking Graham refused the call just as they first denied it, Ray and Mann head back to Iowa and the field of dreams. The unconscious, however, has its own way of working things out. The hitchhiker Ray picks up, saying, "I need all the karma I can get right now," turns out to be the young Graham, pursuing his baseball dreams. Knowing Graham's dream to play the game, Ray starts talking with Terence Mann about his father's dream to play and their uneasy relationship. "He never made it as a ball player. So he tried to get his son to make it for him. By the time I was 10, playing baseball got to be like eating vegetables or taking out the garbage. So when I was 14, I started to refuse. Could you believe that? American boy refusing to have a catch with his father?" To Mann's question, "Why 14?" Ray answers, "That's when I read *The Boat Rocker* by Terence Mann. I never played catch with him again."

In the intimacy of night, Terence asks Ray the question he has probably been thinking of asking since their talk. "What was the awful thing you said, to your father?"

RAY: I said I never could respect a man whose hero was a criminal.
MANN: Who was his hero?
RAY: Shoeless Joe Jackson...The son of a bitch died before I could take it back. Before I could tell him ... you know. He never met my wife. He never saw his granddaughter.
MANN (pointing to the sleeping Archie Graham in the back seat): This is your penance.

Indeed, by taking Graham to the field of dreams, offering another day in which he can fulfill his dream, Ray gets a second chance to do with his father what he did not get around to do while he was still alive.

Two full teams are playing on the field when the three arrive home. With the three tasks completed, the remainder of the movie takes place in the field of dreams. "Hey, Ray. Welcome back," Shoeless Joe calls out. Seeing Shoeless Joes walk up to greet Ray, Terence and Graham cannot believe their eyes. Now that two teams are playing in the field of dreams, the legendary ballplayer invites all three newcomers to realize their dreams, to make their wishes come true.

As in fairy tales, and as in an inning in baseball, Ray is the third one to go to bat.

Archie Graham is the first at bat. He is the first to get a second chance to fulfill his dream, this time playing at the bottom of the inning. Just as Doc Graham had pictured it, after a player slides into third, the young Archie is called to bat. The pitcher he is facing is none other than Eddie Cicotte, the one whose name was on the headlines at the opening montage together with Shoeless Joe. After two pitches aimed at Archie's head — the first one for winking at Cicotte, the second for challenging his fast ball — Shoeless Joe calls time and comes to give the rookie professional (fatherly) advice. "Come on, Arch, it just takes one," Ray calls out from the bleachers, reminding him of his wish. Connecting on the third pitch, Archie drives the ball into center field and the runner home. As he trots back to the bench after his sacrifice, Archie tips his cap to Ray in thanks for helping him make his wish come true. Shoeless Joe rises to congratulate him, as do the other players. "We need it," one of the players tells Archie. From the players' bench, Archie looks at Ray with a grateful smile. He has made his dreams come true. Ray smiles and nods in return, as if saying, you're welcome.

Archie is given a chance to repay Ray the next day, when the magic mood surrounding the game is interrupted by Mark's third appearance. "Ray, it's time to put away your little fantasies and come down to earth," he informs Ray of their dire financial reality, urging him to sign a paper that will salvage his farm. Once again, Karin interrupts their argument with another message from the field of dreams. "Daddy, you don't have to sell the farm." Just as she was the first to see Shoeless Joe and the first to see the other players, Karin (for the third time) is in touch with the dream world, the unconscious, before it becomes real to the grownups. "People will come," she informs them. "It'll be just like when they were little kids, a long time ago. They'll watch the game and remember what it was like." Like everything else in the movie, her words allude to her father's "innocent" childhood, before he "was put to bed at night by stories of ... Shoeless Joe Jackson."

Karin's mysterious words are taken up by the man of words, who elaborates on what the obscure message means. His holding a baseball encyclopedia signals his return to writing and to baseball. In what ensues, Ray has to choose between two voices, that of his hero who believes in the magic of baseball or that of his down-to-earth brother-in-law. "Ray, people will come, Ray. They'll come to Iowa for reasons they can't even fathom. They'll turn up your driveway, not knowing for sure why they're doing it. They'll arrive at your door, as innocent as children, longing for the past." Like Karin, Mann also alludes to Ray's longing for the innocent past. As Mann gets up, the players stop playing and listen to the magic words. He walks towards the baseball diamond, the players walking towards him, as if entranced by his words. "And they'll watch the game, and it'll be as if they dipped themselves in magic waters. The memories will be thick, they'll have to brush them away from their faces."

Rebutting Mark's attempts to persuade Ray to the sign over the farm, shown behind him, Mann walks towards Ray, the players standing behind him, as if agreeing with every word. "The one constant though all the years, Ray, has been baseball. America has rolled by like an army of steamrollers. It's been erased like a blackboard, rebuilt and erased again. But baseball has marked the time. This field, this game, is a part of our past, Ray. It reminds us of all that was once good, and it could be again. Oh, people will come, Ray," Mann sits down. "People will most definitely come."

Weighing the two choices, the two voices, Ray looks at the waiting ballplayers. "Come on, Ray," the voice whispers to him. Out in left field, Shoeless Joe is shown punching his glove. He waits Ray's decision just as he waits a batter at the plate. "I'm not signing," Ray finally decides. In the quarrel that ensues between Mark and Ray, Karin falls from the bleachers. After a brief hesitation, in which Ray calls Annie to "wait" in calling for help, the young Graham runs towards the unconscious Karin until he reaches the gravel that marks the field's boundary. He stops for a moment then drops his baseball glove. As he crosses the threshold, his baseball shoes change to the black shoes of Doc Graham, who is carrying a black medical case rather than the usual umbrella. Having achieved his wish, he no longer needs its reminder. "She is choking to death." He sits Karin up and hits her back a couple times till the hotdog lodged in her throat pops out. "She'll be turning handsprings before you know it," Doc Graham assures in his typical fashion. When Ray thanks him, Graham replies in a fatherly manner, "No, son. Thank you."

The other players show their admiration as Doc Graham heads for the cornfield. "Hey, rookie!" Shoeless Joe calls out to him just before he crosses the threshold. At first Doc seems surprised to be called a "rookie," but then he smiles. Shoeless Joe's "You were good" seems to lift a burden from his heart. He got the acknowledgment that will let him rest in peace. Even in his second chance, he ultimately chooses to be a doctor, like his father. Disappearing in the cornfield, he is a man who got a second chance to fulfill his dream in the field of dreams. His getting his wish, his getting *another day* in the majors, parallels Ray's getting another chance to take back his harsh words to his father, who died before he could tell him he loved him, before he met Ray's wife and his granddaughter.

Home Plate

Shoeless Joe calls it a day, and all the players head for the cornfield. Then he turns back, asking the man who had riveted the players with his evocation of the game's magic, "Hey, do you want to come with us?" Ray, of course, thinks he means him. He cannot believe that Mann is chosen over him. Mann tries to tell him that he is unattached and that Ray has a family, but Ray wants to know what is in it for him. "Is that why you did this?" Joe asks him. "For you?" Ray does not answer, realizing it is against the whole spirit and magic of the field. "There is a reason they chose me just as there is a reason they chose you and this field," Mann tries to explain. "There is something out there, Ray. And if I have the courage to go through with this, what a story it will make. 'Shoeless Joe Jackson Comes to Iowa.'" "Are you going to write about it?" Ray asks, glad to hear of Mann's return to writing. "That's what I do," says Terence, who has come to accept his voice, anticipating Ray's accepting his inner voice regarding his father.

Watching Mann gingerly enter the cornfield, laughing happily like one of the innocent children he evoked, the family of three is shown bunched together as one unit, a shot that recalls another such picture, the first colored picture in the opening montage, which showed the young Ray with his two parents. This picture brings Ray full circle, not unlike a homerun. Where the first such picture showed Ray on the left side, opposite the picture of his father, now, not without significance, he is positioned on the right side, the same side as his father, a sign he has taken his side of the picture.

As Annie and Ray head towards the house, Shoeless Joe keeps looking at them, as if his day's work is not finished. Now that Ray has done his penance, the voice's true meaning is revealed to him. By helping Shoeless Joe, Doc Graham and Terence Mann achieve their baseball dreams, Ray has loaded the bases. Where helping Doc Graham get to bat mirrors his father's dream of playing in the majors, helping Terence Mann get back to writing corresponds to Ray's taking back the awful words he had said to his father. Mann's last words, "Take care of this family," coming right after Karin's near-fatal fall, call Ray to be a good father. To become one, however, he must slay the dragon, the tarnished image of his father that prevents him from becoming his father's son.

"What are you grinning at, you ghost?" Ray echoes his daughter's question upon first meeting Shoeless Joe, anticipating his becoming a son when meeting his father. "If you build it," Joe signals by turning his head to his right, driving the point home, "he will come." He points to the catcher in a Yankee uniform. "Oh, my God," Ray realizes who the player behind the catcher mask is. "It's my father," he informs Annie with a longing look on his face.

Now Ray finds himself in a situation he both feared and longed for. He is given a second chance to heal the wound caused by his relationship with his father. This second chance to come to terms with the introjected father, with the dragon, Samuel Osherson calls "the wounded father."

> One way of healing the wounded father is to plunge into your father's history. A man needs to find ways of empathizing with his father's pain.... We have to understand our fathers' struggle and see the broken connection between fathers and sons as part of the unfinished business of manhood.[1]

In the meeting between father and son there is a striking sense of *déjà vu*. The movie that opened with a "plunge into" the "father's history" now comes full circle, especially as suggested by the similar pictures of John Kinsella in the movie's beginning and end. "It was you," Ray shouts to Shoeless Joe, who is walking to the cornfield. "No, Ray," Shoeless Joe says, turning around to look back at Ray, "It was you." Shoeless Joe's words point to what the voice meant all along. If you build your field of dreams, your dream of atoning with your father will come true. "Empathizing with his father's pain," Ray finally understands what the voice meant with "Ease his pain." And "Go the distance," as Annie chimes in.

The fact that Ray's seeing his father matches the picture (third one in the exposition) of his father is another suggestion that it is all in his head, that it is introjected. It is as if he stepped out of the photograph which showed him as a young ball player, before it was tarnished in Ray's psyche. "My God," Ray says incredulously. "I only saw him years later, when he was worn down by life. Look at him. He's got his whole life in front of him, and I'm not even a glint in his eyes. What do I say to him?" "Why don't you introduce him to his granddaughter?" Annie suggests.

John approaches Ray and his family. "I just wanted to thank you folks for putting up this field, and letting us play here. I'm John Kinsella." He offers his right hand. After the shake of hands and the formal introductions, the ever-intuitive Annie leaves the two to talk as father and son. Of course, as the two walk together, they talk about baseball, echoing the words of Shoeless Joe. Ray's words to his father, "You catch a good game," recall Joe's parting words to Doc Graham; John asking Ray if the field is Heaven repeats Shoeless Joe's very same words. As father and son turn to face each other, the father confesses, "For me it's like a dream come true." Realizing they share the same dream, Ray looks in amazement at his father. "Is this Heaven?" he asks his son, who turns to his father as he picks up his catcher's glove. "No, it's Iowa," he replies. Then, like a little boy asking about Santa Claus, Ray asks his father, "Is there a Heaven?" "Oh, yeah," the father assures his son with a smile. "It's the place dreams come true." Looking at his family on the front porch, the house full of light in the twilight of the evening, Ray concludes, "Maybe this is Heaven."

Ray shakes hands with his father just as he shook hands with Mann, another suggestion that the black boat rocker is his shadowy father. Only after their physical connection through a handshake does Ray call his father "dad," asking him, in a trembling voice, "You wanna have a catch?" "I'd like that," his father replies. Catching the first ball his father throws him, Ray looks at it closely, as if thinking of the magic it worked. Both smile as they throw the ball to each other, connecting as father and son.

As it were, the father's appearance provides the answer to Ray's question before pitching to Shoeless Joe Jackson, "Don't we need a catcher?" He needs his catcher father. And there's nothing like a game of catch to reconnect with a father denied for far too many years. It is what makes the ball field a field of dreams. In Terence Mann's testament to the game's enduring magic, with all the changes that come and go over the years, baseball has remained constant. Much as has remained the son's need to connect with his father, and vice versa.

After three rounds of passing between Ray and his father, Annie comes to the porch, switching on the lights just as Ray had done when Shoeless Joe first appeared, thus connecting the two incidents. Shoeless Joe's coming was only the preparation for his father. While the father and son are shown playing catch from a distance, in the background is an endless stream of car headlights. What they come to see, what the movie has been about all along, from the opening words and picture to the closing play of catch, is the connecting of father and son through the game of baseball. This, after all, is what baseball signifies for many fathers and sons, what it signifies for John and Ray Kinsella. It offers a magical way to connect, a connection that is surely every father's and son's dream.

Recap

Without any reference to psychology, though the word *crazy* comes up many times, part of *Field of Dreams'* great appeal is undoubtedly the healing of psychological wounds between father and son. The wounds are seldom referred to, and never explained, but they are everpresent. Other than the poor excuse that he couldn't forgive a man whose hero was a criminal or that he wanted him to achieve his failed dreams in the game of baseball, Ray never gives a good explanation for his looking for reasons to fight with his father. More than a convenient object upon which to project his anger, his father is a constant reminder of the painful experience the two share. This is part of the pain Ray must ease.

Ray may dismiss his mother's death in one laconic sentence, but the event was surely traumatic for the three-year-old boy. The fact that he never mentions her again, together with his constant talk about his father, suggests that he preoccupies himself with his feelings towards his father so as not to confront the pain of losing his mother. By the age of three, when most boys are still under their mother's wing, Ray was already initiated into his father's world. The color picture of the three Kinsellas, the only picture of the three we see, was replaced by the three Cracker Jack pictures of his father's heroes. This is why Ray's feelings for his father are channeled primarily through baseball. This is why he must build the ball field. The field of dreams is the construct, the dreamworks, of his unconscious. And as in dreams, if to go by the analogous pictures of Shoeless Joe and John Kinsella, the two are one and the same. In the end, his father is Ray's hero just as Shoeless Joe was his father's. This is what the voice is telling him, this is the message of the unconscious. As suggested by the paternal figures of Terence Mann, the shadowy father, the boat rocker, and Doc Graham, the fairy godfather of needy children, and the mention of their fathers, Ray comes to terms with both sides of his father, before and after his mother's death. This is what Mann means when he says that the game "reminds us of all that was once good, and it could be again."

Unlike the father he remembers, who "must have had dreams but never did anything about them," Ray heeds the voice of his unconscious by building the field of dreams. But as in dreams, the unconscious has its own way of resolving conflicts. As Ray's *voice*-over tells us right off the bat, his father was dealt a double blow. While his dream was shattered when the White Sox, a team by which he lived and died, sold the 1919 World Series (dying a little when they lost and dying a lot when the series' scandal was uncovered), his reality must have fallen apart when his wife died. Besides the game of baseball, through which they fight rather than connect, Ray and his father share the loss of the woman in their life. Whereas Ray's reaction to his mother's death may have been repression, his father seems to have fallen into depression, what his son calls "worn *down* by life." Returning to the Midwest, to the cornfield seen in the movie's opening picture of John Kinsella, is Ray's first step in resolving his conflict with his father. In the movie's end he sees him before his depression, before his wife's death, before Ray was "even a glint in his eyes."

Interestingly, the last picture of the opening montage, the home movie of their buying the Iowa farm, shows Annie with a big fish printed on her white T-shirt, a symbol of life and the unconscious. As Ray says while the home movie is shown, "until I heard the voice," until Ray heeded the messages from the unconscious, "I'd never done a crazy thing in my whole life." Up to hearing the voice, Ray has turned a deaf ear to the unconscious just as he has turned his back on his father. In fact, many of his actions, especially the ones related to his father, seem to have been largely dictated by his repressed feelings. But with his return to mother earth, to Annie's home state, comes the return of the repressed. Part of the cornfield, the source of the unconscious, is plowed *under* so that a ball field may be built in its place, just as his unconscious is turned over so that inner transformation may take place, so that it may become conscious. In building the ball field, Ray reconstructs his unconscious playing ground, his *infield*. He brings his painful past up to date where he can see it consciously, where he can resolve his problematic relationship with his father.

In this second chance to atone with his father, Annie (*ani*ma?) helps Ray to summon his repressed feminine spontaneity. As the movie's feminine voice, she persuades Ray to buy the farm and encourages him to build the ball field he *feels* he must. When he comments, "I've just created something totally illogical," she replies, "That's what I like about it." Upon the completion of the field, she also points out his change of attitude towards his father. When Ray first sees Shoeless Joe on the field, she urges him, "Why don't you go on outside?" In the PTA meeting, which she reminds him about, she is the catalyst for his divining the meaning of the voice's second message. The unconscious connection is underscored by their having the same dream. She helps Ray pack for his trip to Terence Mann and keeps in touch with him on his journey to

Moonshine Graham and his return home. This explains why, upon seeing his father, Ray turns to her, asking what to say to him. She suggests that he introduce the two women, the feminine voice, in his life, the missing part in their shared life. While it was Ray who switched the lights on for Shoeless Joe, it is Annie who turns it on for Ray and his father. They play catch, as it were, under her gaze. In Ray's own words, having a family of three once again, "maybe this is heaven." "In Annie's constant support and final motherly gesture and in Ray's finding heaven, we have the final piece, the mending of all wounds. Through the field of dreams and its conquest of death Ray experiences of closeness with the mother he barely knew."[2]

Alongside Annie, who encourages Ray to heed his unconscious, their daughter, Karin, is a herald from the unconscious. She watches the invisible rabbit (a herald himself) on the TV that Ray switches off, the creature that only the hero can see. She is the first one to see Shoeless Joe and the other seven players, and the first to announce that "people will come." In contrast to Ray's interruption of *Harvey*, Karin repeatedly interrupts her father's attempts to deal with his financial reality with messages from the dream world, from the unconscious. Only after she falls unconscious (her voice momentarily suffocated), only after Ray comes close to experiencing what he experienced in losing his mother (and his father losing his wife), does he see and atone with his father.

Ultimately, this atonement between father and son is what touches us most deeply. It reminds us what we need from our fathers. This pressing "need for reconnecting" with one's father, especially for men Ray's age, Osherson calls "naming your father."

> In young adulthood a man may be able to drive through life assuming that things are "worked out" with father or that "my father is who he is, it doesn't matter to me," but as we age into our thirties and forties the need for reconnecting becomes more pressing. The reworking of our image of our father, a deepening of its texture, is part of that great shift in motives and value that mark the middle years— what has been called "the second journey" of adulthood. "Naming your father"— coming to terms with who he really is, stripped of the distortion of childhood — is a key to every man's ability to allow a richer identity to emerge as he ages.[3]

Osherson's words fit *Field of Dreams* as a ball fits a glove. The movie that opened with a picture and the literal "naming" of the father closes with its hero seeing his father as he was, without "the distortion of childhood," before the loss of his wife took its toll, before Ray lost his mother. "Hey, Dad?" Ray calls out to his father in a shaky voice, trying to reconnect. "You wanna have a catch?" As with the other three men, none of which are fathers, Ray gets a second chance to realize his dream of playing catch with his father. This is his "second journey." It is as a father that he gets to rework the tarnished image of his father. It is as a man in his middle years that Ray gets to slay the dragon, the introjected father, that has barred him from reaching home plate in the field of dreams.

Chapter 9

Lone Star
Forget the Dragon

Look, I know you had some problems with your father.
— Hollis Pogue, mayor of Frontera, to Sam Deeds, its new sheriff

Geometrical Triads

Like the three isosceles triangles that make up the five-point lone star, or like the triangle itself, the title of John Sayles' *Lone Star* has three obvious connotations: the Lone Star State of Texas, the star-shaped sheriff's badge, and the movie's *lone star*. Of the three, the "lone star" most significant is the least obvious.

If to go by what Sheriff Buddy Deeds is to those who were under his jurisdiction for "near thirty years," he is the movie's *lone star*. When his name first comes up, he is compared to Martin Luther *King*. The townspeople even build a statue in his image and name a courthouse after him. His son, the current Sheriff Sam Deeds, not only hears of his father's heroics wherever his investigation leads him, bringing to mind Telemachus hearing about his heroic father, he is repeatedly reminded that he does not measure up to his bigger-than-life father. He may follow in his footsteps, but he hardly fills his shoes. As one of his father's admirers remarks about "his son" in typical Lone Star lingo, "He's all hat and no cattle." Sam so much as calls his father a *lone star* when he says, "Won't be another like him."

And yet, however much Sam Deeds is overshadowed by his legendary father, the movie is his story, conveyed from his point of view. It tells how, in the course of solving the crime he believes his father had committed, he resolves his *disagreement* with him. Like the typical private eye, he is a *lone* (solitary) individual who seems most comfortable keeping to himself. But perhaps the clearest indication of his being the *lone star* is the red Lone Star title of the movie superimposed on the sheriff's car in which he makes his first appearance. And if Sam is the movie's *subject*, his father is the *object*, the figure on which he projects his bad feelings. From what Sam hears, Buddy Deeds was more a father to the townspeople than to him. To them he was a good patron, the dragon slayer; to Sam, who sees mostly the *ogre* side of his father, he is a patriarchal dragon, an ominous figure that obstructs him from taking his own course in life.

Like the isosceles triangles that overlap to form the lone star, *Lone Star's* overlapping relationships seem to be structured as isosceles triangles. The most prominent one, and the focus of the movie, is the triangle formed by *Lone Star's* three pairs of fathers and sons. Two of the father-son pairs, the triangle's congruous sides, come from the same family, from the three generations of Paynes. The father-son pair of Buddy and Sam Deeds, whose troubled relationship is the heart of the movie, is the triangle's base. The triangle's three sons are alike in that they all have a score to settle with their fathers.

Another triangle, the *middle-aged offspring-parent,* is made up of the Deeds and Paynes families and the mother-daughter pair of the movie, Mercedes and Pilar. The three not only represent the three *ethnic* groups that make up the border town of Frontera, each family presents a different angle to the parent-offspring relationship. Two of the triangle's offsprings, Sam Deeds and Pilar Cruz, share the same father. Del and Otis Payne, the third pair of the triangle, have their own story of bad blood and hard feelings. As the black side of the *parent-offspring* triangle, their strained relationship reflects the dark side of the relationship between Frontera's past and present lawmen. The two sons, Sam and Del, are alike in that they have returned to the hometown they had left behind, the towns ruled by their respective fathers—one the former sheriff of Frontera, the other the current "mayor of Darktown." Unlike their two fathers, who share a terrible secret, Sam and Del never meet in the course of the movie. Like parallel lines, they share analogous stories that do not cross one another. Del and Pilar, who also never meet in the course of the movie, are opposite legs of the *middle-aged offspring-parent* triangle, in which Sam is its base. In the *Self* triangle, as two sides to Sam's lone base, Del represents the *shadow*, Pilar the *anima.*

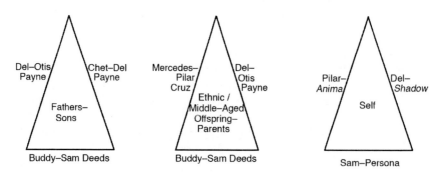

Along with these three prominent triangles, there are three lesser triangles. But however they figure in the movie, all geometric configurations reflect on Sam's disagreement with his father.

Because Buddy Deeds is the prime suspect in Charley Wade's death, at least in Sam's mind, he must investigate his father's history. In the process, bad memories and pent-up feelings resurface, turning Sam's investigation into a quest for the truth about his relationship with his celebrated father. This quest, much more than the investigation, is the underlying force that propels the movie. Like Telemachus' quest for the truth about his absent father, everywhere Sam turns he is reminded of his Odysseus-like father.

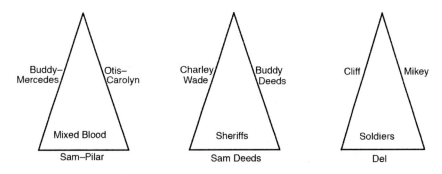

But where Odysseus is alive and thought to be dead, Buddy is dead but very much alive in the minds of the town's citizens. Just as the goddess Athena (who happens to be the name of the black soldier involved in the shooting at *Big O's*), in the guise of Mentor, calls Telemachus to go on a quest for news of his absent father, the discovery of the lone star (together with the Mason's ring and the skeleton) forces Sam to dig up the past that has, in his own words, "seen a good number of disagreements over the years."

Though his presence is felt throughout the movie, Buddy Deeds is shown in only three flashbacks: once at the beginning and once at the end of the movie, both in connection with the murder mystery. In the first he is seen through the mayor of Frontera, Hollis Pogue; in the third through the mayor of Darktown, Otis Payne. Through whose viewpoint the second flashback is seen is not clear. As happens a few times in the movie's flashbacks, which start with one person and end with another, it seems to start with Pilar and end with Sam. It is a brief sequence, and since it takes place in a dark drive-in, we do not really see much. But the event is crucial for both lovers. It marks the time Buddy broke up their relationship, forbidding Sam to see Pilar. They are banished from Eden, their only sin an inter-racial relationship. Or so they think. Together with Sam's only other flashback, this flashback reveals the main source (excuse) for the grudge he holds against his dead father.

Skeletons from the Past

Lone Star's opening shot reveals an arid landscape of cacti and other desert plants, perhaps mirroring the arid and thorny relationship between the movie's fathers and sons. As the camera pans to the right, a middle-aged man is shown consulting a booklet, trying to identify the plants before him. The camera stops to reveal a second man in the background, searching the ground with a metal detector. Both men are investigating. One goes by the book; the other one tries to unearth what lies beneath the surface. What to the man in the background, Mikey, is "lots of cactus and shit," to the one in the foreground, Cliff, each plant has an individual name and an identity of its own, much like the identities of the many of Frontera's citizens. "You live in a place, you should know something about it," Cliff tells Mikey. The skeleton Mikey discovers opens a closed case that no one really wants reopened.

As the movie's exposition, this seemingly inconsequential and brief exchange introduces the subject matter of this epic film: calling things by their rightful names and looking for what lies beneath the surface. Just as Cliff tries to identify the plants above ground, and Mikey searches for treasures underground, in investigating the murder mystery, Sam Deeds undertakes a personal inquiry into his feelings for his father. Mikey also finds the corroded lone star, which Sam, going by the book, places where it was supposedly found, because "we're supposed to leave everything where we found it." Only things do not necessarily go by the book. Once found, there is no putting things back.

That Sam's investigation is about his father is suggested by the subsequent sequence, where, as in the beginning of the *Odyssey,* three old-timers "tell the story of that man skilled in all ways of contending."[1] As Hollis Pogue, the mayor of Frontera, starts to tell "his version" of how Buddy Deeds came to be sheriff, the camera follows his hands, stopping on a basket of tortillas in a red napkin on a red tablecloth. A hand with a Mason's ring, like the one found by Mikey, reaches for the tortillas, lifting a few to reveal a pair of $10 bills. The camera follows the hand with the money to reveal Charlie Wade, a ravenous monster who takes "a healthy bite" from the lives of the citizens under his crooked jurisdiction. Contending with the county's Minotaur, who intimidated its citizens into making regular monthly sacrifices, Buddy Deeds takes up their cause. "There's not a soul in this county who isn't sick to death of your bullshit, Charley. You made yourself scarce, you could make a lot of people happy."

Closing the flashback, Hollis repeats Buddy's last words, "Another beer, please," even though he was no longer there to hear them, suggesting that all is not as it happened, that it is more legend than fact. The camera pans to the left to reveal Sam, riveted by what he hears about his father. The shot that starts with the young Buddy and ends with the middle-aged Sam connects the two, a connection underscored by the abstract painting on the wall behind Sam, showing two figures facing each other. Sam asks to hear about his father because he wants to get the goods on him, as both sheriff and father. What he hears, however, is not what he hoped for. Buddy's kind of law was for the good of the people. As one of his admirers, Fenton, informs Sam, "Charlie Wade was known to put quite a few people in the ground, and your daddy gets eyeball-to-eyeball with him." Whereas the old-timers regard Buddy as a hero who stood up to the county's monster, Sam sees him as a monster. As such, Sam investigates both the *slaying of the dragon* and what for him is *the dragon*, his introjected father.

After introducing the movie's *lone star*, his shadow is introduced next. Like Sam Deeds, Del Payne has returned to Frontera, to his father's turf. Where Sam is in charge of civilian law, Del is in charge of the military. The juxtaposition of his closing words to his soldiers, "The rumors you may have heard that I run a tight operation are not *exaggerated*," with the subsequent shot of Sam looking through a *magnifying* glass at an old photo of his father, not only connects the two, it suggests that his negative picture of his father is also exaggerated, just as is Del's picture of his father. Contrary to how Sam sees his father, throughout his investigation he hears that the rumors about his father "are not exaggerated." At the same time, the magnifying glass, symbol of investigation, signals his starting to take a closer, more *dis-criminate* look at his father.

Sam's studying his father's picture is continued in the very next sequence which opens with a black youth outside Big O's, studying the picture he holds in his hand. As he enters the dark world of Big O's, peopled by African-Americans, he makes his way to the bar, walking between Shadow and Athena and her boyfriend. This shadowy world is overseen by Otis Payne, the mayor of Darktown and Buddy Deed's counterpart, serving his people behind the bar much as the paternal sheriff served the citizens of Frontera. Seeing the king on his throne, the young man pulls out a newspaper advertisement of Big O's Bar-B-Q Sauce, in red letters, showing a drawing of a black man in white chef's outfit, holding a steak with a long fork, not unlike a figure from the underworld. Coming right after Sam's studying the picture of his father, the young man's comparing the man behind the bar and the man in the picture mirrors the difference between the real Buddy Deeds and the picture his son holds. The difference between fact and fiction is further suggested when, in the commotion that ensues after a shot is heard, Big O tells the young man, "You weren't here tonight, were you?" He instructs him to go out the back way, as if he was never there.

Like the movie's other shooting, which initiates Sam's investigation of the murder and of his father, the shooting at Big O's initiates Del's investigation of both the incident and his father. As it were, the two shootings force the two sons to investigate their shadowy pasts, mostly their troubled relationships with their fathers. This is reinforced by the fact that the young man who shoots Athena's boyfriend hails from her past and goes by the name of Shadow, as if he is the return of the repressed.

The three sons' problems with their fathers, the pictures they hold of them, are mirrored by the PTA meeting that is shown next, where there is a big uproar about Pilar's "trying to get across some of the complexity of our situation down here—cultures coming together in both negative and positive ways." Or in another teacher's words, "presenting a more complete picture." The disagreements not only recall Sam's remarking about the disagreements this country has seen, like everything else in the movie, almost every sentence seems to point to his inner disagreement with his father. Especially as put by the white Anglo man (the words *history version* etched on the blackboard behind him) who says, "the story told the way it happened, not the way someone wanted it." Just as each group in this border town refuses to acknowledge "the other side," each of three sons sticks to his version of the past, projecting the unwanted parts on the father.

The movie's three analogous stories start converging when Pilar is called out of the meeting by her daughter. As shown earlier, her son was taken to the police station. It is also where Shadow is shown interrogated about the shooting at Big O's. "Mess with me, that's what you get!" The handcuffed Shadow is tough and unrepentant, as if giving a fair warning: *That's what you get when you mess with the shadow!* Like the skeleton that turned up, and like Shadow who hails from Athena's past, the past catches up with Sam when he catches sight of Pilar, thus encountering the anima right after the shadow. "We haven't talked...." he says to Pilar, who completes his sentence, as if she is his other half. "We haven't talked since high school." "Yep," Sam agrees, not pursuing the matter any further. For the first time in the movie, his detached demeanor is gone, revealing a man who is clearly moved by Pilar's presence. As she leaves with her son, Sam pitches, "It was good seeing you again."

Return of the Repressed

The second chapter opens with the same two men who opened the movie. But while then they were with Sam, now they are with his shadow, running an army obstacle course. Just as their finding the skeleton initiates Sam's investigation (quest), the shooting at *Big O's* starts Del's *quest*ioning the role his father's bar plays in his soldiers' off-duty hours, as well as the role he plays in his own life. For both sons, their return to Frontera turns out to be the return of the repressed, the resurfacing of the past they would like to keep buried. "*Big O's* is the only place in the county that our African-American soldiers are—that they feel comfortable in," Mikey informs Del. Like Sam, Del hears things that go against his image of his father. "You get the feeling he doesn't want to be here?" Cliff asks Mikey when the regimented Del leaves the two to sprint the last quarter mile by himself. As with Sam, Del's return to Frontera brings him face to face with his biggest obstacle, his introjected father, the dragon that holds him captive in his "tight" regimentation.

Sam's investigation is taken up with the showing of the corroded lone star dipped in a solution and pulled out clean and shiny, a visual metaphor of Sam's (and the other sons') quest: to cleanse his perception of his father. In his subsequent meeting with Ben Wetzel, the Texas Ranger assigned to the case, he brings up his father when asking Sam if he remembers "what old Buddy carried for a firearm." Underscoring the father-son relationship, Ben wraps up the meeting with a personal story of his own father and his seeing the Gorgon-like (dragon) Charlie Wade. "I remember Charlie Wade come to my father's hardware store once when I was a little boy. I'd heard stories of how he shot this one, how he shot that one. Man winked at me and I peed in my pants."

In Sam's next meeting, with Mayor Hollis, shown tinkering with his tackle in his fishing boat, a sense of guilt pervades the brief exchange between the two. "I always wondered what you mayors do when you're not cutting ribbons," Sam remarks to Hollis, who admits his guilt, as if referring to his role in the killing of Charlie Wade. Sam's remark alludes to the dedication due to take place the following day, another reminder that he cannot get away from the ghost of his father. Once again, his ongoing investigation of Charlie Wade's murder is accompanied by his *problems* with his father. While Sam claims to "understand why you might want to believe he couldn't do it," Hollis "understand[s] why you might want to think he could." His metaphor in advising Sam to lay off the investigation, his reference to the "old fish," a common symbol of life, "on the bottom of the lake," suggests the unconscious Sam must deal with in his investigation.

The unconscious is continued in the subsequent three scenes, which can be read as Sam's first visit to the realm of the shadow, or Dark Town, as it is called in Frontera. The three scenes are introduced in Athena's interrogation by Cliff and Priscilla, another racially mixed couple, where Shadow is described as coming "from back in Houston ... looking for trouble," another allusion to the return of the repressed.

First, Sam's first station is the former owner of *Big O's*, Roderick Bledsoe's widow. Once again, as if there is no getting away from his father, when Sam introduces himself as "Sheriff Deeds," he is reminded how he measures up to him: "Sheriff Deeds' dead, honey. You're just Sheriff Junior," Mrs. Bledsoe says to set him straight. "Yeah, that's the story of my life," Sam adds wryly, another reminder that his investigation is about his coming to terms with the tall shadow his legendary father casts over his life. Referring to the Gameboy she is playing, Mrs. Bledsoe gives Sam another warning about his quest. "Don't ever start up on 'em, cause once you do you can't stop." But Sam proceeds with his questioning. "Them days, you deal with Sheriff Wade or you didn't deal," Mrs. Bledsoe informs him. "And my father?" Sam asks. "Sheriff Buddy was a different story.... Sheriff Buddy kept his word. That Sheriff Wade, though, he could get ugly.... Had him a smile like the Grim Reaper. He used to sit there with his hand on his old gun acting the kingfish with everybody."

Second, as Mrs. Bledsoe talks, the picture dissolves into a flashback of the club, where Charlie Wade sits with Hollis, eyeing the young Otis Payne who, in Mrs. Bledsoe's words, "had some attitude." Like Shadow, Otis has also "been away up in Houston." His "attitude," his rubbing Charley the wrong way, underscores his personifying for Wade his repressed shadow. "How come you don't look familiar?" Wade asks the young Otis. In terms of the shadow, Otis is unfamiliar to Wade because he is the other, the dark part that he tries to keep a lid on in the county under his jurisdiction. But as repressed shadows tend to do, it assumes an autonomous personality of its own. "You learn how to act your place, son. This isn't Houston," Wade warns Otis, overlooking him from above in a threatening manner, letting him know who calls the shots in Rio County.

By the way the sequence is shot, it is obvious that Wade has it in for darker people such as Blacks and Mexicans precisely because they personify his repressed shadow, which is what makes him so dangerous and unexpected. Like a mythological monster, like the Minotaur or the Sphinx, Wade keeps the county under a reign of terror. Running numbers may be illegal, but it is unhealthy if Wade does not know about it, if no sacrifices are made "on the first of the month, every month." Like the first flashback of Wade's clash with Buddy, his clash with Otis reeks of violence and death. The way Wade uses his gun also reeks of sexual repression. The third time we see Wade in a flashback, he uses his gun to kill in cold blood because no sacrifices were made.

And third, just as the Bledsoes sold their club to Otis, the flashback that starts out as Mrs. Bledsoe's (her voiceover opens the flashback) ends as if it is Otis's. The two are connected by the figure of the black cat in Mrs. Bledsoe's garden and the picture of a big black cat on the wall behind Otis, another reminder of the shadow. After a few questions about Sheriff Wade, Sam asks Otis about his father. But once again, he does not get the incriminating information he seeks. "I don't recall a prisoner ever died in your daddy's custody," Otis tells him. "I don't recall a man in this town — black, white, Mexican — who'd hesitate for a minute before they'd call on Buddy Deeds to solve a problem. More than that I wouldn't care to say."

Once again, in their parallel quests, what Sam hears about his father in his investigation matches what Del hears about his. "Everybody loves Otis — Big O." Apparently Del tries to "run a very tight operation" at home with his son as he does in the Army. "I don't see what the big deal is," Dell's wife, Celia, tells her husband about his troubled relationship with his father. "Go back over, talk to the man, and bury the hatchet, Del." "Why me? He's had almost 40 years and I haven't heard a word from him," Del protests. "You were eight years old when he left.... People change.... We're going to have to see him." "No we don't," Del replies.

Del's ultimate change of mind about seeing his father runs parallel to his loosening control over his son's life. And as Sam's shadow, his letting go is matched, step by step, by Sam coming to terms with his father, letting go of the negative picture he holds on to.

Showing Sam out of uniform (at the "white" bar) is the first sign of his loosening up. The meeting with Pilar and everything else is starting to work on him. The bar and the barman, who labels himself "as liberal as the next guy" (to which Sam counters, "If the next guy is a redneck") are a white version of Big O's and Otis. In his two-bit philosophy on the difference of the races, once again the name of Buddy Deeds comes up. "The lines of demarcation are getting fuzzy. To run a successful civilization, you have got to have lines of demarcation between right and wrong, between this one and that one. Your Daddy understood that. He was, what do you call it? The referee in this damn *menudo* we got down here. He understood how most people don't want their sugar and salt in the same jar." To make his point, the barman motions to the "salt and pepper" sharing drinks in a booth, the black woman (Priscilla) and Cliff, seen earlier in Army uniform interrogating Athena about the shooting. "Take that pair over there in the corner. A place like this, twenty years ago, Buddy'd been on them two. He'd have gone there and give them a warning. Not that he had it in for the colored, but just as a kind of safety tip." Like most of the people Sam encounters, the barman reminds him he will never be like his father: "The day that man died they broke the goddamn mold." The barman's words surely remind Sam how his father had "been on them two" in his relationship with Pilar.

Descent to the Underworld

Lone Star's third section, the *katabasis*, opens with a shot of *Big O's*. Outside the bar, in the bright light of day, Colonel Del Payne, in full uniform, looks at a makeshift sign by the door. "Black Seminole Exhibit Rear Entrance." As in other instances throughout the movie, the sign points to the history that each ethnic group clings to. Walking into the darkness of the club from the light outside, Del removes his hat and puts it by his side to signify that the visit is an official one. He still needs the protection of the official formality and the full uniform. The words of the song playing on the jukebox, "Since I Met You, Baby," can very well refer to both Del and Sam. Their return to their hometown is changing their lives. Del can be seen as Sam's shadow, and Del's venture into his father's "Darktown" anticipates Sam's descent to the underworld south of the border.

"Black Seminoles?" are Del's first words to his father. "Hobby of mine," Otis explains, inviting his son to see the historical exhibit, adding, "Admission is free." But Del declines. He refuses his father's invitation to see his ancestral history just as he refuses to come to terms with his personal history. Much like Sam at the movie's opening, he is on an official visit to the scene of the crime. As a place where their people can "air their grudges out," it seems that Otis's "tightly screwed" son could use some of what his father's bar has to offer.

Like Buddy Deeds, Otis also has a Mexican woman. When Dell is introduced to Carolyn, dressed in red, contrasting Del's dark green uniform, the picture of the black leopard on the wall is conspicuously between them. Del shakes hands with the anima, but there is no handshake between father and son. Del uses his official duty as a shield and an excuse to contact his father. But when Otis asks, "I'm gonna meet that family of yours?" Del shoots back, "Why would you want to do that?" "Because I'm your father," Otis reminds him. Del throws Otis a dark look and walks up to his father who has just acknowledged him as his son, meeting him face to face. "You'll get official notification when I made my decision." The camera overlooks Otis's shoulder as Del marches out the door. Having the last word may be a small revenge against the father he feels has betrayed him, but as his slamming the door on his way out demonstrates, his full uniform and official demeanor cannot hide or protect him from feeling the anger and hurt he harbors inside.

Much like Del airing his "grudges" against his father, in the unveiling ceremony, where once again Mayor Hollis Pogue praises the legendary "Sheriff Buddy Deeds," Sam, introduced as "somebody who probably knew Buddy better than any of us," brings his father down to human size. "Well, you folks who remember my father knew him as a sheriff. But at home he was also judge, jury and executioner. This is a real honor you're doing him today. And if Buddy was around, I'm sure his hat size would be getting a lot bigger every minute. I used to think there wasn't a place in this town you could hide from my old man. And now I'm sure of it." The camera cuts to a medium close-up of Pilar, who nods her head in agreement, smiling over Sam's wry remarks. Perhaps what Fenton comments on the unveiled statue of Buddy, who is depicted putting his arm over a boy's shoulder, "I think he's going to ride that Mexican kid for loitering," best sums up what Sam feels about his father, especially considering the look on his face when he first sees his statue unveiled.

Along with his investigation (his trying to unveil what the two mayors are keeping under wraps), Sam's seeing Pilar again reconnects him with long-buried feelings. Inviting her for a walk after the ceremony is another step in his reconnecting with himself. But even in their walking to a place they visited as teenagers, Buddy Deeds comes up, reinforcing what Sam remarked in the ceremony that there isn't a place in this town you could hide from his old man. Pilar's memory of Buddy recalls what Ben Wetzel remembered about Charlie Wade. As the flashback reveals, Sam and Pilar are still hounded by their parents. As children often do, they misconceive their parents' reason for keeping them apart. By his own words, Sam is still torn between wanting to be like his father and wishing him out of his life. Knowing he cannot take his legendary father's place, his return and taking his old job is an attempt to be his father's son.

Sam's first break in the investigation comes at the break of day, after a night of studying the documented history of former sheriffs, mostly Charlie

Wade's reign of terror, as if familiarizing himself with the dragon. As always, the name of Buddy pops up when an inmate comes to empty the trashcans. "Your father tried to do good for people," he tells Sam. "So I've heard," Sam replies in his usual dry manner. The good side of Buddy Deeds leads to the bad side of Charlie Wade when the inmate informs Sam that Wade "murdered Eladio Cruz," Pilar's "father." Not only that, he gives Sam the name of the man who can verify it. "Chucho Montoya saw it with his own eyes. Shot him in cold blood."

Given this lead, Sam crosses to the other side of the border to verify it in person, making the crossing without his badge. Just as Telemachus sailed for news of his father from the two kings, Nestor and Menelaus, who had fought with him in the Trojan war, Sam crosses the bridge over the Rio Grande into Mexico, to Frontera's darker twin city, to question "the King of the Tires," as he is introduced by his advertisement on the Mexican radio station. If to judge by the King's opening words, "Down here," this crossing the border is Sam's descent into Hades. Montoya's business, retreading tires, suggests what Sam feels next to his legendary father — a retreaded Buddy Deeds, and a poor one at that.

As the King starts telling Sam how he came to see Charlie Wade kill Eladio Cruz, the camera pans to the left from a sign advertising him as the King of the Tires to reveal a bridge where the young Eladio Cruz is shown changing a tire on an old pickup truck. Charley Wade's arrival is shot the same way Sam first arrived at the abandoned rifle range where his bones were found, the camera focusing on the Lone Star painted on the car door. He shoots Eladio Cruz not so much for hauling "wets" across the border as for "making a fool out of Charlie Wade," not cutting him in on the deal. The flashback ends with Sam standing on the very same bridge, his badge back on, lost in thought. If to go by what he does next, the meeting with the King is a significant station in his journey. He returns from "down there" with a new resolve to do something about the people in his life.

Sam's resolve is reinforced by the subsequent flashback, which is initiated by Pilar's reference to her "old high-school heart-throb sheriff," trying to convince herself that "nobody stay's in love for twenty-three years." The flashback takes place in the drive-in where Buddy put a stop to Sam and Pilar's relationship. While on the big screen two identically clad women, one white and one black, handcuffed together, are shown trying to escape their pursuers, Buddy and Hollis are searching with flashlights between the parked cars for young Sam and Pilar, who must feel like the two women on the screen. Torn apart by force, Sam tells his father to stay out of his life while Pilar begs Hollis not to tell her mother. The flashback ends with the grown Sam in the very same drive-in, reliving the traumatic experience together with Pilar. While she is thinking to the *time* they last spoke, he is in the very same *place*, in the drive-in, out of uniform and in his own car, as if he has shed another protective armor.

Having returned to the scene of their separation, the scene of his father's crime, Sam makes a night journey that takes him to a reunion with Pilar. His nocturnal drive is accompanies by a rhythm and blues song that sings about the love ("longer than forever") that he still has for her. Like their shared flashback, which starts with Pilar and ends with Sam, they first get together in her mother's cafe and end in his apartment. "I came back 'cause you were here." Sam turns to face Pilar for the first time. The song Pilar plays on the juke box, which has not changed its songs since she was ten years old, is a Spanish version of the song played at Big O's when Del first came in, another link of the two sons. Their dancing to what must be their song dissolves into their lovemaking in Sam's apartment. Considering that this is (probably) the first time they consummate their love, it is truly a fresh start. Only this time they are adults who had both gone through one marriage. The intimate sequence ends the third part of the movie, with Sam asking Pilar her father's name. "Eladio Cruz," she replies, not thinking much about it, not knowing what Sam is beginning to uncover.

Atonement with the Father

Coinciding with Sam's renewing his relationship with Pilar, Chet returns to Big O, coming in the back way, the same way he left on his first brief visit. The talk about John Horse's staunch stand mirrors Del's proud and stubborn stand against his father, as when Otis replies to his grandson's question why the Seminoles fought other Indians, "They were in the army. Just like your father." Chet's visit to his grandfather not only clears the way for his father to make his own visit, like everything else in *Lone Star*, the exchange between the two, about fathers and sons, reflects on Sam's relationship with his father. Like Chet himself, both Del and Sam are "living proof" of the role the father plays in his son's adult life. "Every time he moves up a rank, it's like he's got to tighten the screws a little more. I mean, just 'cause he didn't, you know, he didn't have...." "Didn't have a father?" Otis completes his sentence. "He is still pissed off about it," Chet adds.

Rhyming with Chet's visit to Big O's, Sam stops by Mercedes' Café, to see if Hollis's memory has returned. "I wish I could tell you I remembered something new, but I can't." Armed with what he thinks is enough incriminating evidence, Sam gives Hollis his "idea what happened," an idea formed by his prejudice towards his father. Once again, it is more a case of the introjected father, the dragon that Sam projects on his father, than the man himself. Hollis, who knows the truth about the murder and Buddy's part in it, points to Sam's preconceived notions. "You lived in the man's house what, seventeen, eighteen years? And you didn't get to know him any better than that."

After hearing from Chucho Montoya the incriminating truth about Charlie Wade, who has come to represent the evil side of Buddy Deeds, Sam hears about the darker side of his father from the Native American Wesley Birdsong. The sequence opens with a shot of a longhorn skull, suggesting that Birdsong's roadside stand, on a "stretch of road that runs between Nowhere and Nothing Much," where "nobody comes by" and full of things nobody wants, is the land of death. Like Odysseus' descent to the underworld to seek advice from the seer Tiresias, Birdsong advances Sam on his journey by revealing Buddy Deeds' other side, suggesting he could have turned out like Charlie Wade. "If he hadn't found that deputy job, I believe Buddy might've gone down the other path, got into some serious trouble. Settled him right down. That and your mother." His adding another piece of information, "Of course, he had that other one later," surprises Sam just as Odysseus was surprised to see the shade of his mother in Hades. Stopping short of revealing "that other's" identity, Wesley picks the dried skin of a rattlesnake, waving its rattle like a medicine man while warning Sam, as did Mrs. Bledsoe and Hollis. "Gotta be careful where you're poking. Who knows what you'll find."

Corresponding to Sam's questioning Wesley Birdsong, Del's interrogating Athena confronts him with the chaotic history that drove him to the regimentation and order of the army. His opening question to Athena, "Are you unhappy in the Army?" is also addressed to himself. And when she asks him, "You really wanna know?" it brings to mind Sam's wanting to know more about his father despite all the warnings. "Please," Del practically asks. Of course, considering what Del comes to know about his father, Athena's question sends him to get to know his father, just as the goddess Athena sent Telemachus to find out about his. As with Sam's visit to Wesley Birdsong, Athena gives Del much more than he bargained for. In an uncharacteristic move, Del drops the official formalities between officer and recruit, what he could not do in his meeting with his father. The informal exchange gets him to see what he was formerly blind to, as suggested by the open blinds behind him. Athena's directness initiates the loosening up of the "very tight operation" that rumors had him pegged for. Adjusting her cap in a fatherly manner, Del offers her a new start, just as she offers him.

Where Chucho Montoya's tale got Sam to renew his relationship with Pilar, Wesley Birdsong's information drives him to his former wife, a scene which also opens with "longhorns." Like Del and Athena, who find a haven from the chaos of life in the Army, Bunny finds it in the game of football. And like Sam and Del, she is a victim of her father. She remains his little girl. Her description of herself as "tightly wound" recalls Del's "tightened screws." The visit offers a picture of Sam's marriage to Bunny, in which, as she put it, "You kind of bought yourself a pig in a poke, didn't you?" "It wasn't just you, Bunny," Sam admits, probably also thinking of his relationship with his father. "No it wasn't, was it? You didn't exactly throw yourself into it heart and soul now, did you?"

Once again, Sam's visit to Bunny corresponds to Del's visit to the home of his father, where they each learn something new about their fathers. Sam learns the name of the "other woman"; Del, who is invited in and "shown around" by Otis's "other woman," learns that his father followed his career from the day he had left home. He may have abandoned him, as Del feels, but he never disowned him. He never stopped caring for him. "When they made you general, Otis just about drove away all our customers going on about it," Carolyn adds. "I'm a colonel," Del corrects her. "Yeah, I know. Man made me memorize the whole damn Army chain of command before he'd marry me." Like Sam's mistaken image of his father, the "shrine" Del sees is hardly what he expected. "My mother said he never asked about me," he confesses. "He never asked *her*," Carolyn sets him straight. Del's abrupt decision to leave suggests that this revelation is too much for him, that he cannot bear to meet his father with this new knowledge, the knowledge that he hasn't forgotten him, that he never stopped loving him, especially as he is not protected by his armor of a uniform. This knowledge creates chaos in his regimented way of seeing. "Tell him I stopped by," he says. "Catch you later, colonel," Carolyn salutes him with a smile. Much like Athena after her meeting with Del, she knows he leaves a different son than the one who first came in.

Indeed, the next time Del is shown he is noticeably changed. Armed with the knowledge that his father did not abandon *him*, he can afford to loosen some of those screws. He can allow a new approach to his son. "You know, the Army isn't *for* everybody. It's not that I don't think you'd be good at it. It's ... you know ... I wouldn't be disappointed if you decided to do something else with your life." Encouraged by his father's uncommon openness, Chet asks, "Are we ever going to see your father?" "Maybe we'll, we'll fix that thing out back, and have a barbecue next weekend." Del has reached some kind of atonement with his father. "We could invite him and his wife over." Seeing the change in his father, Chet adds admiringly, "He makes his own sauce."

Like Telemachus returning from his quest about his father, Sam returns to Frontera from his quest-drive for the truth about his father in search of Hollis, the one person who can tell him what really happened the night of Wade's disappearance. But just as Sam is looking in the wrong place, Hollis is somewhere else. Figuring where else he can be, Sam's drive up to Big O's is shot the same way as when he first made his appearance in the movie. But while then it was in the suspected scene of the crime, now he has arrived at the real scene. Arriving in uniform, but not in the sheriff's car, suggests what his quest has been all along—both official and personal. At Big O's, where he finds Frontera's two mayors, Otis gives Sam the information that *solves* the murder mystery and absolves Buddy of the crime he accuses him of. Hollis, on the other hand, gives him the information that *resolves* his hostile feelings towards his father.

The evidence may have pointed to Buddy's guilt, but Sam's personal antagonism surely had much to do with his judgment. What he had said of his father at the unveiling ceremony, that at home he was "judge, jury and executioner," can be said about his own attitude towards him. Once Sam discovers who did the shooting and understands his father's motives for keeping Pilar and him apart, his hostility diminishes and his long-held grudge disappears. Like his father and the others, Sam decides to keep the truth of the killing. This acceptance of the legend, of the townspeople liking "the story that we told better than anything the truth might have been," which comes in the next-to-last scene of *Lone Star,* recalls the similar acceptance of the legend in the next-to-last scene of *The Man Who Shot Liberty Valance.* Sam's "Buddy's a goddamn legend. He can handle it" is *Lone Star*'s "When the legend becomes fact, print the legend."

Underscoring the two crimes of Sam's investigation, just as the opening sequence was in an abandoned shooting range, the scene of the historical crime, the closing sequence, the epilogue, takes place in an abandoned drive-in, the scene of the personal crime. Pilar's saying that she doesn't "have to ask permission anymore" from her mother mirrors Sam's freeing himself from his father's hold. He is no longer under his shadow. The black-and-white picture of Buddy and Mercedes that he shows Pilar is proof of the terrible truth of their kinship. Knowing the truth, however, does not stop them from resuming their relationship at the very place where it was abruptly stopped. Now they know the reason, the secret, for their feeling connected to one another and for their parents' keeping them apart. But as Otis told his grandson, "Blood only means what you let it." More than connected by blood, Pilar and Sam are soulmates. The fact that they decide to go against their parents gives testimony to their new sense of freedom. The historical obstacles, the dragons, no longer bar their way. "All that stuff and that history," the history teacher proposes, "the hell with it, right? Forget the Alamo."

In a way, the two continue Buddy Deeds' legacy: It may be illegal but it is what his sense of justice calls for. It is the right thing to do. It is what Buddy would have done—find an accommodating way to work it out so both sides are happy. By deciding to continue their relationship, the two accept their parents' covert relationship and its consequence. They see their history for what it is. Unlike Oedipus, who blinded himself after his investigation, Sam and Pilar do not let the historical facts impinge upon the present. They forgive and forget. They forgive their parents; they forget the dragon.

Part IV

⊶⊷⊷⊷⊷

BECOMING A FATHER

Like many profound life changes, becoming a father is a process that extends over time.

— Samuel Osherson, *Finding Our Fathers*

Fatherhood has come a long way since it was portrayed in such '50s sitcoms as *Father Knows Best, Leave It to Beaver* and *Ozzie and Harriet.* Like the sitcoms themselves, the fathers they portrayed are now nostalgia. But back then, despite their silliness and remoteness from reality, these weekly shows assured their audience that the American family had a father at its head. The fathers were usually around the family home, and their role was clear-cut and acknowledged. Fatherhood seemed secure and with a promising future. What is more, as there was very little, if any, literature on the subject, the sitcoms' portrayals of the father were what many Americans saw, and perhaps even accepted, as models of the good father.

Some two decades later, following the enormous changes the American family had undergone in the '60s and '70s, the picture of the good father continued in the person of Bill Cosby, the first Afro-American to star in his own television series. *The Cosby Show,* the '80s throwback to the '50s sitcoms, was the top show in its earlier seasons. Where the '50s fathers were silly, Cosby's character, Cliff Huxtable, was often charmingly goofy. He was a funky father. Still, Cosby himself was taken seriously enough to have a best-selling book about fatherhood. Many people probably bought the book on the strength of his TV persona. The "fact" that he was a doctor, and an obstetrician gynecologist at that, probably played an important part in the book's enormous success. The fact that Cosby was black was also not without significance. He was a good negative of the white original, continuing the fantasy of the all-white '50s family sitcoms. The show's success was a comforting confirmation to the white audience that it had assimilated blacks as part of the American culture.

It had integrated the shadow. And even if the Huxtables were *white* upper-middle class Afro-Americans, they presented a refreshing picture of the American family. It was part of the liberation that the nation was undergoing.

In the early '90s the same liberation paved the way for *The Simpsons*, a cartoon family that nonetheless portrayed the American family in a more realistic light than the earlier sitcoms. The Simpsons may share the name of their hometown, Springfield, with the Andersons of *Father Knows Best*, but the show's father, Homer, is anything but father knows best. His inadequacies and shortcomings seem to reflect the uncertainty and confusion that characterize the '90s father. Perhaps Homer's most redeeming attribute is his sharing his name with the creator of *The Odyssey*. Given the cultural references and parodies that pepper the show, this is surely not without intent. In his own anti-heroic way, Homer is by far the most cunning and adventurous of the TV fathers. He may offer an alternative to the traditional sitcom fathers, but as with the other shows, and as with *The Odyssey*, each episode ends with an affirmation of the family.

Contrary to what was presented in the family sitcoms, contemporary fatherhood is nothing to laugh about. Over the years, ever since the nation started changing from an agrarian society to an urban one, the father's role has been on a decline. Alongside this trend, as young men became more career-oriented in the competitive work world of the city, their interest in fatherhood has also declined. *Becoming a father* was no longer an inevitable part of a man's life. And perhaps even more significant, fatherhood was no longer a sign of manhood. An increasing number of men were unwilling, or unprepared, to exchange freedom of bachelorhood for responsibility, which becoming a father required. In the conflict between the innate impulse to father offsprings and one's more selfish tendencies, the latter seemed to have the upper hand. Ultimately, men were not ready to renounce the pursuit of their own satisfactions for the commitment of fatherhood. In a word, they declined to grow up.

By the turn of the millennium, fatherless families were almost as common as ones with a father. In an aptly titled book, *Fatherless America*, David Blankenhorn comments on this trend:

> As fatherlessness spreads in our society, so do our acceptance and even endorsement of the trend. For as our society abandons the fatherhood idea, we do not simply become "more aware" of children growing up without fathers. We also become "accepting of that." In a culture of fatherlessness, fatherhood becomes irrelevant.[1]

As often happens, this trend did not go unrecognized by Hollywood. In the early '90s, two of Hollywood's most family-oriented filmmakers, Steven Spielberg and Disney, addressed the problem. Spielberg's *Jurassic Park* was the biggest blockbuster in film history, and Disney's *The Lion King* the most successful animated feature of all time (until 2003's *Finding Nemo*). It is not easy to determine how much the subject of fatherhood contributed to the success of these two movies, but the fact remains that they both deal with fatherhood. No doubt these movies were highly entertaining. But it is hard to believe that that was the only reason for their enormous success, especially as the dethroner of *The Lion King*, the animated *Finding Nemo*, is also about fatherhood. Curiously, all three movies take place in the animal kingdom, as if they represent a return to man's more primitive and instinctual nature. *Jurassic Park* ('93) takes place on an island of scientifically resurrected dinosaurs; the '94 *Lion King* is in an animated animal kingdom; 2003's *Finding Nemo* is mostly in the sea, where on his quest for his son the father learns to let go and become a better father. *Nemo*'s clown (fish) father, Merlin, not only recalls the sitcom fathers, the movie's enormous success is yet another reminder that fatherhood is still foremost in our hearts and minds. In their highly entertaining manner, all three movies offer a darker picture of fatherhood than the one presented in the family sitcoms.

When we first meet the heroes of *The Lion King* and *Jurassic Park*, the first two movies covered in this section, they have no intention of becoming fathers. *The Lion King*'s Simba opts for the carefree life as extolled by the "problem-free philosophy" (not being a king/father) of "Hakuna Matata," and *Jurassic*'s Grant is focused on a career of studying creatures that were wiped from the face of the earth. As shown by these movies, fatherhood's biggest adversary is man's shadowy self-centeredness. In *The Lion King* it is personified by the devious Scar; in *Jurassic Park* it is represented by the dangerous dinosaurs. In both movies, which can be read as critiques of contemporary fatherhood, these manifestations of evil, these embodiments of the dragon, have taken over, running rampant, leading to death and destruction.

As already noted, the name Scar is taken from John Ford's *The Searchers*, this section's third and final movie. And as Ford is much more realistic than Disney, or Spielberg, the force of evil in his 1956 western is much darker. The Comanche Chief Scar not only embodies Ethan Edwards' savageness, he represents his unconscious desire to usurp his brother's place with his wife. Ethan's search, for both Scar and Debbie, is his penitence. Between his coming and going he comes to terms with his shadow, which stands in the way of his becoming a father. Only after Scar is dead does Ethan redeem himself by becoming Debbie's (and Marty's) new father, assuming his brother's place without guilt. In the end he may return to the same wilderness from which he came, but he is not the same man. While his coming from the wilderness as "Uncle Ethan" is said outright, his returning to it as a father is conveyed more subtly, through images and metaphors. This is the change Ethan undergoes. He starts his search, his quest, as an uncle and ends by becoming a father.

The Lion King and *Jurassic Park* may not measure up to *The Searchers* in complexity and depth, but in all three movies the cinematic heroes undergo similar journeys into fatherhood. Only after dealing with what represents for them the shadow, the dragon, do they embrace some form of fatherhood. And what is perhaps more significant, in embracing fatherhood the three achieve a fuller measure of manhood. They do what all good fathers do—they give of themselves to others.

Chapter 10

The Lion King
A Picture of Fatherhood

This is just for you and your daddy. You know, a sort of father-son thing.
— Scar to Simba

A Moving Epic

Fatherhood may have been in dire straits in America of the '90s, but in the mythical animal kingdom of *The Lion King* it is a cause for celebration — at least in the movie's beginning and ending. Between these bookends, between the movie's two ceremonial celebrations of fatherhood, Disney's animated feature charts its hero's rite of passage from denying patriarchy to its acceptance and fulfillment. In outlining how the spirit of the father and the wisdom of the shaman initiate the young lion into his rightful throne as both king and father, the movie offers an engaging model for the rite we must undertake in becoming our fathers' sons and becoming fathers ourselves.

Speaking (in the DVD supplement) of *The Lion King*'s unprecedented success at the box office, one of its creators points out that the movie "had something that appealed to people on a deeper and more fundamental level." And calling attention to what that "something" is, immediately after this observation the movie's hero, Simba, is shown running after his father's fading image in the clouds, beseeching him, "Don't leave me." While the son's plea, no doubt, speaks to many of today's fatherless sons, Disney's movie, like Mufasa's words to his son in this brief sequence ("Remember! Remember!"), urges us to remember our responsibility to our fathers and to ourselves as potential fathers.

Along with its depiction of the father-son relationship, the creators of *The Lion King* attribute its great success to the *creative process* and *collaboration* that went into the animated film. This collaboration, they maintain, had much to do with "creating something that has moved people." Like the movie's opening song, proclaiming that the Circle of Life "moves us all," *The Lion King* moves us because, coming from the collective work of its creators, it addresses our collective imagination, the wellspring of myths. It moves us in ways we hardly expect from an animated film. We are fascinated by this movie because its characters are conceived as archetypes, as primordial images that mirror different parts of our shared psyche.

The movie's primary archetype, of course, is the king-father, personified by King Mufasa. He is portrayed as an ideal father, fulfilling the traditional role beyond reproach. He is wise, patient and understanding. As king, as patriarch of Pride Land, he represents the Logos principle. His word is the law of the land. He is the source of his kingdom's order and harmony. Like the sun, he is the center of the animal kingdom and its source of life; like the Fisher King in the myth of the Holy Grail, when *he* goes, so does the kingdom.

Notwithstanding its African setting, *The Lion King* also fits right in with what Robert Jewett and John Shelton Lawrence call *the American Monomyth.* Like the movie that begins with a harmonious Pride Lands and ends with its restoration,

> The American monomyth begins and ends in Eden. Stories in this genre typically begin with a small community ... living in harmony. A disruption of harmony occurs, and must be eliminated by the superhero, before the Edenic condition can be re-established in a happy ending.[1]

As Jewett and Lawrence point out in their examination of Disney's body of work, "Disney's efforts to create a sanitary form of happiness were regarded as the finest examples of educational entertainment."[2] Disney's movies were created according to Walt's vision of a wholesome and sanitary America. *The Lion King*, however, is somewhat of an exception. Perhaps because it came out 28 years after Disney passed away in 1966, or perhaps because the story was created in the '90s, the movie turned "educational entertainment" to adult entertainment. In the words of one of its creators, *The Lion King* "crossed the barrier from children entertainment to entertainment." The movie may have conformed to Disney's wholesome vision, but it was far from sanitary. As film critic Hal Hinson noted, "Of the 32 animated films Disney has produced, this story of a young African lion's search for identity is not only more mature in its themes, it is also the darkest and the most intense. Shakespearean in tone, epic in scope, it seems more appropriate for grown-ups than for kids."[3]

However understated (or unconscious), another element that surely contributed to *The Lion King*'s unparalleled success with grown-ups is its portrayal of fatherhood — its past, present and future. In its entertaining manner it shows what fatherhood had once been, what it is today, and what it could and should be. As did myths in the past, this filmmyth shows its audience, kids and grown-ups alike, what the son must do to reclaim the father's rightful throne and become a father himself.

Mufasa's reign is what fatherhood had once been, when fathers were accessible and played prominent roles in their offspring's lives. Fathers who were wise, warm and always around — model know-best fathers such as Ozzie Nelson of *Ozzie and Harriet*, Ward Cleaver of *Leave It to Beaver* and Jim Anderson of *Father Knows Best*. Until his last breath, Mufasa is what David Blankenhorn calls "the Good Family Man."

> As a father, the Good Family Man is not perfect, but he is good enough to be irreplaceable. He is married. He stays around. He is a father on the premises. His children need him and he strives to give them what they need, every day. He knows that nothing can substitute for him. Either he is a father or his children are fatherless. He would never consider himself "not that important" to his children.[4]

The death of Mufasa together with Scar's bachelorhood and self-serving reign, which brings disaster upon Pride Rock, is a portrayal of our ever-growing fatherless society, where the "failure to sustain or create compelling norms of fatherhood amounts to a social and personal disaster."[5] This trend is reflected by the *social* disaster of Pride Rock under Scar's evil rule and by Simba's *self*-exile and carefree lifestyle. Like many of today's young men who deny the paternal impulse, Simba lives in the here-and-now without care or responsibility, a far cry from his own father who put his family first. Somewhat like Peter Pan or Ibsen's Peer Gynt, he mistakes *being for himself* for *being himself*.

Simba's return to Pride Rock (and himself), his assuming responsibility and his father's throne, and becoming a father, point to what is required to change the disastrous status of contemporary fatherhood. It entails coming to terms with the introjected father, embodied in myths and fairy tales by the dragon.

Celebrating Fatherhood

The Lion King opens with the dawning of a new day. Amidst the sounds of nature's many animals, a lion's roar is heard in the darkness. As the sun rises, one by one the animals raise their heads and look up. All start heading towards the rising *sun*. But as we soon see in a tour-de-force of sights and sounds, they are going towards their king's newborn *son*, their future king, whose birth is one more link in the continuing Circle of Life. Standing proudly on Pride Rock, symbol of his throne, Mufasa looks at the gathering members of his kingdom. Rafiki, the shaman mandrill, makes his way towards Mufasa's throne. He is an honored figure who mediates between the every-day and the eternal Circle of Life, between the known and the great unknown. Climbing up to Mufasa, his staff leading the way, Rafiki raises his arms and the two embrace warmly. The day they have been waiting for has arrived. So begins the celebration of fatherhood, *The Lion King*'s model picture of what fatherhood once had been.

The shaman has come to play his part in the ceremony of christening the future king and presenting him to his future subjects. Mufasa leads him to

Simba lying snugly in his mother's arms. The shaman shakes his staff above him, breaking a large round gourd and anointing his forehead with its red-brown insides, the same color as Mufasa's mane. Then he counters it with a sprinkle of soil. Considering what ensues, it seems to represent the two sides of life and death, the two sides represented by Mufasa and his dark brother Scar.

This part of the ceremony completed, the shaman takes the next in line from his mother to the tip of Pride Rock and lifts him up for all the gathered animals to see. They are joyous. They have a future king. The Circle of Life will continue. A high angle shot of Rafiki holding the newborn swings around to show the bewildered expression on the cub's face. Just then a shaft of sunlight breaks through the morning clouds, shedding its light on Pride Rock, as if the heavens are partaking in the ceremony. The animals bow in veneration. The closing shot, pulling away from Pride Rock, shows the shaman holding Simba, this time with his father and mother lying together behind them. All seems picture-perfect at Pride Rock, where everything has its time and place.

As suggested by Rafiki's two-part anointment, the subsequent sequence opens with a black screen, a dark hole from which a small mouse emerges to the light of day, evoking a dark image of Simba's birth. The mouse is immediately snatched by Scar, Mufasa's dark brother. The picture of his holding it by its tail is a dark rendering of Rafiki holding up Simba. His words to the dangling mouse, "You see, well, I shall never be king, and you shall never see the *light* of another *day*," reveal what he would like to do to the newborn, whose birth inflames his desire to be king. As long as Mufasa did not have a son, as long as his brother was not a father, he was next in line.

In the first of several rescues, which start with the tiny rodent and end with the young Simba, the hornbill Zazu rescues the mouse from Scar's teeth. "Didn't your mother ever tell you not to play with your food?" he chides Scar in the movie's only reference to the brothers' mother, suggesting that Scar is mama's boy, which is supported by his bachelorhood and effeminate mannerisms. He never made the transition from the mother to the father because the place with the father was already taken by the older Mufasa. Darker and with a black mane, Scar is the archetype of the shadow. The scar over his left eye, which gives him his name, marks him as the Cain of the two brothers. He is the *black sheep* of the family, the *other*, the part that Mufasa denies and represses, as demonstrated by his absence in the celebration of his brother's first born. Mufasa may want Scar at the ceremony because of his pride, but considering the noble and sterile way he explains the Circle of Life to Simba, he does not leave much room for the shadow. Ironically, it is Scar's presence, not his absence, which allows Mufasa to appear as the all-good king and ideal father. He appears in such bright light because all the dark unacceptable traits are projected onto Scar.

Scar's reaction to Mufasa's timely rescue of Zazu, the first of his three rescues, "Why, if it isn't my big brother descending from on high to mingle with the commoners," underlined the *high* versus *low* embodied by the two brothers. One is the high consciousness; the other the low unconscious. This is reinforced by the *light* and *darkness* in their face-to-face confrontation, in which the screen is clearly divided into shadow and light. Framed by the dark opening of the cave, Mufasa appears against a light background; the darker Scar is shot against the darkness of his cave. Their difference is also emphasized by Scar's reaction to his brother's show of strength. "Well, as far as brains go, I got the lion's share. But when it comes to brute strength, I'm afraid I'm at the shallow end of the gene pool." From Mufasa's point of view, Scar is a brother to be tolerated, but also one who needs to be kept in line. As the shadow that Mufasa denies, he brings out the worst in his brother. And typical of the shadow, left to itself in some dark corner, or cave, it takes on a life of its own, striking when the moment is ripe. "Perhaps you shouldn't turn your back on me," Scar both threatens and warns his brother, who takes it as a "challenge." As Jewett and Lawrence point out, "The action of the American Monomyth always begins with a threat arising against Eden's calm."[6]

Having introduced the two sides of the father-king, the change in the weather foreshadows the changing of "Eden's calm." Following the three shots of the African savannah, the camera slowly nears what seems to be an African baobab tree, known as the "tree of life," which plays an important role in African mythology and folklore. Inside dwells the shaman Rafiki. Using what may very well be the tree's "money fruit," he draws an icon of the cub Simba. His painting his brow with a reddish stripe completes the ritual commenced on Pride Rock. His divining the name "Simba" transports us to a picture of an older Simba standing on Pride Rock as a new day is about to dawn. The theme of light versus darkness comes into play once again when the impatient Simba wakes up his father, who reminds the mother, "Before sunrise he's your son." Considering the earlier comment about Scar's mother, Mufasa's words are another reference to Scar and himself, as if in their family the light Mufasa belonged to the father, and the dark Scar to the mother.

In what may very well recall the young Mufasa and his father, Simba reminds his father that he "promised" to show him his kingdom, the outer world of the father. Unlike many mothers who cling to their sons, Simba's mother nudges him lovingly towards his father, the figure who traditionally initiates the son into what lies beyond the mother's domain. Simba is his father's for the duration of the day. The scene's closing shot shows the mother looking on with great pride as Simba follows his father up to Pride Rock, going out together to encounter the new day.

In this portrait, Mufasa seems the ideal father. However, in his explaining to Simba about the delicate balance in the Circle of Life, without mentioning the dark side that counterbalances the light side, Mufasa presents a one-sided picture — ideal but not real. When the curious Simba asks "about that shadowy place," Mufasa explains, not without a warning, "That's beyond our borders. You must never go there, Simba." Of course, Mufasa may be protecting his son, who is too tender for such grownup darkness.

Mufasa's denying the dark side is evoked during the bird's morning report, when a gopher distracts Simba by popping up from various holes in the ground. Seeing his son's attempts to catch the *under*ground creature, Mufasa asks, "What are you doing, son?" "Pouncing," Simba replies. Like his father denying his shadowy brother, Simba tries to keep the gopher below ground. "Let an old pro show you how it's done," says the father, seizing the opportunity to initiate his son into another part of *becoming a man*: repression. As a king who cannot do certain things, Mufasa has his son do to Zazu what he would like to do to Scar. In keeping with Mufasa's bright side, the pouncing lesson is given in a playful and humorous mood. Mufasa's real intentions, to keep Pride Rock sanitary, are revealed when he receives the more serious news, "from the underground," that hyenas, creatures from the "shadowy place" and Scar's natural allies, have crossed into Pride Lands. He drops everything and sets out to drive them from his kingdom. The naive Simba asks his father to come along, but where Mufasa is going is no place for a young cub. He has some growing up to do. As Zazu assures him, "One day you will be king" and then he can chase after those hyenas "from dawn until dark."

Unlike his father, Simba's uncle does not forbid him from crossing to the shadowy parts. In fact, he encourages him. With the screen divided into shadow and light, Simba in the light half and Scar in the shadowy half, the "weird" uncle asks his nephew if his father showed him what is beyond his kingdom. Stepping into Scar's shadowy part, Simba replies that his father forbids him to go there. Scar makes out as if he supports the father's opinion, saying, "It's far too dangerous." But he adds cunningly, "Only the bravest lions go there."

This is all the encouraging Simba needs. "Come on, I just heard about this great place," he runs to tell Nala, his playmate. On their way to the elephant graveyard, he imagines that the life of a king means maximum freedom and minimum responsibility, where he is "free to run around all day ... free to do it all my way." The song, "I Just Can't Wait to Be King," presented in strong colors and many African patterns, is his fantasy of what it will be like to be king. As he tells the chaperoning Zazu, who remarks that he has "never seen a king of beasts with quite so little hair," under his reign the first thing to go will be tradition. To a naïve cub it is an obstacle to freedom rather than a framework that keeps the kingdom together. But as he tumbles into the shadowy graveyard, not before Nala shows him who is really on top, Simba gets his first taste of harsh reality, of the shadow.

Despite Zazu's reminding him that he is still "fuzzy," that they are "way beyond the boundary of the Pride Land," and that they "are all in very real danger," Simba sees himself as above it all. "I laugh in the face of danger," he announces proudly, only to be echoed by the eerie laughter of the three hyenas, agents of the ominous shadow, who emerge from the darkness of an elephant's skull, showing Simba he is no match against them. With his back to the wall, Simba tries to scare the hyenas off with a "roar," but all that comes out is a weak yowl. "That was it?" one of the hyenas taunts him. On his second try, much to everyone's surprise, a full-grown roar is heard. It is Mufasa. He has come to the rescue at the last moment. After a brief fight, part of which is shown as shadows cast on the cave wall, Mufasa pins the three hyenas to the ground, warning them, "If you ever come near my son again." And turning to his son, he reprimands him, "You deliberately disobeyed me!"

As Simba and company leave the Burial Ground, the camera tilts up slowly, stopping on the figure of Scar, who casts a huge shadow on the wall. What he has witnessed from his shadowy throne gives him food for thought. The fact that he does not raise a finger to save his "favorite nephew" reveals his true nature. In contrast, his brother, always the mentor, makes the most of this incident. "I've got to teach my son a lesson," he says, turning to him sternly, and sending Zazu and Nala home. Simba cringes, walking shamefully in obedience towards his angry father. Stepping into a small ditch, he is surprised to see that it is his father's huge footprint. It is another shock of recognition, demonstrating how far he has to go till he reaches his father's size. Looking down at his small paw then looking up at his father, who now, in his anger, looks even bigger, Simba is reminded of his true size. But despite his disappointment in his son, and his son's disobeying him, Mufasa likes the fact that Simba was only trying to be brave like him, that he is a role model for his son. The two joke lightly about the fact that "nobody messes with your dad," though having seen Scar's true face, we know better.

Under the starry sky, as if sensing his impending death, Mufasa tries to correct Simba's illusion that he will always be around. "Simba, let me tell you something that my father told me. Look at the stars. The great kings of the past look down on us from those stars. So whenever you feel alone, just remember that those kings will always be there to guide you." The father and son are shown as silhouettes against the starry night sky. "And so will I."

In complete contrast to the starry sky above, the camera slowly descends to the lower depths to reveal the three hyenas, who feel they are "dangling at the bottom of the food chain." Likewise, in a shadowy version of Simba's "I Just Can't Wait to Be King," Scar's song celebrates the return of the repressed, emphasized by the many eruptions from the inferno below. Like a shadow that turns dangerous when denied for too long, Scar sings that respect and justice will come in the future. Throughout the song that celebrates evil with fascist imagery, the shadow, both Scar's and the hyenas,' is most prominent. Towards the song's ending, Scar is raised higher and higher by a jutting rock that rises from the infernal fire below, singing that he will be the king, recognized and revered. As the camera pulls back in the closing shot of the sequence, it reveals a shadowy Scar against a crescent *moon*, a maternal symbol that signals the new dark phase that is about to replace the paternal *sun-throne* of Mufasa.

Having detected his brother's Achilles' heel, Scar does not waste any time carrying out the revenge of the repressed. He twists Mufasa's sense of responsibility and Simba's fascination with the dark side to his advantage. "This is just for you and your daddy," he tells the naive Simba about the surprise he has for him and his father. "You know, a sort of father-son ... thing." Once again, as he had wanted to go with his father to chase off the hyenas, Simba wants to go with Scar. But the uncle leaves his nephew to wait for his father, suggesting that he "work on that little roar of yours."

Simba's third attempt at roaring, at proving his masculinity, makes him think he started the stampede. But as already shown, behind it all is the devious Scar. He knows what it will take to get his brother to come to his son's rescue. And sure as the sun comes up each new day, Mufasa comes just in time. The rescued Simba sees his father leap on the ledge of the gorge, thinking he is safe. But when he comes around the mount of rocks to get a better view, missing the part where Scar refuses to help his brother, tossing him down below with "Long live the king," Simba sees his father tumble to his death. Realizing something is terribly wrong when he sees his father's body lying still under a broken tree, Simba cries for help. But the only help he gets is the "help" his father got, when he too called for help. "Simba, what have you done?" Scar asks accusingly, pronouncing "the king is dead," then quickly adds, "And if it weren't for you, he'd still be alive." Making the most of this tragic moment, Scar inflames Simba's sense of guilt. "Oh, what will your mother think?"

The guilt-stricken Simba turns to Scar, "What am I gonna do?" "Run away, Simba!" he advises. "Run away and never return!" Heeding his uncle's advice, Simba runs from the irreversible tragedy he has brought about. Like Oedipus, he survives his designed death but carries the guilt for the death of his father. And like many of today's sons, whose absent fathers are not around to initiate them into manhood, Simba's initiation into the Circle of Life is disrupted by this traumatic event of losing his father. With the death of his father, Simba's ideal picture of fatherhood is shattered to pieces.

Fatherless Kingdom

Under a crescent moon, Scar confesses his "personal loss" and proclaims the throne of his dead brother his own. Whereas Mufasa, like the sun, ruled the day and his entire kingdom was in his light, now Pride Rock is taken over by his dark brother who, like the moon, governs the night. As his dark vision reveals, his reign is evil and self-serving. Pride Rock under his rule becomes a fatherless kingdom.

In complete contrast to the opening sequence, when the animals flocked to Pride Rock, now the camera pulls back to reveal the gathering hyenas. The shaman Rafiki is shown shaking his head in lament for Pride Rock. As the background changes to his tree house, he smears the painting of the young Simba, his bright future cut short by the forces of darkness. Considering that Mufasa was mostly portrayed as a father, his death and the abdication of the son mirrors the present state of contemporary fatherhood, where fathers are largely absent and a growing number of sons opt for a trouble-free existence in which becoming a father is no longer an option. As such, Scar's self-serving reign and Simba's "trouble-free" lifestyle can be seen as a metaphoric picture of "Fatherless America," especially in view of the disaster that overtakes the Pride Lands.

> The most urgent domestic challenge facing the United States at the close of the twentieth century is the re-creation of fatherhood as a vital social role for men. At stake is nothing less than the success of the American experiment. For unless we reverse the trend of fatherlessness, no other set of accomplishments — not economic growth or prison construction or welfare reform or better schools — will succeed in arresting the decline of child well-being and the spread of male violence. To tolerate the trend of fatherlessness is to accept the inevitable of continued societal recession.[7]

Cast out of the familiar world of his childhood, Simba is shown lying motionless under the hot desert sun. Though seemingly dead, his death is a symbolic one. What dies is the innocent cub. Simba himself is saved by a pair of outcasts, the meerkat Timon and the warthog Pumbaa. Characterized as *brain* and *brawn*, recalling his father and uncle, they are his new family. They are the *male group*, the group (gang) that frequently replaces the family for many fatherless boys during their transition from adolescence to young adulthood. It is what many boys do, how they compensate themselves, when there are no fathers around to initiate them into manhood.

> In a psychological sense, the masculine mysteries are learned in the male group. With the assistance of the powerful libido of the group, the individual male is helped to pull free from strong, regressive Oedipal forces. The group serves as a kind of second parent. It is a way-station for the developing male from which he goes on forays in the fearsome world of adult power. Here in the group he can relax, so to speak, while he builds up his strength and courage for the next, and more difficult, steps in his individuation journey — separation from the mother *and* father archetypes, the male group itself, and finally, encounter with his individual Self.[8]

Simba may have been saved from death and accepted as a fellow outcast, but what needs to be revived is his spirit. In Timon's words, "he's depressed." Rather than mourn and deal with what he believes is his part in his father's death, Simba's opts for his two new friends' wonderful solution: repression. Somewhat like his father's denying the shadow, the two's "trouble-free philosophy" tempts Simba to repress his guilt for his father's death and his (Oedipal) desire, however unconscious, to replace him as king.

Objectionable as it may seem, in his desire to replace his father as king, Simba is much like Scar, which may explain part of his fascination with his "weird" uncle. As expressed in their parallel songs — Simba's "I Just Can't Wait to Be King" and Scar's "Be Prepared" ("For the death of the king") — the two are impatient to replace Mufasa at the throne. Of course, unlike his cutthroat uncle, Simba does not contemplate his father's death when he *can't wait to be king*. And yet, as long as he is alive Simba cannot be king. What is more, it is Simba's birth that hastens Scar's seizing the throne.

Scar and Simba are also alike in their shared view of the king's sovereignty. Whereas the childish Simba says to Mufasa, "But I thought a king can do *whatever he wants*," Scar declares before Sarabi, "I'm the king. I can do *whatever I want*." But while in Mufasa's death Scar is fully aware (conscious) and active, Simba is unaware (unconscious) and passive. As such, Scar may well carry out Simba's repressed (unconscious) desire for his father's throne.

Without his father to guide him, and going against what he taught him, Simba accepts his newfound companions' Hakuna Matata of turning your back to the world. As Pumbaa informs him, "these two words will solve all your problems." When asked what he did, Simba only replies, "Something terrible. But I don't want to talk about it." With the pain too great to bear, Simba protects himself by shutting it out, by repression. Like the bugs he learns to eat, however hard to swallow, it is what he needs to survive. But just as his food has been narrowed down to something that a lion would never eat, in accepting the duo's lifestyle, his life is reduced to a hollow existence. He seems to have regressed to a life of oral gratification centered on the intake of food (and the anal pleasure of passing wind). In contrast to the hunger at Pride Rock under Scar's rule, Simba is "stuffed" with "slimy" food. But as shown next, like many of today's self-serving men who stuff themselves rather than give of themselves to their offsprings, Simba's *spirit* is far from satisfied.

In something that recalls "a gathering of men," the three outcasts are shown lying on their backs after a hearty meal. Simba is in the foreground gazing up at the starry night sky. "Ever wonder what those sparkly dots are up there?" Pumbaa asks Timon. After exchanging views, the two turn to Simba. At first he is reluctant to go along, but they do not let up. When he finally shares his view with his pals about the star-studded heavens, as if it were a Rorschach test, the camera focuses on his face, the closest he is shown since he grew into a lion, the closest to himself since repressing the memory of his father. "Well, somebody once told me that the great kings of the past are up there, watching over us." He recalls his time with his father under a similar starry sky. When he finally says what he didn't "want to talk about" in their first meeting, he is ridiculed by his two pals. Especially the smarter Timon, who tries to keep their *be-here-now* existence at all cost. "Who told you something like that?" he roars in laughter. Simba tries to make on as if it is "pretty dumb" after all, but after years of blotting out his painful memory, his repressed feelings are stirring back to life. He looks up at the stars, as if asking his father to guide him, as he said he would, because right now he "feels alone." He feels alone because he does not belong with the two, because he is without his father.

As often happens, Simba can live in a state of denial for only so long. His return to himself begins with the return of the repressed memory of his father. Disheartened by the experience with his pals, Simba walks away from the two. It is the first time he is shown alone since teaming up with his new circle of friends, which has replaced his father's Circle of Life. Gazing up at the night sky, he seems to question what his father had told him, collapsing to the ground in frustration. His fall stirs up dried leaves and milkweed floss that are swirled by a spirited wind, perhaps the spirit of his father.

The camera follows the floss as it is carried across the desert and to Rafiki's baobab tree, where he snatches it out of the air. He sniffs it, grunts, and bounds down into his tree, sifting it around in a big tortoise shell in one of his shamanic rites. "Simba?" He can hardly believe what he sees. "He's alive!" he laughs joyfully. Coming from a shaman, these divining words herald Simba's return from the dead, his coming out of the death-in-life of Hakuna Matata. Rafiki marks Simba's *return* to life by painting a full grown mane on the smeared image on the wall. "It is time," he pronounces, as if it is all part of a preordained pattern. And in a way it is. A father can take a son only so far. As in many shamanic initiations, Simba has to die to one state before he can be reborn to another. He may not know it, but it is time for him to return and take what is rightfully his, time to return to Pride Rock and the Circle of Life. But before he returns to face what he turned his back on, Simba is visited by three figures from his past, three figures who remind him what he knows in his heart he must do.

As suggested by the song Timon and Pumbaa are singing, "The Lions Sleep Tonight," the first one to wake Simba from his sleep of forgetfulness, the first one to awaken his inner father, is his childhood playmate Nala. His first shock of recognition comes when she pins him down as she had done in the past. "Nala?" He is surprised and happy to see her. Her question, "Who are you?" foreshadows Rafiki's identical question. But presently Simba is still in a state of denial. His sense of guilt and shame are stronger than anything Nala can say. And yet, with her appearance Simba senses that something is wrong. "What? What is it?" he asks her. "It's like you're back from the dead. You don't know how much this will mean to everyone. What it means to me." But however Nala tries, she cannot budge Simba from denying his true calling. "No, I'm not the king. Maybe I was gonna be, but that was a long time ago." Nothing she says can offset his reluctance to forsake his adopted lifestyle and return home. Not even their mutual declaration of love or her informing him that the future of the Pride Lands depends on him. "What's happened to you? You're not the Simba I remember," Nala admonishes him. "You're starting to sound like my father," Simba says, walking away. "Listen, you think you can just show up and tell me how to live my life? You don't even know what I've been through!" After the ridicule he got from Timon and Pumbaa, Simba is not about to risk talking about the reasons behind his refusal.

Whereas in the past he was a cub who tried to be a lion, now he is a lion who behaves like a cub. Confused and feeling so low he can only look up, Simba turns to his father in the starry heavens. "You said you'd always be there for me! But you're not. And it's because of *me*," he lowers his head in shame. "It's my fault. It's my fault." Simba's confession is a good step in the right direction. But like many fatherless young men, he needs to be acknowledged by his father before he can overcome his doubts and fears and return to face the past and his feelings of guilt and shame.

Witnessing all this from the height of a nearby tree, Rafiki, portrayed as a cross between an eastern guru and Castaneda's Don Juan, has come to release Simba from the spell he has fallen under. Like a wise trickster, he arouses Simba's curiosity by his provocative antics. He acts as a *reflector*, throwing Simba's questions right back at him, ultimately getting him to look beyond his own reflection, to look at what he has become.

It begins when Simba, walking away from Rafiki's senseless chanting, lies down by a pool and gazes listlessly at his image in the water's reflecting surface. Rafiki keeps annoying Simba by throwing a nut into the water that reflects his image, stirring up the way he sees himself, making waves in his unconscious. When Simba asks him who he is, Rafiki throws it right back at him. "The question is, 'Whooo ... are you?'" "I thought I knew," the dejected Simba replies. "Now I'm not so sure." But the shaman has a few tricks up his sleeve. "I know who you are. You're Mufasa's boy." Hooking Simba with this bait, Rafiki starts reeling him in by running away. "Wait!" Simba calls after him, crossing a wooden bridge over a stream, a small but significant threshold. He chases after the shaman, whom he finds sitting in a lotus position on a black rock like a holy guru. The mention of his father is the turning point. When he asks if he *knew* his father, Rafiki corrects him, "I *know* your father." And when Simba, lowering his head in disappointment and dejection, corrects him by telling him that he died "a long time ago," the shaman replies, "Wrong again!" Standing at the entrance to the dark forest, he continues. "He's alive! And I'll show you. You follow old Rafiki. He knows the way. Come on!"

As Rafiki leads the way into the dark forest, the unconscious, Simba looks apprehensively through the cave-like entrance. His passage through the dark forest is conveyed as a *rite of passage* through the dark night of the soul. Commenting about this passage on the DVD supplements, the movie's creators point out that indeed it was "to reflect Simba's unconscious mind. It was literally going back, peeling through the layers to the center of the problem, where he had buried and suppressed the whole thing about his father."[9]

Having made the passage through the forest, through the unconscious where his introjected father dwells, Simba is ready for what Rafiki is about to show him. The shaman parts the growth of reeds; Simba looks down, but all he sees his reflection. "That's not my father. That's just my reflection." Rafiki, standing right behind Simba, entreats him. "No. Look harder." He puts his finger in the still water. "You see?" he whispers softly, as Simba looks at his reflection in the rippling water, his stirred unconscious: "He lives in you."

Simba suddenly sees his *inner father*, the father he tried so hard to forget, to repress.

Mirroring what Simba sees in the water, Mufasa's voice is heard calling Simba's name from afar. "Father?" Simba looks up. He is shown at the bottom right corner of the frame, reduced to the mere speck he has become, as a ghostly image of his father slowly forms in the approaching dark clouds that fill up the frame. "Simba, you have forgotten me." He speaks like a heavenly father. "You have forgotten who you are, and so have forgotten me. Look inside yourself, Simba. You are more than what you have become. You must take your place in the Circle of Life."

Hearing his father's words may induce Simba to go back, but as his father never taught him how to confront the shadow, he does not know how. The only time Simba saw his father and uncle together was when Scar killed his father, and he did not even see that, only the results. In true-to-life form, no longer a ghostly image, Mufasa tells his son what he, like many of today's abandoned sons, so desperately needs and fears to hear. "Remember who you are. You are my son, and the one true king." Simba is shown bathed in his father's golden light. "Remember who you are." Having said what his son needed to hear, Mufasa's image grows dark again. Simba chases after his fading image, pleading with him not to leave him. In his reply, Mufasa reminds his son to *remember* what he tried so desperately to forget, what he repressed from consciousness—that he is his father's son.

Acknowledged by his father, and realizing he lives in him, frees Simba to go back and confront his father's dark side, the obstacle that stands in his way of assuming the throne. This dark side, the ogre side of his father, and all the guilt he harbors inside, is the *dragon* he must slay. Presently, however, Simba is torn apart. "I know what I have to do. But, going back means I'll have to face my past. I've been running from it for so long." Like a Zen master who knocks sense into his disciple's scull, the mischievous Rafiki whacks Simba on the head with his staff. As an archetypal trickster, he is the liberator of the repressed. "Whereas the father is the lawgiver, and stands for order and even repression, the trickster is the lawbreaker who represents the expression of instinctual desires."[10]

Rafiki's unexpected whacking frees Simba from the invisible (unconscious) shackles of the past. Like a paradoxical therapist, he enlightens Simba. "The past can hurt. But the way I see it, you can either run from it, or ... learn from it." And to make his point, Rafiki swings at Simba with his staff again. Only this time Simba ducks, taking Rafiki's staff and tossing it aside, running off and shouting back to the shaman, "I'm going back!" As Simba disappears in the horizon, his return is accompanied by shooting stars crossing the skyline, the heavens once again taking part in the prodigal son's return just as in his birth. Rafiki is shown laughing joyfully in the foreground, holding the staff above his head in celebration. In getting Simba to go back and face what he must, Rafiki brings about what Robert Bly calls "the inner warrior," the one who "is in service to a purpose greater than himself: that is, to a transcendent cause. Mythologically, he is in service to a True King."[11]

Fatherhood Reclaimed

Much like Dorothy in her journey to meet the Wizard of Oz, in his decision to return to the Pride Lands Simba is helped by his three friends. As they assure him, they are with him "to the end." In deciding to return, to accept his role as his father's son, Simba has clearly changed from a follower to a leader, becoming one with the royal blood that runs in his veins. He has become his father's son to such an extent that his mother and Scar mistake him for Mufasa when he appears after Scar hits her for reminding him that he is not "half the king Mufasa was," another reminder that Scar is his brother's other half. Their reaction — Scar's negative "No, you're dead!" and Sarabi's affirmative "You're alive?" — suggests that Simba has returned from the dead. Scar is relieved it is not Mufasa, but as Simba informs him, with assertiveness that recalls his father, his days as king are over. "The choice is yours, Scar. Either step down or fight." In confronting Scar, Simba does what his father never did. He confronts the shadow head-on.

Realizing he does not have a fighting chance against the fully grown Simba, if only because he looks and talks like Mufasa, Scar resorts to another one of his shadowy tactics. Like a prosecutor before the lionesses in a courtroom, and the hyenas in the gallery, he aims for Simba's most sensitive spot, his feeling responsible (guilty) for his father's death. Smelling blood, the devious Scar stalks around Simba, accusing him of causing Mufasa's death and extracting from him an admission of guilt, all the while driving him back to the ledge of Pride Rock, with the hyenas right behind him. "It was an accident," Simba defends himself. "Oh, Simba, you're in trouble again. But this time Daddy isn't here to save you. And now everyone knows why!" With these words Simba slips over the edge, clinging to the ledge by his forepaws. Just then, as if bigger powers are at work, lightning strikes, igniting the dried shrubs below. While Scar savors the moment of Simba's life hanging by a thread ("This is just the way your father looked before he died"), the fire spreads, creating a fiery image of an inferno. But Scar's treachery backfires. His arrogance, his pride, gets the best of him. Confident he has Simba's life at his grasp, he seizes him with his claws as he seized his father, whispering into his ear, "And here's my little secret. I killed Mufasa."

As the only one who witnessed what really happened, and the one who caused it all, Scar is the only one who can set Simba free. In a brief flashback, which repeats Simba's seeing his father's fall to his death, the camera closes in on his stunned eyes, just as it had formerly closed in on his father, dissolving into the shot of his father's fall. Set against the fiery inferno of the present, it underscores Simba's re-experiencing the traumatic event that drove him into exile and repression. It is reinforced by the dissolve into a shot of the cub Simba seeing his father's death. Back then the camera zoomed away from his eyes; now it is reversed, zooming in, as if what he repressed has returned to his consciousness. His cry of pain in reliving the trauma frees Simba from the past. It gives him unexpected strength to bounce back from what seems certain death, stopping short of following his father's fate. In one great leap he pounces on Scar, pinning him to the ground. "Murderer!" he accuses Scar, getting him to admit his crime before the gathered lionesses and hyenas. His public confession, "I killed Mufasa!" shocks Sarabi and ignites Nala, who pounces in Scar's direction, setting off an all-out fight between the forces of good and evil.

As always, the decisive battle is between the two archrivals: Simba literally dealing with the dark side of his father. True to the coward that he is, Scar sneaks off, climbing the same cliff where Simba, as a cub, told him he is "going be king of Pride Rock." At the summit, a dead end with only a fiery inferno below, Simba closes in on Scar. "Murderer!" he accuses him again, reversing Scar's charge against him. With his back to the wall, as Simba was in his first venture to the shadowy graveyard, Scar can only beg him to "have mercy." When this doesn't move Simba, Scar tries to put the blame on his cohorts, the hyenas. But Simba is no longer the naïve cub. Unable to kill his father's brother, however, he gives Scar some of his own medicine, hurling back the very words that sent him to exile: "Run. Run away, and never return." But Scar has one last trick up his devious sleeve. With the words, "As you wish, your Majesty," he throws fiery embers into Simba's face, pouncing on him with renewed viciousness.

The slow motion of the ensuing fight, set against the infernal background, transforms it into a clash of two primeval forces, two archetypes, of good and evil. As Scar knocks Simba down on his back and leaps at him through the flames with murder in his eyes, the close-up on Simba's astonished face recalls his father. But somehow, as in jujitsu, he uses Scar's momentum to kick him with his hind legs over the edge of the cliff, where his three partners in crime confront him. What they do to him is suggested by the shadows on the wall, once again underscoring what Scar has been throughout the movie. As flames engulf the screen, what is destroyed is the shadow that has turned the Pride Lands into a wasteland. With Scar's demise, Pride Rock is shown going up in flames, marking the end of his shadowy reign.

As in the myth of the Holy Grail, where the healing of the Fisher King brings about the restoration of his kingdom, the rain coming down, putting out the flames, signals the beginning of a new era, the revival of the wasteland. The shadow that had fascinated Simba while his father was alive, and plagued him since his death, is out of the picture. Now Simba can take his rightful place as Pride Rock's new king. The sequence ends with Rafiki motioning to the throne that Simba is to assume. As he had done with his father, the shaman bows to the new king before the two hug, pronouncing, "It is time."

Simba slowly climbs to the summit of Pride Rock through the life-restoring rain. Once again, the stormy clouds slowly part, revealing a starry sky. "Remember," Mufasa's voice is heard from above. True to his father's guidance, Simba remembers who he is. He responds with a great roar that echoes his father in the movie's opening, a roar he tried twice before when his father was alive. Likewise, in a panoramic shot of Pride Rock that recalls the shot of Mufasa standing at its summit, the wasteland dissolves into a flourishing kingdom. Not only has life returned to the kingdom, a new life has come into the world in Simba's newborn son, who is held up by Rafiki as he had held up his father at the beginning of the movie. In becoming a father, Simba continues the Circle of Life, like his father and all the fathers before them.

As is often the case, with the Circle of Life coming full circle there comes a change. Whereas in the beginning, when Rafiki presented Simba, the sky was dark, now, when he presents his son, it is blue and white. However subtle the distinction, it is not without intention. The bright sky is a last reminder that the denied shadow that hounded Mufasa and was always in the background has been confronted and dealt a deathly blow. Integrated in the new Circle of Life, it is no longer an autonomous dragon that plots to dethrone Pride Land's king and father.

Chapter 11

Jurassic Park
Fatherhood Repressed

You can't just suppress sixty-five million years of gut instinct.

— Dr. Alan Grant

The Repressed Recreated

Is it a mere coincidence that Steven Spielberg's three most successful movies, *Jaws*, *E.T.* and *Jurassic Park*, all star uncanny creatures? Is there a connection between these creatures and the movies' unprecedented success? And if so, what is the great attraction?

Coming from the deep sea, outer space and man's recreation of the distant past, the creatures are all unconscious projections. They all emanate from the cinematic heroes' repressed unconscious. But more so, they mirror the repressed unconscious we share with the cinematic heroes. This is why they so fascinate us. This is the big attraction. Whether benevolent as in *E.T.*, or malevolent as in *Jaws* and *Jurassic Park*, we somehow recognize these unconscious creatures from our dreams and nightmares. Like Hitchcock before him, Spielberg understands our attraction to the unconscious and its creatures. And his extraordinary ability to project all this on the screen surely plays a big part in his movies' unparalleled success.

Curiously enough, or maybe not, our great attraction to the unconscious is pondered by Herman Melville in *Moby Dick*, the book from which *Jaws* draws its basic story.

Why is almost every robust healthy boy with a robust healthy soul in him, at some time or other crazy to go to sea? Why upon your first voyage as a passenger, did you yourself feel such a mystical vibration, when first told that you and your ship were now out of sight of land? Why did the old Persians hold the sea holy? Why did the Greeks give it a separate deity, and own brother of Jove? Surely all this is not without meaning. And still deeper the meaning of that story of Narcissus, who because he could not grasp the tormenting, mind image he saw in the fountain, plunged into it and was drowned. But that same image, we ourselves see in all rivers and oceans. It is the image of the ungraspable phantom of life; and this is the key to it all.[1]

Juxtaposing *Moby Dick* and *Jaws* makes you wonder: Is it by chance that the Great American Novel and the most successful film of its time deal with (and are named after) creatures that dwell in the ocean's depth? Or is it another case of our attraction to the unconscious and the creatures it harbors?

If needing further proof of our attraction, the enormous success of *Jurassic Park* seems proof enough. Like the unconscious ocean in *Moby Dick* and in *Jaws*, the backdrop of the primeval world of Jurassic Park is used by Spielberg to deal with man's unconscious forces. But where the appearance of Jaws from the ocean's depths is the return of the repressed, in Jurassic Park, where the dinosaurs are securely fenced in, it is *the repressed recreated*. The world that John Hammond has created, a sort of Spielberg Disneyland, which he dreams "will send kids right out of their minds," is nothing less than the repressed objectified, the unconscious made conscious for all to see. The dinosaurs that break free from confinement represent the autonomous forces that erupt from the hero's repressed unconscious, as suggested early in the movie, when the hero identifies with the raptors while attacking the boy who questions their ferociousness.

But as with *Jaws*, and more so with *E.T.*, there is another story in *Jurassic Park*. While showing what happens when man starts fooling (genetically) with Mother Nature, Spielberg also takes a hard look at what happens when men go against a vital part of their nature. Through the movie's hero, Alan Grant, a man who hates children, Spielberg shows what happens when men repress their paternal impulse, when they refuse to become fathers. As with *Moby Dick* and *Jaws*, it is the old tale of the hero slaying the dragon. The dinosaurs are the dragons that turn against Grant, punishing him for denying his paternal impulse, "for what is not consciously developed remains primitive and regressive and may constitute a threat."[2] In his own special way, Spielberg is showing that unless men like Grant become fathers, unless they slay their inner dragons, the future of humanity could be no different than the dinosaurs he is so busy unearthing.

Having dealt with the absent father in *E.T.*, and becoming a father himself in 1985, by the early '90s Spielberg was ready to deal with fatherhood, one of America's growing problems. In his first three movies of the decade, *Hook* ('91), *Jurassic Park* ('93) and *Schindler's List* ('93), the focus is on fatherhood and becoming a father. The three make up Spielberg's "Fatherhood Trilogy," rounding out what he started in his first feature, *Sugarland Express*, a movie essentially about motherhood. Spielberg, after all, is almost always dealing with the American family.

In *Hook*, the first of the three, the hero learns to be a father to his two children. His happy thought, which enables him to fly, is "I am a father!" The hero in *Schindler's List* becomes a paternal figure to the persecuted Jews whose very lives hinge upon his humaneness. Among other things, the movie chronicles his becoming a *mensch. Jurassic Park*'s Grant undergoes a similar journey into fatherhood, in a place that Hammond, a father and a grandfather, regards as his "baby." It is while dealing with the park's recreated creatures that Grant has a change of mind and heart towards children. And it is Hammond's grandchildren, particularly the boy Tim, who bring about this change. Representing the future, they force Grant to face and deal with his repressed past and become a father.

The Repressed Revived

Nothing better demonstrates Spielberg's mastery of filmmaking than his cinematic expositions. And the three-part exposition to *Jurassic Park* is no exception. While introducing both the hero and the movie's subject matter, it reveals the problem he needs to resolve: his preoccupation with extinct creatures from the past and his "hate" of children who embody the future.

First, evoking the repressed unconscious and its unseen threat, *Jurassic Park* opens with a black screen and eerie music, followed by a shot of something hidden approaching with a menacing rumble from behind rustling bushes. In the first of three shots-reverse shots that open the sequence, the camera cuts to a close-up of a black man in a red hard hat, revealing only the lower part of the "Jurassic Park" logo on its front. He is looking in the direction of the commotion, where an undisclosed source of light is coming though the dense growth. In a second "people" shot, a group of men with the same red hard hats, the "Jurassic Park" logo now fully visible, are all looking at whatever is out there and getting closer. Unlike the first two stationary "people" shots, in the third "people" shot the camera slowly dollies in on a white man, who holds a huge rifle and sports a light fedora. He is surrounded by men holding electric shockers, all poised for whatever is approaching through the bushes.

What finally emerges is a huge forklift, carrying an equally large steel cage. As the forklift transports the cage to the fortified gate of the "prison," there is a sense of urgency. Then, through a rectangular slot in the cage, like a rectangular movie screen, among four red-helmeted men who are shown from the point of view of whatever is locked inside the cage, which seems powerful and dangerous, the white game warden (Muldoon) comes into the center of the frame as if singled out by the caged beast. Ordering the "loading team" to "step away," the game warden calls for the "gatekeeper," who climbs to the top of the cage. Once again, we get the beast's viewpoint, this time of the "gatekeeper" who follows the game warden's order to "raise the gate." Suddenly, as if refusing to be imprisoned, the beast charges forward inside the cage with a wild shriek. The cage slides away from the prison gate, toppling the gatekeeper to the ground. A second later, the beast drags him by his feet towards the cage. While the men with the guns try to stop the beast by shooting into the cage, the game warden grabs the upper part of the gatekeeper's body. In a rapid series of three extreme close-ups, we see the beast's inhuman, snake-like eye, followed by the game hunter's horrified eyes, which bare a resemblance to the eye of the beast. Then it is back to the beast's eye. They seem to recognize each other, each one the other's *other*.

This primeval rivalry continues by the tug of war between the two, the beast pulling the gatekeeper by the *lower* part of his body, the game warden by the *upper*. Each time the game warden orders his men to "Shoot her!" his open mouth is shown in an extreme close-up, the teeth suggesting that he is just as carnivorous as the beast inside the cage. But the game warden is no match for the beast. The gatekeeper's hand slips through the game warden's grip and into what must be the beast's mouth.

Thus ends the first part of the three-part exposition. The caged beast, like the repressed unconscious, cannot be contained forever by man's modern technology. The beast's wreaking mayhem with the opening of the gate anticipates the mayhem that erupts in the hero's life when the park's security system is turned off, forcing him to deal with the father impulse that he denies so vehemently.

Second, by first showing the white man (Gennaro) on the raft reflected in the water, and then tilting upwards to show him in reality, the opening shot of the second sequence evokes the lower and the upper, the conscious and unconscious. The dark-skinned man pulling the white man ashore continues the motion of the beast pulling the gatekeeper into the cage. That same accident brings the man to this out-of-the-way mining site, in search of Hammond, the man who dreamed up Jurassic Park. Before we see him, Hammond is depicted as a father by the fact "that the accident [that] has raised very serious questions about the park," as Gennaro puts it, takes a back seat to his helping his daughter in her time of need.

A worker interrupts the two, informing a local man (Juanito) that they have found another mosquito. The camera cuts inside the mine where workers with mine helmets with lights on the front (contrasting the "Jurassic Park" logo in the previous sequence) are chipping the walls. Having mentioned Hammond in the light of day, now Grant's name is mentioned inside the dark mine, another suggestion of the conscious and unconscious. "If two experts sign off on the island, the insurance guys will back off," Gennaro informs Juanito. "I've already got Ian Malcolm, but they think he's too trendy. They want Alan Grant." Juanito is handed a yellowish chunk as he answers Gennaro. "Grant? You'll never get him out of Montana." He calls the workers to shine their lights on the chunk he is holding in his hand, just as the game hunter ordered his men to shoot the beast. "Why not?" Gennaro asks. "Because Grant's like me." The camera closes in on the lighted translucent yellow chunk. "He's a digger." In the extreme close-up, we see a mosquito trapped inside the translucent yellowish chunk Juanito is holding for everyone to see.

This last shot, of the mosquito trapped in the fossilized resin, parallels the beast trapped inside the steel cage. As we soon learn, this tiny insect is the germ of the beast's creation. Moreover, the mosquito trapped in time mirrors the hero's preoccupation with the past. And just as the act of pulling transported us from the opening sequence to the second sequence, the picture of the trapped mosquito transports us to the exposition's third and final sequence.

Third, the third part of the exposition opens with a shot of a brush brushing away the earth from a black object buried in the ground. As if sexually caressing the black object it uncovers, the phallic brush reveals the raptor's claw that represents Grant's aggression towards children and perhaps hints at his attraction to the dinosaurs he is busy uncovering. Rather than procreate offspring, Grant digs for remnants of the past.

The second shot shows another brush, brushing away the earth to reveal a vertebral column, then different hands unearthing a set of animal jaws. The third (high-angled) shot shows three more hands, brushing away the earth covering the same set of jaws. Over a second high-angled shot, which reveals a circle of people clearing away the earth to reveal a strange-looking skeleton, the names with ominous meanings, Badlands, Snakewater, Montana, appear on the screen, telling us where we are, geographically and otherwise. The person in the center of the frame is Grant, who picks up the claw that opened the sequence. Next to him is his co-worker and girlfriend, Dr. Ellie Sattler, a paleobotanist (a botanist who studies plants of former geological periods, chiefly through fossils).

"Dr. Grant. Dr. Sattler. We're ready to try again," says a voice as the camera cuts to a man walking towards the people we have just seen. This call repeats the worker calling Juanito to see the mosquito. Answering the man's call, Grant rises in the foreground, his light fedora, like one worn by the game warden, leading the way. "I hate computers," he mutters, suggesting that he himself is a "dinosaur." Ellie (*elle*?) comes into the picture, tying a red bandana around Grant's neck as a mother to a boy. Significantly, Grant wears this scarlet noose, which divides his head (masculine thinking) from the rest of his body (feminine intuition), throughout most of the movie. He first appears without it (we do not see him take it off) after a pivotal event in his journey to fatherhood, which signals the beginning of his connecting head and heart.

During the computerized "digging," Grant's hate for children is revealed in his sadistic *spiel* about the Velociprator's cunning viciousness to the boy who spoke when he should not have. Grant assaults the boy like a vicious monster, not unlike the caged and unseen beast that opened the movie, especially emphasized by his use of the raptor's claw, as if to remind us that the raptor is his projection. "Hey, Alan, if you wanted to scare the kid, you could've just pulled a gun on him." Ellie underscores his exaggerated response (his projection).

And Spielberg deliberately points out that to Grant children are "noisy, they're messy, they're expensive. They smell." In short, unlike the dead dinosaurs, and unlike Grant, they are alive.

As if Grant said something he should not have, a man-made bird, a whirly-bird, descends from the sky, its gust of wind creating havoc in the camp, antic-ipating the havoc in his psyche, particularly his attitude towards children. Because at heart he has remained a kid for whom digging is fun, a child frozen in time just like the mosquitoes in the fossilized resin, Grant hates computers (progress) just as he hates children who signify the future. Having kids would mean an end to his *fun*. But all this begins to change with the helicopter that brings John Hammond, the man in white, who functions as Grant's fairy god-father, and who plays God in recreating (resurrecting) the dinosaurs. Despite what Juanito had told Gennaro in the previous scene, that he would never get Grant out of Montana, Hammond gets him to come to Jurassic Park by offering to continue funding his digging (his fun) for three more years.

Opening the three-part exposition with Muldoon and closing with Grant, who bear a resemblance to one another, Spielberg suggests that the two mir-ror one another. One's job is to keep the dinosaurs confined, the other keeps his paternal impulse confined. As subtly conveyed by Spielberg's cinematogra-phy, whether confined in a cage, sealed in time, or buried underground, all three creatures mirror Grant's repressed paternal impulse.

Once Hammond gets Grant to leave his diggings and come to Jurassic Park, to the revived past "right up your alley," so that he can give his endorse-ment to satisfy the investors, the camera cuts to Costa Rica. In this transitional sequence, another man with a light straw hat arrives in what is to him a for-eign world. The man he is meeting in this Central American café, Nedry, is a ravenous infant who betrays the father of Jurassic Park. Just as he wolfs down the food on his plate, he has a voracious appetite for money. He considers the generous Hammond, who "spares no expenses," *cheap*, yet he himself is too cheap to pay for his meal immediately after getting a large amount of money. As he warns the man delivering the money, while stuffing another piece of food in his mouth, "Don't get cheap on me, Dodgson. That was Hammond's mis-take." Nedry's greed initiates the havoc that brings destruction to Jurassic Park. As such, he is the "gatekeeper" who initiates the breaking free of the caged dinosaurs and of Grant's repressed paternal impulse.

After two shots of the flying chopper, the third shot shows Grant playing with the "bird of prey's" black claw. In crossing the threshold to Jurassic Park, where the dead past has been revived, Grant carries a relic of that past and sym-bol of his hate for children. The camera pulls up to show the black-dressed Dr. Ian Malcolm sitting opposite the white-dressed Hammond, another pair of opposites, not unlike the conscious and the unconscious. Hammond calls Mal-colm a mathematician (order); Malcolm considers himself a chaotician (dis-order). Their clashing colors mirror their disagreement over Jurassic Park's chances of survival. While Hammond insists that everything is in order, the chaotician Malcolm sounds a warning. "John doesn't subscribe to chaos, particularly what it has to say about his little science project." The two men face one other from either side of the frame. Between them there is a rectangular window, not unlike a movie screen, divided horizontally by the light sky above and the dark sea below, another allusion to the conscious and the unconscious.

"There it is," Hammond announces, as the island comes into view. The helicopter is shown approaching a valley enclosed by two slopes that seem like two legs. The shot showing the helicopter flying through the uterine passage adds to the feeling that we are entering a feminine world. This is reinforced by the revelation that there are only female dinosaurs on the island. "Hold on! This can be a little thrilling," Hammond warns the passengers about the landing, but also about what they are about to experience in Jurassic Park. His warning seems to apply mostly to Grant, who, after some scrambling with the seat belt, manages to tie two *receptive* (*female*) ends together in a simple knot, leaving Ellie to fend for herself without a seat belt. It is a sign of his ineptness with modern objects but also of his infantile self-centeredness and lack of masculine attributes.

Upon landing, Hammond takes Ellie and Grant by the arm, escorting the two to the start of their journey. Crossing another threshold in the small bridge with a security gate and a guard on each side, there are warning signs of danger. In fact, almost everything they encounter is a form of warning. Especially Gennaro's warning the confident Hammond, "Let's get something straight, John. This is not a weekend excursion. This is a serious investigation of the stability of the island." Like everything in the movie that points to the hero, it is also a serious investigation of Grant's psyche, as suggested when the camera slowly zooms in on him when he spots one of the dinosaurs. Likewise, Malcolm's response to Hammond's confidence about containing the creatures refers to Grant's efforts to contain his paternal impulse. Particularly as it is addressed to a grandfather and to the father "present for the birth of every little creature on this island." "John, the kind of control you're attempting is not possible. If there's one thing the history of evolution has taught us, it's that life will not be contained. Life breaks free. It expands to new territories. It crashes through barriers. Painfully, maybe even dangerously ... life finds a way."

By breeding Velociprators, giving birth to extinct creatures, Hammond unleashes a monstrous force he cannot contain. The sequence ends with the camera coming for a close-up of the newborn raptor in Grant's open hands. It is an image of a father holding his newborn baby, a visual metaphor for the father impulse that is about to see the light of day. That Grant's problem with fatherhood is about to be resolved through his dealing with the raptors is reinforced by Muldoon, the game warden who has "dealt with the raptors more than anyone," informing the guests, mostly Grant, that they "show extreme intelligence, even problem-solving intelligence." Of course, Muldoon is also talking about the "extreme intelligence" of the "problem-solving" unconscious, as when he maintains that the Velociprators, like the repressed unconscious, are too dangerous to roam freely in the park's grounds. Like the Minotaur in the labyrinth, they have to be contained in fortified cages.

Hammond, the King Minos of Jurassic Park, gets a warning from each of the three experts about the modern-day labyrinth he has just built to contain the monsters he has created. And like the labyrinth itself, the warnings suggest the unconscious. As Malcolm sees it, the park is an outcome of Grant's hubris. "The lack of humility before nature that's been displayed here staggers me.... Don't you see the danger, John, inherent in what you're doing here? Genetic power is the most awesome force ever seen on this planet. But you wield it like a kid who's found his dad's gun." Ellie takes the position of the mother that will do anything to protect her offspring. "You picked them because they look good, but these are aggressive living things that have no idea what century they're living in and they will defend themselves. Violently, if necessary." Grant's warning to Hammond foreshadows the events that force him to mix with the children. "I don't want to jump to any conclusions, but dinosaurs and man, two species separated by 65 million years of evolution, have just been suddenly thrown back into the mix together. How can we possibly have the slightest idea what to expect?"

No sooner said, Grant gets an unpleasant surprise when Hammond is notified that his grandchildren have arrived. Walking to greet them, with his guests following behind, Hammond's words are still another foreshadowing of what Grant is about to undergo. "You four are gonna have a spot of company out in the park. Spend a little time with our target audience." In their excitement to see their grandfather, the grandchildren knock him down, just as their presence knocks Grant off his adamant stance against children, against fatherhood. Ellie smiles back at the reticent Grant, who holds his hat close to his chest, the head protector protecting his heart. Ellie's smile, which seems to say "Isn't it wonderful?" turns sour when she sees Grant's negative reaction. Once again she is confronted with the fact that Grant and children do not mix. Interestingly, the hat, symbol of the paternal repressor, is the first of three items that Grant parts with in the course of his journey of becoming a father.

Repressic Park

Before the departure into the recreated world of Jurassic Park, Grant stops dead in his tracks when confronted by the boy who shares his interest in dinosaurs. His bringing up Grant's theory that dinosaurs turned into birds recalls the sequence in Montana, especially his remark about dinosaurs not looking like birds. Unlike the intimidated boy whose remark he echoes, however, Tim does not let Grant have his way. His relentless pestering suggests a father hunger, which only adds to Grant's uneasiness.

As the sequence between Grant and Tim demonstrates, Grant is not ready to deal with the boy. Sensing this, Ellie suggests that the girl Lex should go with him. "She said I should ride with you because it'll be good for you," Lex informs Grant, who prefers to go without the kids altogether. But true to Ellie's words, it is in the course of saving Lex from the Tyrannosaurus rex that Grant loses his hat, a clear sign of dropping his armor, the object with which he earlier shielded his heart. In fact, Grant seems to be less averse to the girl than he is to the boy, who surely reminds him of himself as a fatherless boy. Aside from Grant's masculine hat, the two are identically dressed — beige pants, brown belt and a blue shirt. Like Grant, Tim also sports a bandana around his neck, a blue one to Grant's red. This sequence ends with the camera once again coming for a close-up of Grant, who seems to sense that this visit is not what he expected.

The tour-adventure, the initiation, commences with the flashing "Tour Initiated" on all four sides of the car's computer screen and with the computer technician starting the tour vehicles with a last warning, "Hold onto your butts!" Riding with Ellie and Grant, Malcolm smells trouble: "God help us. We're in the hands of engineers." And when they pass through the entrance to the primeval world of Jurassic Park by two enormous, primitive-looking gates, with fire torches all around, Malcolm wonders, "What have they got there — King Kong?" It is another reminder of one of man's failed attempts to contain the beast, to repress its unconscious forces.

The announcer's words of caution in the cars' speakers, "You are now entering the lost world of the prehistoric past," announces the hero entering the primordial realm of the unconscious. By the time "they are approaching the Tyrannosaur paddock," having gone through a connecting (uterine) tunnel, Tim and Grant are sitting in corresponding places, each in his respective car, equally disappointed in not seeing anything beyond the electrified fence. Even the offering of a sacrificial goat does not bring the creature out. "T. rex doesn't want to be fed," Grant mutters to himself, once again voicing his objection to Hammond's project, all but calling it "Repressic Park." "He wants to hunt. You can't just suppress sixty-five million years of gut instinct." At this point in the movie, he does not see that "you can't just suppress" your inherent paternal impulse.

Moving towards the third station, Grant is shown in the foreground, peering outside the car's window. As if entranced by the "siren's" song, he opens the door and exits the moving car, getting off the charted course, with the two children right behind. Contrary to the way Grant treats Tim, who keeps vying for his attention, when Lex falls down, he helps her up, enquiring if she is okay. Lex keeps holding Grant's hand, much to Ellie's delight. When Grant tells the others to wait and proceeds alone to the source of the sounds, Tim follows.

Coming up to the source of the noise that he is drawn to, the Triceratops lying on the ground, clearly the most maternal of the park's creatures, Grant is ecstatic. "She was my favorite when I was a kid," he confesses to Ellie. "And now she's the most beautiful thing I ever saw." From the way he reacts to the sick female, the way he puts his head against her heaving belly (and with Lex looking on approvingly like a young Ellie), she obviously represents the good mother. And if she is the good mother, the vicious creatures in the prehistoric park represent the devouring mother. This notion is underscored by Grant's reply to Malcolm's commenting that Ellie is tenacious, "You have no idea," as if alluding to her maternal instinct, or to his own mother.

As if proving his words about her tenaciousness in not letting him go, up to now Grant and Ellie have been shown together. This explains Ellie's response to Malcolm's deduction ("God creates dinosaurs. God destroys dinosaurs. God creates man. Man destroys God. Man creates dinosaurs"): "Dinosaur eats man. Woman inherits the earth." Aside from her feminist fantasy, it is another reflection of Grant's psyche. He is in the clutches of the Terrible Mother, unable to produce children who will inherit the earth. But in Ellie's wanting to stay behind, to care for the sick animal like a mother, she lets go of Grant, allowing him to deal with his problem without her. "I'll catch up with you if you go on," she says, sending him on his way. Underscoring this momentous event, the sound of thunder signals the beginning of the storm and the turbulence that Grant is about to experience.

The next time we see Grant, he shares the back seat with Malcolm, his double, who holds opposite opinions about wives and children. A sign that Grant is beginning to change is his asking Malcolm, "You got any kids?" For once the talk is not about dinosaurs. It is also Grant's first un-derogatory remark about children. Malcolm's reply about his three kids, "Anything at all can and does happen," is another warning of what Grant is about to experience with Hammond's grandchildren.

Rebirth

The subject of birth is suggested when the camera cuts to Nedry stealing the embryos. His shutting off the computers, so that he can proceed with his plan, initiates Grant's series of trials. "What did I do?" Grant asks when the car comes to a stop, just as he did earlier at the digging site when the computer did not work. Rather than being his doing, it is Nedry's shutting off of the park's security, which signals that Grant's own security system, the defense mechanism containing the paternal impulse, is about to change. Grant's rebirth commences when he leaves the protective womb of his car. Typical of this movie, and of fairy tales, his rebirth comes about in *three* sets of trials, in which *three* things are repeated: (1) he sheds a symbolic object; (2) a man is sacrificed; (3) he saves a life.

(1) Having come to a stop, the tour car, much like the womb that Grant has outgrown, becomes a death trap. At the first sign of danger, which is mostly

experienced through the children, their accompanying adult, Gennaro, leaves the two to fend for themselves. "He left us. He left us," the hysterical Lex says incredulously, perhaps suggesting what happened to Grant as a young boy with his father. The next time we see her, as the T. rex is getting closer, she calls for "Dr. Grant," as if sensing his embryonic paternal instinct. Unlike Grant, who knows that the beast's "vision is based on movement," Lex turns on the flashlight she finds in an emergency box. "Turn the light off. Turn the light off," Grant says in his car, a sign of his growing care. In their own car, Tim repeats Grant's words, another suggestion that he is a young version of him. Interestingly, both the T. rex and the twin raptors are always after the two kids, particularly Tim, except when Grant and Malcolm draw them away from the children with their torches. In this act Grant emerges from the womb, risking his life to save another, a most fatherly act. Chasing after Malcolm, the T. rex comes upon Gennaro, eating him in one big bite. Immediately after this first sacrifice, Grant loses his hat while saving Lex.

(2) By the brief exchange between Grant and Lex, it is obvious that he has undergone a change. "Lex, I'm right here," he says, trying to calm the hysterical girl. "I'm going to look after you, but I have to go help your brother," who is trapped in the demolished, womb-like car. Crying "He left us. He left us," the still hysterical Lex repeats what she said in the car. "But that's not what I'm going to do," Grant assures her in a fatherly manner.

Despite his aversion to climbing trees, common symbols of life (which, unlike his digging, grow upwards from mother earth), Grant climbs a gigantic (phallic) tree to help Tim. Up on the tree with Tim, the implied change in Grant is now apparent in his attempt to free the trapped boy. With "Give me your hand," he reaches out to Tim, connecting with the boy. "It's just like coming out of a tree house. Did your dad ever build you a tree house, Tim?" As they share with one another, as father and son, neither one's father built his son a tree house where he could play in a world of his own, a world separate from the mother. But like the relentless monster, the womb-car (mother) seems to be after them as they make their escape down the tree. "We're back in the car," Tim comments when they find themselves inside the toppled car, sharing the womb. "At least we're out of the tree," Grant replies. Not having a father to initiate him to adulthood, to offer an alternative to the mother, Grant acts as a father in freeing Tim from the maternal womb.

When Ellie and Muldoon come to help, the gigantic T. rex chases them away, as if the initiation is Grant's alone. He has to learn to like children. He has to deal with what represents his paternal impulse by himself.

Out on their own, and out of the womb, Grant and the two children seek refuge for the night on top of a gigantic tree. Their new harmony is mirrored by the friendly brachiosauruses and by the two children nestling in Grant's arms. Significantly, the Velociprators claw unearthed in Montana makes his sitting uncomfortable. When he takes it out of his pocket and looks at it, Tim asks him, "What are you going to do now if you don't have to dig dinosaur bones any more?" "I guess we'll just have to evolve too," Grant replies, putting into words what he is already undergoing. His assuring Lex that he will keep an eye on them throughout the night gives further testimony to his growing father impulse. His letting go of the claw is another sign of his evolving. The close-up of the discarded claw, the last shot of the sequence, concludes the second stage of Grant's evolution, which is reinforced by the sacrificial death of the infantile Nedry.

(3) The third and last stage of Grant's evolving has three different *revivings*: the return of electricity, Tim brought back to life by Grant, and Grant's emergence as a father. Hammond opens this part with reassuring words to Ellie across the dining room table, commenting on Grant's growing paternity. "Who better to get the children through Jurassic Park than a dinosaur expert?" When shown the following morning, Grant is still awake, as he promised Lex he would be, the two kids asleep in his fatherly arms. The trio makes physical contact with the friendly dinosaur, connecting with the Good Mother. They see the "big cow" from up close and even touch her, as their grandfather dreamed kids would do in his park. The new life motif that controls this *rebirth* stage is introduced when Grant finds hatched dinosaur eggs. Saying "Malcolm was right. Look, life found a way," he shares his thoughts with the two children.

The cross cutting to the park's control center introduces the *resurrection* motif as Hammond realizes that the only way to get the system working again is to turn it off and restart it. When the electricity does not come on after the computer technician Arnold goes to turn it back on, Ellie, who senses that something is wrong, volunteers to go. Aware of the danger, Muldoon joins her, arming himself with the same rifle he used in the opening sequence. Once outside the shelter, they realize the raptors have broken free. As Muldoon informs Ellie, "We're being hunted." Where Grant and the kids are hounded by the giant T. rex, they are hunted by the more intelligent Velociraptors.

Like the female dinosaurs who found a way to reproduce life, the two females of the new family are the ones that bring the park back to life, when Ellie turns on the power and when Lex gets the computers working again. Where Hammond instructs Ellie on the walkie-talkie, Grant guides Tim over the perimeter fence. The two shots, the written Perimeter Fence on the electric board and Tim climbing the very same fence underscore the connection between the two. Another connection between the two scenes is turning the electricity back on. As if uttering the magic words, "Mr. Hammond, I think we're back in business," a raptor attacks Ellie, who is punished for restoring life. Her restoring the electricity literally hurls Tim into Grant's open arms. Bearing in mind that the two are electrocuted by the same perimeter fence, one symbolically (playfully) and one for real, it is yet another sign that they are one.

While Grant's playing a prank demonstrates his playfulness, Tim's electrocution initiates the father's breathing new life into the son. In bringing Tim back to life, Grant frees himself from the past, from the hold of the devouring mother that keeps him from growing up and becoming a father. Significantly, it comes right before Muldoon, the keeper of the paternal impulse, meets his death — the third and last shown sacrifice. Taking off his hat, symbol of his role as game warden, just as Grant lost his, Muldoon confronts the beast. The raptor, which had made eye contact with the game warden in the opening sequence, finally gets his revenge. Saying "Clever girl," Muldoon acknowledges the raptor's intelligence just before it devours him. As the controller of the beast, as a projection of Grant's introjected father, Muldoon represents the obstacle whose demise allows Grant's emerging fatherhood.

Family Reunited

When shown emerging from the jungle, from the unconscious, Grant is without the red bandana that Ellie had initially tied around his neck — the mother's symbolic strangle, which separates his head from his heart. Like the newborn raptor breaking through the egg's shell to the light of day that he held in his hands, Grant breaks off from the devouring mother's hold that kept him in a limited and heartless existence. Once again, life finds a way. In bringing the kids to the seemingly safe visitors' center, a semblance of home, Grant has become a father. His calling Tim, "*Big* Tim, the *human* piece of toast," just before he leaves the two "to find the others," may very well be his commenting on his own condition. Like a true father, he reassures the two, "I'll be back. I promise."

Left to themselves, the two kids find a display of food much like what Hansel and Gretel, another brother and sister abandoned by their parents, must have found in the witch's house made of sweets. Unbeknownst to them, the two raptors that killed Muldoon are now after them, as if they have a score to settle. The raptor's first appearance as a silhouette underscores its shadowy role. Just as the witch represents the dark side of Hansel and Gretel's mother, the two raptors must represent the dark side of the two's parents. They are the unconscious forces the two siblings must confront and come to terms with.

Whereas in the beginning Grant attacked the boy with the raptor's black claw, now, having returned with Ellie, thus replacing the siblings' divorced and absent parents, he finds himself protecting the kids from the very same creatures. However much his knowledge of dinosaurs may have helped him deal with the T. rex, the encounter with the two raptors is another story. As Grant had informed the kid at the digging site, the "bird of prey" is not to be mistaken for a T. rex, whose "visual acuity is based on movement." It is "a pack hunter," attacking its victim from the side in "coordinated attack patterns." As father protector, Grant tries to shield the two kids and Ellie from the two raptors that are closing in on them. Only the last-minute intervention of the T. rex saves them from certain death. Once again, natural selection wins the day.

A bigger monster kills the two smaller ones, killing the dark side of the children's parents. In the process, the skeletal remains of the past are destroyed and the banner that reads, "When Dinosaurs Ruled the Earth," comes toppling down. While the skeletons' destruction mirrors Grant's inner world, the T. rex's triumphant roar can be read as his triumph over his fear of becoming a father. His last words of the movie, "Mr. Hammond, I've decided not to endorse your park," is concurred with by Hammond: "So have I." Bearing in mind that Grant has become the children's father, his at-one-ment with their grandfather is truly atonement with the father. In rejecting the monstrous park and all it represents, Grant slays the dragon that guarded his paternal impulse.

When we last see him, Grant is in the same helicopter that brought him to Jurassic Park, flying (fleeing) away. The picture that opens this sequence, a close-up of the trapped mosquito inside the amber that Hammond fashioned on top of his walking cane, suggests that he is back where he started. As he turns to contemplate what remains of his world, the camera pans to show the equally shocked Ellie and Malcolm. In the silence that accompanies the traumatized survivors, Ellie, who now sits between the white clad Grant and the black-dressed Malcolm, herself in gray, smiles admiringly as she looks at Grant with the two kids asleep in his arms. All this is shown in one shot, underscoring the united family they have become. Considering that the last time the two children nestled in his arms was up on a tree, Grant is now a tree of life (rooted in mother earth) in whose branches the brother and sister find comfort. And if so, Grant is not unlike a tree house that he and Tim never experience in childhood.

Looking at Tim and Lex, Grant smiles back at Ellie, whose look seems to ask, "Doesn't this feel good?" Grant concurs. He has had enough of dinosaurs for one day. Instead of searching for their remains in the *past*, he turns his head, together with Ellie, towards a flock of birds flying over the waters, recalling his comment upon first seeing the dinosaurs, "They move in herds."

The last shot of Grant shows him leaning back, at peace with what he holds in his arms. His gaze follows a lone bird, his free spirit, flying alongside the "whirlybird" that is taking him away from Jurassic Park and to a new life. The closing shot of the helicopter heading towards the sunset, brings to mind countless endings of Western heroes riding off into the sunset after their work is done, after they have restored order by gunning down the shadowy villain, by slaying the dragon. To paraphrase Ian Malcolm, the movie's shadowy father, the paternal impulse "finds a way." In his becoming a father to the fatherless siblings, Hammond's grandchildren become Grant's children.

Chapter 12

The Searchers
Slaying the Dragon

SAM: You are wanted for a crime, Ethan?
ETHAN: You asking as a captain, or a preacher, Sam?
— Ethan Edwards and Sam Clayton before setting out on their first search.

Invisible Signs and Meta-Fords

When casting John Wayne in *The Searchers*, John Ford must have had in mind Howard Hawks' *Red River*, a Western in which Wayne, a favorite of both filmmakers, first portrayed an anti-hero. "I never knew that big sonofabitch could act," Ford remarked upon seeing Wayne's darker side in Hawks' first Western. Having launched Wayne's career in his first talking Western, the 1939 *Stagecoach*, Ford saw that the masculine actor was more psychologically complex than he had cast him in his earlier Westerns. Eight years later, when making *The Searchers*, Ford seems to have borrowed liberally from Hawks' Western. Tom Dunson's brief fight with the Indian who killed "the only woman he ever loved" is taken up in *The Searchers* by Ethan Edwards' five-year search for Scar, the Comanche chief who raped and killed the woman he loved. The two Indians, who personify both heroes' "other half," wear their tokens of love — a double headed bracelet in *Red River* and a war medal in *The Searchers*. In both Westerns, but much more so in *The Searchers*, the Wayne character denies his "other half" by projecting it on his surrogate son. Tom Dunson projects it on his adopted son Matt Garth, Ethan Edwards on his adopted "nephew" Martin Pawley. All in all, just as *Red River*'s cattle drive is the working-out of the ambiguous relationship between Dunson and Matt, the search in Ford's Western traces the working-out of the strained relationship between Ethan and Marty, between father and son.

Notwithstanding these borrowings, *The Searchers* has the unmistaken stamp of a John Ford Western. Even more than his other classic Westerns, from *Stagecoach* to *The Man Who Shot Liberty Valance*, *The Searchers*, Ford's masterpiece, is like his well-known introduction, "I'm John Ford. I make Westerns." Both convey much more than he would have us think. Just as he dismissed attempts to ascribe artistic intentions in his movies, in making Westerns Ford employed what he called "invisible technique" that was meant to make the audience forget they were watching a movie. In *The Searchers* he reached such mastery in using the "invisible technique," we hardly notice the scores of elliptical signs and metaphors that give the 1956 Western great depth and complexity.

Ford may very well allude to *The Searchers'* "invisible technique" when he has *Look* leave an arrow sign, which receives a close-up, and has Marty commenting (in voice-over), "Maybe she left other signs for us to follow." Like Look's sign, Ford's framing and shot composition leaves countless visual "signs for us to follow." We only have to look.

In another instance, Ford all but "draws us a picture" when he has Ethan inform Marty that *Nawyecky*, the name of Scar's tribe, means going one way when meaning another. Like the unconscious that Scar embodies, which communicates through metaphors that say one thing when meaning another, *The Searchers'* many visual signs and metaphors reveal a dark tapestry, a sort of Rorschach inkblot that, like the shadowy Ethan, "fits a lot of descriptions."

Among its "lots of descriptions," *The Searchers*, which Ford described as a "psychological epic," fits the myth of the hero slaying the dragon. Ford uses this archetype, that "fits a lot of descriptions," to reveal the dark side, the repressed unconscious, of his Western hero. Ethan Edwards' five-year search for Debbie, who is held captive by Scar, the dragon of the movie, is an epic quest of expiation for the savage crime carried out against the woman he loved by the agent of his repressed unconscious. Only after he scalps Scar, after he slays the dragon, does Ethan take Debbie in his arms, repeating what he first did inside Martha's home, before she was contaminated in his mind. As J. A. Place notes in *The Western Films of John Ford*,

> The action can thus be seen as a manifestation of Ethan's psychological tensions, with which Ethan cannot come to terms in his conscious mind but which he can resolve through their transference into symbolic events. In such an interpretation, Scar becomes the agent of Ethan's unacceptable unconscious desires to invade and destroy the home of Martha and Aaron, from which he feels so excluded, and (presumably) to rape Martha. The close association between Scar and Ethan has its basis here. The Indian's very name may be an expression of Ethan's rather disfigured psyche. The "search" of the film thus becomes the seeking out and destruction of Ethan's unacceptable desires, and only after Ethan's ritualize mutilation of Scar can he finally accept Debbie.[1]

Considering that early in the movie Ethan expresses his love for Martha through his affection for Debbie, in taking her in his arms he "come[s] to terms in his conscious mind" with his repressed love for his brother's wife. But before

Ethan comes to hold the "woman" he believes to be Scar's wife (as Martha's was Aaron's), he must work out his guilt for his "unacceptable desires" for Martha. This he does through his growing relationship with Marty, through whom he expresses his "unacceptable desires" for Martha by his obvious disdain. It is not for nothing that the two share the first four letters of their names. In Ethan's mind, in his unconscious, the two are connected. And as such, Ethan works out his forbidden desires for Martha by becoming a father to Marty. To use Place's words, Ethan resolves his "unacceptable unconscious desires ... through their transference into symbolic events."

A Psychological Epic

Ford's "invisible technique" in conveying how Ethan comes to terms with his forbidden feelings for Martha is probably best demonstrated by the movie's first few scenes, particularly the opening, which sets up the tense relationship between the two. This brief scene is quintessential Ford, revealing his mastery of cinematic storytelling through framing and visual composition. Considering the subtle information it conveys, this cinematic *tour de force*, like much of the movie, is best appreciated when examined shot by shot.

Opening with a black screen, Ford gives us a sign of things to come from the very first shot. Like the meaning of *Nawyecky*, Ford seems to say one thing when meaning another. We think the dark screen is a brief break between the opening credits and the start of the movie, when in fact it is the dark interior of the Edwards' frontier home. Between this darkness and the matching one that ends the movie, between the movie's bookends, the only other time the screen goes black is between Scar's blowing the bull's horn that signals the start of the massacre and Ethan's seeing its outcome, suggesting a connection between the two, as if it is Ethan's projection.

Still in the same shot, accompanied by the music of the song "Lorena," "which functions instrumentally as the theme for Ethan's brother's family, including — and specifically — Martha,"[2] the camera follows the woman as she opens the cabin door to the light of day, stopping momentarily in the doorway, gazing at an approaching horseman. As she steps outside to the porch, her black silhouette changing into a clearly defined figure in a light blue dress and white apron, the camera stops together with her. She places her right hand on one of the roof's supporting posts, dividing the frame into two halves, evoking an image of the two's relationship — sharing the frame and separated by frames. The woman is in the foreground, to the left of the supporting post; the approaching horseman is in the background, on the right side of the post and frame, a dark phallic butte behind him in the distance. This famous opening shot, virtually repeated in the movie's closing shot, exemplifies Ford's cinematography and his use of Monument Valley's primal beauty in conveying with images what cannot be said by words.

The second shot shows the woman from the front as she looks at the man approaching her home. Her shielding her eyes from the glaring sunlight underscores the contrast between the dark interior and the sunny outdoor. Her hopeful but troubled gaze suggests she has been waiting for his arrival for some time.

Following the first of three identical shots that show the approaching figure, with phallic buttes on either side of the frame, the woman is joined by a man, to whom she turns with a distressed look on her face. "Ethan?" he asks uncertainly, not sure who it is, or perhaps not knowing what to make of his arrival.

The ensuing shot shows three children gathering on the porch, all looking in the direction of the approaching horseman. Together with the man up front, they form a four-cornered square with the woman at its center, underscoring her place in the family and in Ethan's heart. The barking dog draws attention to the little girl at the far end of the porch, who is singled out by the following shot, showing her holding a rag doll. Saying "Quiet, Chris," she tries to suppress the dog's excitement, as if he sniffs Ethan's repressed desire for Martha.

In the second identical shot of the approaching Ethan, he rides up to the porch, dismounting as the man of the family steps forward to meet him. The camera cuts to the older girl and her brother. "That's your Uncle Ethan," she informs her brother. With her announcement comes the tune "The Bonnie Blue Flag," "a patriotic Confederate anthem, obviously meant to suggest Ethan's Confederate past and (like his relationship with Martha) another lost cause."[3] In contrast to the bewildered man and woman, the two are excited to see their uncle. Having learned the man is Uncle Ethan, it is not clear whose brother he is.

The third identical shot shows Ethan holding a saber and saddlebags in his left hand, walking towards the man of the family, who extends his right hand. The two shake hands silently. Ethan turns to look at the woman.

The next shot shows the whole family in the front of the cabin, the two supporting posts dividing the frame into three parts. The children are on the porch — the little girl and the dog are on the left side, the two older siblings on the right side. The three adults are in the foreground, closer to the camera and occupying the center "frame," underscoring their centrality in the exposition and in the movie itself. Moreover, Ethan is significantly positioned between the man and woman at the center. In this symmetrical shot, the man of the family is on the right side with his son and older daughter. On the left side is Ethan, the woman and her younger daughter, positioned in a straight line, as if suggesting (or anticipating) a connection between the three. Ethan removes his hat as he starts walking towards the woman. Just as she extends both her arms towards him, to touch him as much as to keep a distance between them, the two are shown in an intimate shot. This extending and holding back defines their relationship. Furthermore, their sharing the frame recalls the earlier shot of the husband and wife in the only time they share the frame, suggesting that Ethan is replacing (usurping) the husband.

"Welcome home, Ethan," the woman greets him. When Ethan reaches to kiss her forehead, she closes her eyes. She seems to want more, but he only gives a light kiss on the brow. It is another image, another sign, of their relationship. The minute she takes her hands from Ethan's arms, the music associated with him stops, returning to "Lorena," continuing until he lifts Debbie inside the house. It is the first of several associations between the song and the mother and her younger daughter. Unable to take her eyes off Ethan, the woman leads (or draws) him into the house. Aside from the opening shot, this shot of the two is the longest of the dozen shots the make up the sequence, underscoring the two's role in the movie.

The closing shot, repeating the one showing the front porch, shows the woman entering the dark inside, followed by Ethan and the other man, the children right behind them, ending the movie's brief but telling exposition.

The subsequent scene inside the home, much longer than the opening, is shown in three well-orchestrated shots. All are low-angle shots that stress the oppression of the ceiling's wooden beams, reflecting the mood that Ethan's arrival has brought about. The three-shot sequence first shows the whole family, then the three adults, and finally the two men.

In the first shot, Debbie is once again singled out, this time by Ethan lifting her up. His mistaking her for her older sister Lucy reveals how long he has been gone and anticipates his associating Debbie with Martha, as underscored by Martha's theme ("Lorena") on the soundtrack. The music stops when Ethan walks to the family table, Debbie in his arms. As in the family portrait on the porch, in the gathering around the table, Ethan, the woman and Debbie are on one side, the rest of the family on the other, as if now that Ethan has returned the woman is his. Ben's saying (with Ethan's phallic saber in his hand) about Lucy, "She got a fella, kisses him, too," is another allusion to the woman's love for Ethan. Especially as the two women, the one referred to and the one alluded to, chime in with "Ben!" in another attempt at suppression. What is more, Ben asks Ethan most suggestively about "what he's gonna do with his saber."

The second shot, which includes the three adults (with the children in the background), shows Ethan in the middle, once again coming between the man and the woman, standing beneath the crossing of two huge ceiling wooden beams, as if a fulcrum in this uneasy balance. When the man asks him about California, Ethan replies that he "ain't been to California," looking directly at the woman. "I don't intend to go, either." He continues looking at her, as she had earlier looked at him, suggesting that he came to stay (with her). Before things get too uncomfortable, the woman is quick to change the subject: "Supper will be ready as soon as you wash up." Then she turns to Ethan, "Let me take your coat for you," helping him with his gray Confederate coat. The way she touches the coat and the way Ethan, together with the camera, follows her as she takes this part of him into her bedroom, is another picture of the suppressed eroticism between the two.

In the third and last shot, the camera shows the two men. The man extends his hand to Ethan, repeating the woman's welcoming words. Ethan takes his eyes off the woman and looks at his outstretched hand. The two shake hands once more, acknowledging one another. "Thanks, Aaron," Ethan replies with a slight smile, as the sequence fades out. The introduction of Aaron together with Mose Harper, mentioned off-handedly, suggests that the two are brothers.

The shot of Marty's arrival, which opens the next sequence, repeats the shot of Ethan's arrival through the frame of the open door, implying a connection between the two right from the start. But unlike Ethan, who slowly dismounted his saddled horse, Marty leaps off his bareback in one clean bound. He is free and loose. As he enters the home, briefly shown as a silhouette much as Martha was initially shown upon Ethan's arrival, the family is shown sitting around the supper table. In contrast to the first two scenes that focused on the suppressed love between Martha and Ethan, this one focuses on Ethan's disdain for Marty.

Surprised to find Uncle Ethan, Marty stiffens as he walks to the woman's side. "Good evening, Uncle Ethan," he greets him, reminding Ethan of their family relationship. His "Welcome home, sir," recalls the woman and Aaron's welcoming words. The "home," much to Ethan's displeasure, is another reminder that Marty is part of the family. The disdainful expression on Ethan's face as he looks at Marty brings the woman to think (hope) that he does not remember him. But Marty, suffering Ethan's rebuffing in a medium close-up, seems to know what Ethan means. Much as Ethan's arrival intrudes on the constellation of the family, Marty is an intrusion in "his" family. Ethan cannot take his eyes off him just as earlier he could not take them off Martha. His first words to Marty, "A fella could mistake you for a half-breed," exaggerates his Indian blood, underscoring Ethan's uncalled-for disdain, which he expresses in each of the four shots he is shown. In projecting on the "half-breed" his other half, Ethan truly "mistakes" him for what he really is. The fact that in all shots Ethan shares the frame with Martha is the first sign that his disdain is connected to his repressed love for her, particularly as later he does not show any objection to the "half-breed's" romantic relationship with Laurie. For Ethan, the "half-breed" Marty is a convenient object on which to project his frustration in regards to Martha.

In his apology to Martha for being late, which reveals her name, Marty may very well remind Ethan of his own lateness in regards to her. Trying to ease the tension, Aaron immediately reminds Marty (and Ethan) that it was Ethan who found him after his folks had been massacred. But Ethan rejects the affiliation between the two ("It just happened to be me. No need to make more of it"), as one rejects an unwanted part, revealing to the others that he is not the uncle they were expecting. That his blatant disdain to Marty is connected to his latent desire for Martha is underscored by the fact that once she is raped and murdered by the Comanches, Ethan's disdain begins to gradually diminish. The more Ethan comes to accept Marty, the closer he gets to make amends with his unacceptable desire for Martha. As a "half breed," Marty is also a mediator between Ethan and his "other half," the Comanche chief who carries out his dark desires. "If in Ethan the forces of savagery and civilization are locked in battle, in Martin Pawley they are peacefully combined."[4]

With Marty shown briefly on the porch, ostracized by Ethan's disdain, the attention returns inside, to the tense triad of Martha, Aaron and Ethan. Just as Ethan could only express his repressed desire for Martha through his disdain for Marty, now, sitting in the rocking chair before the fireplace, he expresses his love for her through her children, particularly Debbie. When Debbie asks her uncle for a token of his love, Martha tries to suppress her, as if she knows it is Ethan's way of expressing his love for her. And indeed, as suggested by the accompanying "Lorena," the medal Ethan gives Debbie is an expression of his repressed love for Martha, who protests softly, "Ethan, I think she's too young." "Oh, let her have it," Ethan cuts her short. "It doesn't amount to much." It amounts to what Ethan can give to express his love to Martha. That is why the thought of Debbie as Scar's squaw, not to mention his wearing the medal, so enflames Ethan. It reminds him of his forbidden desire for Martha.

The camera stays with Ethan and Aaron sitting in facing chairs, with Martha significantly positioned between them in the background. When Aaron starts talking about Martha not letting him quit as did the two mentioned families, she comes to Ethan's side, unable to take her eyes off him. The two are shown together again, facing Aaron. As if hinting that he knows more than he lets on, Aaron looks squarely at Ethan. "Ethan, I saw it in you before the war. You wanted to quit. You wanted to clear out. You stayed beyond any clear reason. Why?" The unspoken answer, of course, is Martha, who stands behind Ethan.

True to her nature, Martha tries to suppress Aaron's probing, but his question touches a raw nerve in Ethan. "Are you asking me to clear out now?" Ethan stands up, taking side with Martha as he faces Aaron, who remains in his chair, keeping it formal with "You're my brother, Ethan." Only now, in this tense moment, it is revealed whose brother Ethan is. "You're welcome to stay here as long as you have a mind to," Aaron turns briefly to Martha. "Ain't that right, Martha?" When the proud Ethan asserts that he will pay for his stay, tossing Aaron two bags of freshly minted Yankee dollars, which raises questions how he obtained them, Martha steps between them, reaching for the lit kerosene lamp hanging above the fireplace in the center of the frame. The taller Ethan reaches to help her, wrapping his hand around hers, as Aaron notices that the money is "fresh minted, ain't a mark on it," bringing him to speculate on what Ethan did during those three years since the end of the Civil War. "So?" Ethan challenges him, slowly removing his hand from Martha's, as if feeling guilty of more than one crime. Still in the same shot, Ethan follows Martha as she takes the lamp to her bedroom. When she is out of his sight, another shot shows him from another angle, slowly walking outside, not saying a word to Aaron, who is by the fireplace stashing away the money.

In the brief three-shot sequence that ends the first day of his return, Ethan is shown sitting on the same front porch steps where Marty sat earlier (another connection between the two). With Debbie's dog as his companion, he is alone with his "animal" desire for Martha. This is suggested by the reverse shot sandwiched between the two shots of Ethan, which shows what he sees through the cabin's open door. His *seeing* Aaron closing their bedroom door recalls his eyes following Martha to their bedroom — once with his coat and once with the kerosene lamp. It is a forbidden chamber he cannot enter. As such, and as emphasized by the movie's recurring doorway shots that show Ethan on the porch looking in, he is truly on the outside looking in, his love for Martha held back by the social order he is not part of. Having been repressed for so long, however, it returns with a vengeance the very next day.

The return of the repressed is evoked by the following morning's opening shot of galloping horses, common signifiers of the sex drive. Considering the closing shots of Ethan on the porch and the repeated references to his repressed desire, the six men (like the six members of the Edwards family) riding towards the Edwards home with the smoking chimney, can be read as an extension of Ethan's released emotions. Particularly as one of the phallic buttes that was in the background upon his arrival looms large behind the chimney, and as the very next shot shows Martha, the object of his desire, by the fireplace, from which the smoke emanates. As if sensing the return of the repressed, the dog is heard (not seen) barking once again just before four hard knocks are heard and Sam Clayton's calls out, "Aaron, open up!" These words, which recall Ethan's seeing Aaron closing the bedroom door, may well be the words of his repressed desire, of his unconscious. As if sensing the danger, Martha calls Aaron to open the door.

Clayton's unexpected arrival is not unlike Ethan's, especially as he wears a coat and stands between Martha and Aaron just as Ethan had done the day before. While he swears Aaron and Marty, the males of the family, to a search posse, Ethan, the third male, emerges from behind him. The camera, stationary up to now, comes in towards Clayton as Ethan approaches him, coming to rest on the two. "Captain. The Reverend Samuel Johnson Clayton," Ethan says, surprising the man with the two titles. "Well, the prodigal brother. When did you get back?" Clayton, like Aaron before him, questions Ethan's past. "I ain't seen you since the surrender. Come to think of it, I didn't see you *at* the surrender." Of course, what Ethan has not surrendered is his desire for Martha, as his reference to his phallic saber suggests. That Ethan wants to take his brother's place with Martha is subtly suggested by his wearing a red shirt, blue trousers and light suspenders just like Aaron, and by his insisting on taking his brother's place in the posse. Aaron protests weakly, not speaking up again for the remainder of the sequence, as if his replacement is complete.

"Stay close, Aaron," the experienced Ethan instructs his brother, as the camera cuts to Martha and Aaron, who are shocked at what Ethan hints is behind the *stealing*, recalling Aaron all but accusing Ethan of a similar crime. In Ethan's words, it "could be Comanche." But it could also be his repressed desire. As if sensing this, Martha immediately sends the kids to another part of the house. Her fears mount when Clayton (positioned between Ethan and the couple) proposes to swear-in Ethan, who replies, "No need to. Wouldn't be legal anyway." "Why not?" Clayton confronts him. "You are wanted for a crime, Ethan?" Martha and Aaron are shown together for the second time, anxious over what Ethan may have done in the years since the war. Their present reaction recalls their initial reaction to his arrival. Martha, more shocked than Aaron, perhaps because the alluded crime is connected to her, tries to suppress things by offering Ethan coffee. But Ethan answers Clayton's question with one of his own. "You asking as a captain, or a preacher?" His words suggest a crime both legal and moral. What is more, when Clayton replies "You fit a lot of descriptions," the camera cuts for the third time to Martha and Aaron and their distressed reaction to Clayton's accusation. All three shots showing their reactions suggest that Ethan's crime, that "fits a lot of descriptions," is his unlawful desire for his brother's wife, and that Martha and Aaron know it.

Accompanied by "Lorena," the indoor sequence is concluded in one shot, showing Clayton averting his eyes from catching sight of Martha through the doorway of her bedroom, gently caressing Ethan's Confederate coat. Then, together with the un-mindful Clayton, who sees but does not look, the two are shown alone for the first time since Ethan's return, as Martha silently hands him his hat and coat, an act which allows them a bit more display of emotions. When Ethan bends to kiss her chastely on her forehead, just as he had done on his arrival, Martha seems softer and more compliant, returning his gesture with a tender touch of her hand. The two exchange looks before they part, Ethan cutting it short. As he walks silently out the door, Martha follows him with outstretched hands, stopping at the doorway.

Closing out the first part of the movie, the lone farmhouse is shown in the wilderness, a dark cliff hovering ominously above it in the background. Among the men of the search party, Ethan is the last one to leave. Martha is shown gazing at him riding away just as she gazed at him coming in the movie's opening shot, with Debbie coming to her side. The two watch Ethan ride away as if they were his wife and daughter, as if Ethan has taken his brother's place in the family just as he has in the search party.

The Crime

With the start of the search, Ethan's relationship with Martha (and Debbie) is replaced by his relationship with Marty — one relationship engenders the problem, the other resolves it. Riding side by side behind Clayton, the two are more alike than Ethan cares to admit. The two's likeness and difference is suggested by the Western's two familiar icons of masculinity. The similar covered rifles they both hold point to their likeness; their different hats, Ethan's black and Marty's light one, point to their difference. As their father-son relationship changes in the course of the movie, so do their hats, becoming more alike.

The nature of the two's relationship is established in their very first exchange, when Marty points out, "Somethin' mighty fishy about this trail, Uncle Ethan," and Ethan cuts him short, not for pointing out his suspicion, but for calling him "Uncle." He lets him know who is in charge, all the while denying their kinship. When Ethan does ask him ("Now what's so mighty fishy about this trail?"), before Marty can answer, they are cut short by the other son of the search party, Brad, who calls out to his "Pa," to "look" at the slain cattle. As if recognizing his projection, Ethan comes to realize that stealing the cattle is a ploy to clear the way for Scar's carrying out his repressed desires. Once again, Lars and Brad Jorgensen, the father-son pair of the search party, offer an alternative to the denied connection between Ethan and Marty, particularly as their two homes are thought to be under attack. When Lars calls his son to race home with him, "Brad! Brad! Son," Marty, shown in a close-up, waits for a similar response from Ethan. "Well, are you coming or ain't ya?" he turns to Ethan, who declines. "That farm is 40 miles from here, boy. And these horses need rest and grain." Where Lars called Brad "son," Ethan calls Martin a derogatory "boy."

As Marty rides off, Ethan stays behind with Mose Harper. Having unleashed the murder raid, he throws him his rifle, as if disowning the phallus. His kicking the dancing fool (accompanied by the rhythm of Indian tom-tom drums on the soundtrack), saying, "Break out the grain," is another expression of his suppressed emotions that *break out* as the Comanches' raid. The next shot, a lingering medium-close-up of Ethan wiping the lather off his horse's back with an Indian blanket, staring blankly up ahead, shows him envisioning the worst yet holding it all inside. Where up to now all transitions between sequences were marked by dissolves, now it cuts from Ethan right to his brother Aaron, suggesting that what is shown is a projection of his psyche: his forbidden desire for Martha *breaks out* as a shadowy savage. "The use of 'Lorena' as accompaniment here, performed low in the violin's register and cast into the minor, anchors Ethan's close-up specifically around Martha and foreshadows her fate."[5]

At the Edwards homestead, all signs suggest that the coming massacre is linked to Ethan's arrival. Aaron's words to the barking dog, "Quiet, boy," echo Debbie's words upon Ethan's arrival. Martha also senses that something ominous is out there, as she opens the door to look outside, just as she did then. The look she and Aaron exchange as he comes inside recalls their reaction to Ethan's unexpected arrival and to his alleged crime. Clearly afraid, Martha goes to the door to look again. What she is unable to express is expressed by Ben, who comes in with Ethan's saber, an extension of his phallus, saying "I wish Uncle Ethan was here. Don't you, Ma?" It is another sign that what is out there is Ethan's projection. Lucy's scream, which echoes her excitement at Ethan's arrival, is one more sign that what is out there is Ethan's double.

The only one unaware of the threat is Debbie. Sent outside through a side window, she barely sits down by a pair of twin tombstones (of the brothers' parents), when she looks up and sees an approaching figure, whose shadow falls on her and the tombstone, a sign that it is Ethan's shadowy double. The next shot shows the war-painted face of an Indian looking down at Debbie just before he blows a bull's horn, an image of released sexual passion that signals the start of the massacre.

By not showing the massacre, Ford leaves it to our imagination, to imagine together with Ethan what is unleashed by his repressed unconscious. Ford shows Ethan's and Marty's different reaction to the "spectacle" in identical three-shot sequences, once again underscoring their similarity and difference.

In the first shot, coming to where he can see the burning Edwards homestead, Ethan stops next to a phallic butte, which is also in the frame in the following close-up. The shot/reverse-shot of Ethan and the burning farmhouse confirms that it is seen through his eyes. The repeated close-up reveals Ethan's pent-up rage. His whipping the scabbard off his rifle, as he starts racing to the scene of the crime, mirrors the sexual turbulence he harbors inside.

In the second shot, Marty, like Ethan, is shown seeing the burning farmhouse. Only he is without a horse and a rifle, two common symbols of sexual desire. Unlike Ethan, whose desires are unacceptable and therefore repressed, Marty's reaction is emotional.

Arriving at what is left of the burning homestead, Ethan calls out Martha's name, leaving no doubt who is on his mind. Martha's bloodstained dress leads him to the log shelter partly buried in the ground. Together with a "tragic" variation of "Lorena" on the soundtrack, he is shown as a silhouette from inside through the doorframe, recalling the movie's opening shot. Seeing what he feared most, his head and body collapse in grief, recalling Martha's own collapse in parting from Debbie. As Arthur M. Eckstein points out in his introduction to the book, *The Searchers*, a collection of *Essays and Reflections on John Ford's Classic Western*, Ford deliberately emphasized the sexual aspects of this sequence.

> [I]n Ford's finished version of the film, we see Ethan and Martha's blood-soaked ripped-open blue dress amid the smoking ruins of the Edwards household. It is an awful sign, to the audience and to Ethan, of what has happened to Martha — that she was raped by Comanches before being killed. This scene, too, with its terrible implications, we now know was not in Frank Nugent's shooting script, but was added later on location by Ford himself, to emphasize the sexual focus of the film.[6]

Where prior to Martha's rape and murder Ethan repeatedly displayed his disdain for Marty, now the movie starts to focus on the developing relationship between the two, between father and son. In fact, Ethan's first fatherly act immediately follows his discovering Martha's body, when he does not let Marty (who also calls out for "Aunt Martha") go inside and see the horror. When Marty refuses to listen (again), Ethan knocks him down, protecting him like a father. As he tells Mose, "Don't let him look in there, Mose. Won't do him any good."

Another sign of the change in Ethan's relationship with Marty comes in the subsequent graveyard scene, where Martha's name is the only one heard in Reverend Clayton's eulogy over the singing of "Shall We Gather at the River." Where up to now the "uncle" denied any connection to Marty, and earlier had rejected his call to head back to the Edwards homestead, after Martha's burial he calls out to him by name, for the first time in the movie, as he is about to embark on his search, echoing Marty's very words to him. "Well, come on, if you're going with us."

The sequence's closing shot shows Marty parting from Laurie, the couple sharing the frame with the shelter where Ethan found Martha. The camera tracks after Marty as he rides away, stopping on the face of Mrs. Jorgensen, who follows the men's departure, just as Martha had followed Ethan's departure on his first search. Likewise, Lars and Laurie enter the frame just as did Debbie. Laurie, who is shown only after Martha's funeral, replaces her in the center of the frame and in the ensuing drama. Just as the Jorgensens' father-son relationship offers an alternative to Ethan's relationship with Marty, this visual rhyme is the first sign that Marty's and Laurie's relationship is an alternative to the suppressed relationship of Ethan and Martha. This budding relationship runs parallel to, and mirrors, Ethan's working out his guilt-ridden relationship with Martha, which he resolves through his developing relationship with Marty as father and son.

The Search for Penitence

The start of the second search repeats the opening of the first, as once again Ethan's and Marty's likeness and difference are underscored by their sitting on their horses but facing different directions. By having them share the frame, we see both Ethan's thirst for revenge in his shooting the dead Indian's eyes and Marty's reaction to his sadistic act. As if initiated by his shooting the eyes, it is the first time Ethan is shown through Marty's eyes. From here on out, the movie (and Ethan) is increasingly seen from Marty's point of view. As Douglas Pye points out, "Increasingly, and in ways that seem entirely controlled, the film detaches us from Ethan so that we are required to perceive the neurotic and irrational nature of his attitudes and actions."[7]

Ethan's changing attitude towards Marty is subtly suggested by his reaction to Marty's siding with Captain Clayton against his line of attack. "What does a quarter-breed Cherokee know about the old Comanche trick of sleeping with his best pony tied right by his side?" Considering his hate is linked to

Marty's Indian blood, calling him *a quarter-breed* still exaggerates his true "eighth part," but it is an improvement on his calling him a "half-breed."

A more obvious sign of change, in both Ethan and Marty, comes up after the search party "unsurrounds" itself from the Comanches by crossing to the other side the river. The sequence focuses on Ethan, but as anticipated by Mose's "I've been baptized, Reverend" (in answering "How far is the river?"), Marty undergoes a baptism by firing. His horror at killing another human, as confirmed by Mose's "You got him, Marty!" is in complete contrast to the sadism of Ethan, who clearly enjoys the killing. Marty breaks down briefly, but comes back up shooting. Having been initiated, from innocence to experience, Marty henceforth becomes increasingly the *other* hero of the movie.

If up to now there were subtle signs that Scar is Ethan's shadowy double, in their first encounter it is made clear by the twin medium close-ups of the two, each holding a rifle. Once Ethan confronts his double, he can no longer go by Clayton's command, which represents law and order (gun and Bible). When he decides to continue the search by himself, Marty, together with Brad, insists on going with him. At first Marty does not know what to call Ethan — Uncle Ethan, Ethan or sir. But by the time he agrees to follow his orders, he starts calling him by his first name, another sign of their changing relationship.

Ethan may give the orders, but it is Marty who discovers the trail that leads him to Lucy's body. In view of the shape he is in on his return, the solo search is a turning point for Ethan. He is clearly a changed man. The way he throws his rifle and slumps to the ground recalls Marty's reaction to his first killing. His stabbing the ground with his knife expresses part of the emotions he tries to keep under control. Finding Lucy's body must remind him of what he unconsciously wanted to do to Martha. That is why he takes it so hard when the inquisitive Brad wants to know the meaning of the "buck wearing Lucy's dress." "What do you want me to do? Draw you a picture? Spell it out?" Of course, this could also be Ford's asking us, or one of his interviewers, the very same questions.

Left to imagine what happened to Lucy, much as Ethan imagined what happened to Martha, Brad goes mad. When he takes off with a gun towards the camped Comanches, and Marty tries to stop him, Ethan trips Marty with his foot, catching him from behind by his shirt when he runs after Brad. The two are shown sharing the frame as Brad is killed up ahead, Ethan placing a paternal hand on Marty's shoulder.

Following Brad's death, the subsequent scene opens with two shots that show Ethan and Marty traveling together in two different seasons and in two different directions, which marks the passage of time and the futility of their search. Then, in one shot, the two are shown in what is their first civil conversation. Having lost the Comanche's trail in the snow, Marty, wearing a white hat, wants to give up. "Well, why don't you say it? We're beat, and you know it." But Ethan, wearing a black hat, refuses to see it as a defeat. "Our turning back don't mean nothin.' Not in the long run. If she's alive, she's safe. For a while, they'll keep her and raise her as one of their own until ... until she's an age to...." Ethan cannot finish the sentence. His thoughts are too terrible to utter. His referring to himself as "a critter who'll just keep coming on" can very well refer to the undying persistence of the unconscious, a force that keeps coming on no matter how repressed.

Taking a break from their search, Ethan's and Marty's first return to the Jorgensen homestead is a virtual re-enactment of Ethan's return to the home of Martha and Aaron. Only now, as initially suggested after Martha's funeral, the relationship between Ethan and Martha is replaced by the one between Marty and Laurie. The analogy between the two relationships is emphasized by Mrs. Jorgensen's emerging from the doorway just as in the movie's opening sequence it was Martha who emerged from the doorway. In blue dress and white apron, Mrs. Jorgensen is dressed like Martha. She even shades her eyes from the sun and receives a close-up just as did Martha. Coming from behind, Laura, unlike the restrained Martha, smiles happily and removes her apron upon seeing Marty. Shown twice by herself, she calls his name, rushing to kiss him. "Probably forgettin' all about you," Mrs. Jorgensen remarks upon seeing Marty's reaction, which recalls Martha's remark when reminding Ethan who Marty is. But Marty, in complete contrast to Ethan, is much more forthcoming. "Her name is Laurie," he answers Mrs. Jorgensen, practically unable to take his eyes off Laurie. "But I fairly forgot how pretty she was." He looks at Laurie, who takes him by the arms and leads him inside the house much as Martha drew Ethan inside her home. This displacement of one couple for another, which plays a significant part in the story, seems to take off the edge of Ethan's guilt, as if it is transferred to Marty and Laurie.

While Ethan is mostly shown with Lars and Mrs. Jorgensen, talking about the search for Debbie, which is ostensibly a re-enactment of his meeting with Aaron and Martha, Marty is coupled with Laurie, in an intimacy unimaginable between Ethan and Martha. As if mirroring what happened between the two, Laurie wants Marty to stay, but she unwittingly gets him to leave by reminding her father of Futterman's letter, which was delivered earlier by Charley MacCorry. Unlike Marty, who bathes and is cleansed after his first killing, Ethan's hate mounts after seeing a piece of Debbie's dress sent with the letter. It is another reminder of the raped and murdered Martha and Lucy, starting Ethan to think of killing the defiled Debbie. This is strongly suggested when, holding the piece of the dress, Ethan answers Mrs. Jorgensen's "Have they found her yet?" with "Not yet," repeating the words slowly to himself as he ponders the cloth he runs between his fingers.

What Ethan merely suggests, Marty says outright the next morning when he explains why he must go with him. "He's a man that can go crazy wild. And I intend to be there to stop him in case he does." In serving Marty breakfast, stealing for him Futterman's letter, and giving him her "own good horse,"

Laurie helps Marty continue his journey, though not without warning him, as the more reserved Martha probably never warned Ethan, "Don't you count on findin' me here when you get back." As Marty rides off, Laurie is shown in medium close-up. Having replaced Martha as the dominant woman in the film, she is the last one shown upon Marty's departure just as Martha was shown upon Ethan's.

Marty soon catches up with Ethan, for the two are shown in the transaction with Futterman. Ethan (in a dark hat) does most of the talking, but it is Marty (in a light hat) who is singled out (twice) by medium close-ups, once in identifying Debbie's dress and once while repeating the name of the Comanche chief who holds her captive. His "Scar?" recalls Aaron's "Ethan?"— another sign of the link between the two. The dress Futterman sells them sends them north after Debbie, "captive child of Chief Scar," the dragon who holds her captive.

By showing the subsequent segment of the search through Marty's letter to Laurie, delivered by Charlie MacCorry, who has "come a-courting," we get a good look at Laurie's frustration with Marty's lack of personal involvement. Her losing hope in Marty may very well be Ford drawing us a picture of what Martha must have felt. In writing about getting himself a wife, and an Indian one at that, Marty practically pushes Laurie into Charlie's arms, much as Ethan must have pushed Martha into Aaron's. For the most part, in two of the letter's three flashbacks, Marty's "marriage" to Look functions as a lighter side of the darker relationship of Debbie and Scar, particularly in Ethan's mind. It is another sign that Marty and Scar are two conflicting sides of Ethan. Marty mentioning Scar's name scares off Look, but not before she leaves an arrow sign for the two to follow.

Where the first two flashbacks focus on Laurie's reaction to Marty's impersonal words, the third and longest flashback focuses on the way Marty comes to see Ethan's growing madness. "We were heading north through buffalo country when somethin' happened that I ain't got straight in my own head yet." Marty cannot fathom Ethan's senseless cruelty, in shooting madly at the stampeding buffalos. As the sensible voice, Marty tries to stop Ethan the same way Clayton stopped him from shooting the retreating Comanches. But Ethan knocks Marty down, something he would never do to the older Clayton.

Over the sound of Ethan's shooting, Marty hears the cavalry's bugle from afar. He yells repeatedly for Ethan to "listen," to the voice of reason, to law and order, represented by the approaching cavalry. Suggesting that Ethan does not listen to the cavalry's "horn," the sequence's closing shot lingers on the two, framed by the branches of a withered tree, which looks like a pair of buffalo horns, recalling the one blown by Scar to start the massacre on the Edwards home. As one of Ford's pictures of the two's psyche, the "horn" Marty is grasping is whole; the one on Ethan's side is broken, not unlike his world since Martha's death. Ethan holds a rifle and wears a black hat just as when he found

Martha's body, while Marty is without the two just as he was then. Moreover, when the two catch up with the cavalry, the aim of each one's search is revealed in two separate but identical shots. Ethan is shown sitting on his horse, holding a rifle; Marty is shown sitting on a horse taking out Debbie's rag doll from his saddlebag and stuffing it inside his coat, close to his heart.

Ethan and Marty do not find Debbie or Scar at the fort they come to, only evidence of what could have happened to her in Scar's captivity. To the cavalryman's remark about two rescued white girls who could easily have been Lucy and Debbie, "It's hard to believe they're white," Ethan replies ominously, "They ain't white. Not any more." These words are complemented by the way Ethan, unshaven and shadowy, looks disgustingly at the mad woman (the "Martha" to "Lucy and Debbie") when he hears her cries as she clutches Debbie's doll. This brief three-shot sequence, which first shows Ethan, then the woman, then Ethan again (recalling the same three-shot sequence of his seeing the burning Edwards farmhouse), underscores the fact that it is his viewpoint. Considering it is Marty's letter, however, it is his seeing how Ethan looks at the mad woman who reminds him of Martha. Her cries, especially when Ethan is shown, sound like the moaning during sexual intercourse. This perhaps explains the horrified look on Ethan's face, which the camera moves in on. The thought of miscegenation, the projection of his repressed unconscious, horrifies Ethan and drives him mad.

The Katabasis

Following the sequence of Marty's letter, Ethan and Marty are shown continuing their search against a red setting sun, a fitting image for opening what may be called *The Searchers' katabasis,* the descent to the underworld, to the unconscious, the domain where the dragon dwells. As often happens in such descents, in their subterranean journey Ethan's and Marty's relationship undergoes a noticeable change.

The first sign of change, however subtle, is the identical hats the two wear (Ethan on his head, Marty stringed on his back). It is emphasized by the sombrero Ethan spots on a horse's head outside the Mexican cantina, the way station to their descent. Another small sign is their two identical checkered shirts, though of different colors. Inside the cantina they find Mose, who literally jumps for joy at seeing the two. Like them, he wears a checkered shirt, his dark blue and white much closer to Marty's black and white than Ethan's red and white. Mose may be a mad fool, but he does not have Ethan's madness. As he says early in the movie, "Mose knows." Somewhat like Tiresias pointing the way home to Odysseus in his descent to Hades, Mose leads Ethan to the Mexican man who "knows where little Debbie is." When this man, present in the cantina, introduces himself and invites the three for a drink, once again Ethan excludes Marty, telling him, like a father to a son, "Wait till you grow up."

Like Charon, the old man who ferries the dead to the underworld across the river Styx, the Mexican leads Ethan and Marty to Scar's camp. That in his descent to Hades Ethan meets his dark double, his unacceptable "other half," is establish by the shot of two "identical" Indians—identically dressed, each holding a rifle in an identical position. The double motif is further emphasized by the twin animal skulls that stand guard, like two gargoyles, before the entrance to Scar's tepee, warning signs of the dragon's lair.

When they finally meet, the two adversaries stare each other down in identical shots—Ethan from slightly below, Scar from slightly above. It is followed by an identical shot of Marty. As this three-shot sequence demonstrates, Scar (who is shown with fire and smoke in the background) is the mirror image of Ethan's dark unconscious. Less obvious is that Marty is the *other* side of Ethan, Scar's opposite. In this "psychological epic," he is the Superego to Scar's Id.

"Scar, huh?" Ethan walks up to "the great Cicatriz war chief," confronting him face to face. "Plain to see how you got your name." Scar follows suit, calling Ethan by the name they have given him, "Big Shoulders." Equally arrogant, the two archenemies recognize their mirrored image in one another, as suggested by their echoing each other's words about their ability to "speak pretty good" the language of the other. When Scar invites the three to his tepee, Ethan once again tries to exclude Marty, but much more forcefully. "You stay out of here!" But this time Marty stands his ground. "Not likely!" he says with equal force, a sign of his becoming more of a match for Ethan.

The confrontation outside Scar's tepee continues inside. Following a brief introduction by the Mexican, informing Ethan and Marty that Scar's "sons are dead, so his wives sit on the honor side of this lodge," the remainder of the sequence is between Ethan and Scar. Unwilling, or unable, to address Scar directly, Ethan talks to him through the Mexican. But Scar speaks directly to Ethan, telling him what happened to his *two* sons and why he kills whites. "Two sons killed by white men. For each son, I take many...." The Mexican completes his sentence, "scalps." This thirst for revenge is another connection between the two.

When Scar calls one of his wives, twice, to show them the lance from which scalps hang like trophies, Ethan and Marty look up in unison to see Debbie, which shocks the two much more than Scar's scalps. As the lingering shot of Debbie reveals, she is even more shocked than they are. The experienced Ethan nudges Marty not to let on that he recognized her, but Scar is not fooled. The emotions are too great to conceal. "We've seen scalps before," Ethan says, downplaying his shock. "This before?" Scar taunts him by holding the medal he gave Debbie, dangling from his neck. As he did with his desire for Martha, who was alive when he gave Debbie the medal, Ethan holds back his rage. In fact, both antagonists clearly suppress their shared hostilities for one another. But seeing the medal on Scar is too much for Ethan, who gets up to leave, remarking to the Mexican as if Scar is not present. "I came to trade, not to admire his collection." Agreeing to trade the next day, but neither side really meaning to, Ethan exits the tepee. The Mexican and "He That Follows" are right behind him.

With the Mexican departing because he does not want "blood money," Ethan asks Marty deridingly, "Do you want to pull out too?" Marty, looking down at Ethan, counters by repeating what Scar called him, mocking his masculinity. Then, as Marty walks away, he sees Debbie, unseen by Ethan, running towards the two. She has come to warn them about the inevitable attack that Ethan was sure would come. Marty tries to make her remember back to the time they played as big brother and little sister. "Don't you remember me, Debbie?" His words break through to Debbie, who replies in English, "I remember. From always." As a memory from *always*, Debbie's words may very well echo what Martha must have felt waiting for Ethan, particularly as Ethan is shown hearing her words to Marty. "First I prayed to you, come and get me. Take me home. You didn't come." Likewise, Marty's reply, "But I've come now, Debbie," may express the reason for Ethan's return to his brother's family, to reclaim Martha.

Debbie telling Marty he has come too late, "These are my people," is all Ethan needs to hear. He draws his gun and orders Marty to "stand aside." But Marty, knowing what Ethan has in mind, shields Debbie with his body, protecting her as Ethan failed to protect Martha and her family. "No you don't, Ethan!" He draws his own gun, confronting him as an equal. With the two guns poised against each other, recalling the earlier meeting between Ethan and Scar, Ethan advances, trying to intimidate Marty, ordering him once again to "Step aside!" But an Indian's arrow stops him by piercing his "big shoulder," his masculinity, stopping him from committing another crime, this time a very real one. Marty turns around to shoot the Indian, as the attack Debbie had come to warn them about commences. The two clear out on their horses, Marty shouting Debbie's name as he and Ethan had earlier shouted Martha's.

Framing Ethan and Marty through the opening of the dark cave they scramble towards to take cover from the pursuing Comanches, the shot recalls the movie's first image of Martha framed by the doorway. Once again, as in the first attack across the river, Scar is shown going through the rite of putting on his crown and Ethan's bullet topples him off his horse. This time, however, Marty is no longer shy with his gun. He has come a long way since the first encounter.

The shot of the retreating Comanches dissolves into a shot of Marty in the womb-like cave, filling his canteen with water. Like the water streaming down from the rocks, the subsequent shot slowly reveals (from top to bottom) the mountainside where the cave is lodged, the camera lingering on its dark opening. If to go by the imagery and by what transpires next, Marty emerges from the cave's uterine opening reborn. His rebirth is suggested by background in his confrontation with Ethan, which is much like a woman's vulva, particularly the dark opening at the center of the frame.

Aside from this rather long shot, most of the other shots of the sequence are mirrored shots of Ethan and Marty. Where Marty is reborn, Ethan is obsessed by Debbie being Scar's squaw. The shooting angle of these shots, Ethan from slightly above and Marty from slightly below, which recalls the shots of Ethan meeting Scar, is a first sign that the roles in their relationship have begun to change. Another sign is Marty's giving Ethan (who sits half-naked on a rock, his body slumped in exhaustion and defeat) the life-giving water, just as he had done after Ethan came back broken in spirit from finding Lucy's body. In return, Ethan acknowledges Marty as "blood kin" in the only way he knows, by making him the sole beneficiary of his will.

Reading slowly what Ethan had written, Marty stops to question his being "without any blood kin." But perhaps he should question the preceding phrase of Ethan "being of sound mind," as hate and the need for revenge have poisoned his mind, driving him to virtual madness. Having seen Debbie as a full-grown woman, the sexual implications are too much for him to bear; since she has been defiled by Scar, at least in Ethan's mind, Ethan disowns her. But where Scar (Id) plays on Ethan's dark desires, Marty (Superego) plays on his sense of humanity. "What kind of a man are you, anyway?" He throws the will back at Ethan, reminding him of his aim to shoot Debbie. "She's been livin' with a buck. She's...." Ethan stops short of uttering Debbie's sexual relationship with Scar. "Shut your dirty mouth!" Marty draws a knife on Ethan. "I hope you die!" is all he can say. "That'll be the day," Ethan responds with his familiar arrogance. But as anticipated by Marty taking out the poison from Ethan's wounded shoulder, what ultimately dies is his burning desire to kill Debbie. And what is born in due course is his becoming a father, to both Marty and Debbie.

In taking out the poison from Ethan's wounded shoulder, as Samuel Osherson points out in *Finding Our Fathers*, Marty may very well detoxify his own "inner image" of the "wounded father." "Healing the wounded father means 'detoxifying' that image so that it is no longer dominated by the resentment, sorrow, and sense of loss or absence that restrict our own identities as men."[8] In other words, Marty slays the dragon, the introjected father that "restricts" his growing identity. This is underscored by the fact that from this point on, Marty "is no longer dominated by [Ethan's] resentment." That he is no longer under the dragon's shadow is suggested by his not repeating Ethan's mistake in letting the woman he loves marry the wrong man.

Two Pairs

As if evoking the detoxified Ethan, the mood changes abruptly with the music of the wedding celebration. The opening shot of two sets of legs (of two men playing two different musical instruments) and the symmetrical shot of the men dancing on one side and the women on the other introduce the *pair* motif that dominates this segment of the movie. The music and dancing stop as Captain Clayton makes an entrance that recalls his entrance into the Edwards home. In fact, the whole sequence is a re-enactment of Clayton's first appearance at the Edwards home. Charlie MacCorry, who "can't hardly recognize" himself, is a ridiculous Aaron; Marty is a bright version of the dark Ethan. Martha's presence is evoked by the singing of "Shall We Gather at the River," sung at her funeral. The first part of the sequence ends just as it had started, in another symmetrical shot of Reverend Clayton at the center, men on one side, the women on the other, about to commence the rite of uniting man and woman before the eyes of God and their community.

Cutting to the outside (and outside the community), Ethan and Marty are shown driving up in a carriage, probably due to Ethan's wound. Like the shot that opened the preceding sequence, the first outside shot shows *two pairs* of twos: Ethan and Marty and the two horses. Their sharing the wagon is another sign of their growing atonement, as is their wearing, once again, identical hats. Where up to now it was Ethan who "held the reins," "giving the orders," now it is Marty. The change in Ethan is apparent in the tone of his now-familiar response, "That'll be the day," to Marty's naïve question on hearing the song inside the Jorgensen house, "Hey, you don't suppose they're throwin' a party for us, do you?" (Of course, considering what transpires next, and as if celebrating their coming together as father and son, the party is for them.) The arrogant tone that characterized Ethan's previous responses, such as his last line before Marty took the poison out, is now more relaxed. He even allows Marty to help him step down from the carriage, something he would never allow prior to Marty taking the poison out of his shoulder. Ethan is in an uncommonly giddy mood throughout the sequence. This change, this lightening up, allows Ethan to experience what would have happened had he returned in time to stop Martha from marrying his brother. Ethan speaks from personal experience when he says to the equally surprised Laurie and Marty as she comes down the back stairs in a white wedding gown, "Looks like you two have a lot to talk about."

Stepping inside the house, Ethan disrupts the wedding proceedings just as he had disrupted his brother's family life and their funeral, taking great pleasure in informing Charlie that Marty is with him. "Yep," he smiles to himself, stepping up to the bar as if to celebrate Marty's return in time. Three men join the father of the groom for a drink, the one in the center welcoming him back. The shot of the four, with Ethan looking at the man on the left side of the screen, cuts to a mirror shot of Marty and Laurie standing by the wooden "bar" above the fireplace. The two's declaration of love for one another may well be Ethan's wishful thinking of what might have been, particularly as Marty, like Ethan, looks at Laurie on the left side of the screen, and Laurie, like the man at the bar, is glad to see Marty back. Unlike Ethan and Martha, who suppressed their expression of love for one another, Marty and Laurie are open and direct. "One letter in five years. I read it till the paper dried up and the writing faded out," Laurie confesses, turning her back to Marty. "Might at least said you loved me. You might have asked me to wait for you. At least that'd be something." In his reply, Marty could very well voice Ethan's unsaid words. "But I always loved you. I thought you knew that without me havin' to say it." This pair of mirrored shots (one showing Ethan in his most cheerful mood, the other showing Marty and Laura working out their love for each other) is another sign that the coming together of the young couple reflects Ethan's coming to terms with his guilt-ridden relationship with Martha.

The high point of this dramatic sequence comes when Marty suggests that the best thing for him to do is to go away, thus choosing the course taken by Ethan. Laurie responds with, "If you do, Martin Pawley, and I'll just die," words that express what must have been on Martha's mind but remained unsaid. Likewise, Marty's reaction in learning that Laurie intends to marry Charlie, who intrudes upon the two, must have been what Ethan felt when Martha married his brother, though he probably did not "say it." Moreover, just as Ethan's past was questioned by Aaron, now Charlie reminds Marty of his crime and "that Indian wife you took." With all the suggested similarities, however, Marty is not like Ethan, nor does he repeat his mistake. He is not guilty of killing Futterman and his men, he took a wife unknowingly (naively), and he does not intend to let the woman he loves marry the wrong man without a fight. On the other hand, Marty does not have to fight his own brother, which makes his conflict much simpler.

In their fight, Marty swings at Charlie when he insinuates that Look "is not the first squaw you ever...." As with Ethan's thoughts of Debbie (and Martha), it is the sexual aspect that enflames Marty. The staging of the fight sequence, in a space that "joins" the two parts of the house, is another sign that it is between two sides. Laurie enjoys seeing Marty finally fighting over her, as Ethan never fought his brother for Martha; Charlie, unlike Aaron who silently abided the feelings he saw between Martha and Ethan, will not proceed with the wedding "till we get a few things cleared up around here."

The pair motif continues inside the house, as *Reverend* Clayton declares the wedding dissolved and turns his attention to Ethan as *captain*. "I'm talking to you as a ranger. Not as a preacher." Ethan gives up his gun without a word when the captain asks for it, something he would not have done in the past. Marty, on the other hand, does not give in so easily. This difference in the two is another sign that things have changed. Just when he stands up and announces he does not intend to cooperate, a young lieutenant, Marty's comical double, enters with surprising news. As the butt end of Clayton and Ethan's "funnin'" about the colonel being his *pa*, the young lieutenant's appearance, aside from providing the turning point in the search by finding Mose, reinforces the idea that the wedding was the bringing together, the atonement, of father and son, especially "considering nobody got married." This explains Ford casting John Wayne's son, Patrick, in the role of the young lieutenant.

Once again, it is Mose who advances the search for Debbie and Scar. But whereas in the cantina he talked to Ethan, now he only tells Marty of their whereabouts, another sign in the change of Marty's relationship with Ethan. What is more, it is Marty who recognizes the place Mose describes.

Expiation

However detoxified, seeing Scar's camp enflames Ethan's need for revenge. The two shots of his gazing from his vantage point overlooking the camp below is a first sign that, once again, what transpires is his projection. The close-up shot of a disturbed Ethan not only recalls the look on his face when he realized what was in store for Martha in the Comanches' massacre, the profile shot of Clayton chewing on something also recalls the one that showed his catching sight, while drinking coffee, of Martha brushing Ethan's coat. There Clayton witnessed Martha's love for Ethan; now he witnesses Ethan's madness when he answers his question about how many Indians he figures are down there: "About a dozen each. Enough to go around."

Contrary to Ethan's thirst for blood and disregard for Debbie's life, Marty insists on saving her before they begin their attack. For the first time since the search began, Marty stands up to Ethan and Clayton, the two father figures of the search party. Nothing Ethan says breaks his resolve to save Debbie. Not even when he tries to work on his sense of revenge by telling him that one of the scalps he saw "strung on Scar's lance" was his mother's. "It don't change nothing," Marty rebounds after a brief emotional setback. Just as he did not heed Laurie's harsh words about Martha wanting Ethan to "put a bullet" in Debbie's brain, Marty does not fall into Ethan's trap. He does not share his need for revenge.

Apparently, if to judge by Ethan's subsequent actions, in this confrontation, shown in a single shot, Marty earns his respect — not an easy thing to come by. Despite his being against it, when Clayton agrees to allow Marty to "go right ahead" and rescue Debbie, Ethan agrees in the only way he knows: "It's your funeral." And just before Marty goes off, on a cliff that has two "fathers" in Clayton and Ethan, and two sons in Marty and Charlie, Ethan puts a fatherly hand on his shoulder, as if saying "Good luck, son." He even helps Marty descend towards the Indian camp, thus advancing him on his quest. These are small gestures on Ethan's part, hardly noticeable, but they reveal his change of heart towards Marty and anticipate his change of heart towards Debbie.

Once again, following an establishing shot showing the Indian camp from where Ethan is standing, the shot showing Scar coming out of his tepee may be read as another of his projection. Half-naked, wearing the medal Ethan had given Debbie, Scar searches for whatever is making the dog bark, which doubles for Debbie's dog barking when Ethan returned at the movie's opening. Cutting back to the search party, the shot showing Ethan looking in the direction of Scar's camp, followed by the shot showing Marty stealing into Scar's tepee, is yet another sign that it is his projection (particularly as the shot of Scar's lower body coming to the teepee's entrance recalls the shot of Ethan's lower body when he found Debbie's shawl and doll). Before Ethan can get to his shadowy double, his other side kills him with three shots, which start the search party's attack.

The first shot of the attack, which once again shows the "twin" Indians in identical positions, each taking a shot at the coming attackers, reinforces the double motif. Ethan is shown riding on his horse into his double's tepee, where he finds him already dead. He is last shown pulling Scar by the head and drawing out his knife. The next time he is shown, he comes out of the tepee holding Scar's scalp, no different than his despised double. That scalping his savage double is a crucial rite for Ethan, a slaying of the dragon that allows him a change of heart towards Debbie, is suggested by the fact that no one is killed in the attack.

The change in Ethan is first apparent in the way he calls Debbie's name when chasing her from the top of his horse. His tone of voice seems to say, "Debbie, I don't want to hurt you." Shown through the dark opening of the cave, which recalls the movie's opening shot of Martha, together with the Martha theme coming on the soundtrack, Ethan's lifting up Debbie is a clear sign that he has come to terms with his feelings for his brother's wife. His lifting Debbie recalls the time before Martha was raped and killed, when Ethan could only express his repressed love through her children, particularly Debbie. With Ethan's "Let's go home Debbie," which echo Martha's first words in the movie, "Welcome home, Ethan," the two embrace as Ethan and Martha never did, perhaps because now it is between father and daughter. At last Ethan is part of what remains of Martha's family without the guilt that accompanied his desire for his brother's wife. In accepting Debbie, in becoming a father, Ethan slays the part in him that, like the dragon that Scar represents, wants revenge for the crime carried out against Martha. In delivering Debbie from the dragon's captivity to her new home, Ethan delivers himself from his "unacceptable unconscious desires" that have driven him to virtual madness.

That Ethan has become a father is reinforced by the opening shot of the very next scene of Captain Clayton and the young lieutenant, and by the appearance of the colonel, the lieutenant's father. Considering this sequence does not advance the narrative, it underscores, once and for all, the father-son motif that accompanies *The Searchers* from start to finish. Ironically, the father congratulates his son, "Good work, son," when the only "good work" he did was wound Captain Clayton with his careless sword. Coming after Ethan scalps Scar, Captain Clayton's feelings for the young lieutenant, comical but negative, seem to "absorb" Ethan's disdain for Marty, whose "good work" killed Scar and saved Debbie.

The mood of atonement is evoked in the two identical shots of the closing sequence, showing Mose rocking in his rocking chair on the Jorgensens' front porch, happy to see Ethan returning with Debbie and Marty. As Aaron's brother, Ethan is like the Biblical Moses, which suggests that Ol' Mose represents the part of him that longs for the Promised Land of home and family, symbolized by the rocking chair by the fire. This is emphasized by *The Searchers'* next-to-last shot, which singles out Mose in the rocking chair promised by Ethan when they find Debbie. He smiles contently, as if that that part of Ethan finds "peace of mind."

The final sign of Ethan's atonement for the crime against Martha is the meeting of Marty and Laura. Unlike Martha, who waited for Ethan to come to her, Laurie rushes to Marty as Martha's theme comes on for the last time in the movie, stopping just before she reaches him, as if waiting for a sign from him before she gives herself again. This time Marty does not hesitate. He rides towards her, reaching to her with his hand. It is all the sign Laurie needs. She comes up to him, taking his hand. Having displaced Ethan's and Martha's relationship, their finally coming together suggests that Ethan has made amends with his mixed feelings for Martha. This is corroborated by the absence of phallic buttes that loomed large in the exposition and in much of the movie.

Following the shot of Mr. and Mrs. Jorgensen, the new mother and father to Debbie (and future parents-in-law to Marty), Ethan is singled out as he dismounts and takes Debbie down from his horse, just as the song that opened the movie comes on the soundtrack. Closing out the movie, the song's last verse sums up what the search has been about: "A man will search his heart and soul." Indeed, from the moment he first arrives, and more so after Martha's death, Ethan has been searching his heart and soul, or in terms of this "psychological epic," his repressed unconscious. As demonstrated by the similarity between this wordless closing sequence and the movie's opening, the story has truly come full circle.

Framed by the porch's twin supporting poles, the closing shot of the movie, a mirrored shot of the opening, shows Ethan handing Debbie to the welcoming arms of Mr. and Mrs. Jorgensen. When she is escorted inside the Jorgensen home with her new mother and father, the camera draws back *inside* the dark interior of the house, just as it had moved *out* in the opening shot, so that Ethan, standing on the threshold, is framed by the doorway. He steps aside to allow Laurie and Marty, the new couple, to enter through the door. Bearing in mind that in the shot that opened the movie Martha came out towards the approaching Ethan, the entrance of Marty and Laurie completes their replacing, their displacing, the two's uneasy relationship, as if finally putting it to rest.

Perhaps Ethan standing outside the door, briefly gazing inside and slowly walking away with his back turned to the dark interior of the home, is best explained by the closing lines of the same song that opened the movie. In finding and bringing back Debbie (and Marty), Ethan may have atoned for his crime of passion, and scalping Scar may have cleansed his poisoned psyche, but his search does not bring him peace of mind. Like the closing words of the song, his search must continue.

If on his first return Ethan came home to stay, now he has no home to return to, and no Martha to welcome him. What started in darkness ends in darkness, though not of the same home, a last sign that something has changed. Having arrived in the movie's opening as "Uncle Ethan," and to Marty not even that, part of Ethan's consolation, "his peace of mind," is his becoming a father.

Notes

Introduction

1. James Hillman, *A Blue Fire* (New York: Harper Collins, 1989), 218.

2. Joseph Campbell, *Myths to Live By* (New York: Penguin, 1972), 253.

3. Geza Roheim, *Fire in the Dragon*, (Princeton, New Jersey: Princeton University Press, 1992), 5.

4. James Hillman, "The Great Mother's son, Her Hero, and the Puer," in *Fathers and Mothers*, ed. Patricia Berry (Dallas: Spring, 1990), 169.

5. Samuel Osherson, *Finding Our Fathers* (New York: Ballantine Books, 1986), 27.

6. Robert Bly, *Iron John: A Book About Men* (Reading, Mass.: Addison-Wesley, 1990), 95.

7. Erich Neumann, *The Origins and History of Consciousness* (Princeton: Princeton University Press, 1954), 170–71.

8. David Blankenhorn, *Fatherless America* (New York: Basic Books, 1995), 13.

9. Bly, 117.

PART I

1. Ray Raphael, *The Men from the Boys* (Lincoln: University of Nebraska Press, 1988), xxi.

Chapter 2

1. Robert Bly, *Iron John: A Book About Men* (Reading, Mass.: Addison-Wesley, 1990), 99.

2. Samuel Osherson, *Finding Our Fathers* (New York: Ballantine Books, 1986), 227.

3. William Shakespeare, *Hamlet*, in *The Complete Plays and Poems of William Shakespeare* (Cambridge, Mass.: The Riverside Press, 1942), 1057.

4. Bruno Bettleheim, *The Uses of Enchantment* (London: Thames and Hudson, 1976), 106.

5. James Joyce, *Ulysses* (New York: The Modern Library, 1961), 34.

6. Homer, *The Odyssey*, translated by Robert Fitzgerald (Garden City, N.Y.: Anchor Books, 1963), 11.

7. Woody Allen, dir., *Crimes and Misdemeanors* (DVD, MGM, 2001).

8. Ibid.

Chapter 3

1. Edith Sullwold, "The Ritual-Maker Within at Adolescence," in Betwixt & Between: Patterns of Masculine and Feminine Initiation, ed. Louise Carus Mahdi, Steven Foster and Meredith Little (La Salle, Il.: Open Court, 1987), 119.

2. John G. Cawelti, *The Six-Gun Mystique* (Bowling Green, Oh.: Bowling Green State University Popular Press, 1984), 82.

3. Erlling B. Holtsmark, "The Katabasis Theme in Modern Cinema," in *Classical Myth and Culture in the Cinema*, ed. Martin M. Winkler (New York: Oxford University Press, 2001), 25–26.

4. Joseph Campbell, *The Hero with a Thousand Faces* (New York: Meridian Books, 1956), 69.

5. James Hillman, *The Dream and the Underworld* (New York: Harper & Row, 1979), 29.

6. Warren Steinberg, *Masculinity* (Boston: Shambhala, 1993), 83.

7. Sullwold, 120.

8. Ray Raphael, *The Men from the Boys* (Lincoln: University of Nebraska Press, 1988), 6.

PART II

1. Will Wright, *Sixguns & Society* (Los Angeles: University of California Press, 1975), 4.
2. Jane Tompkins, *West of Everything* (New York: Oxford University Press, 1992), 6.

Chapter 4

1. James Wyly, *The Phallic Quest* (Toronto: Inner City Books, 1989), 80.
2. Joseph Campbell, *The Hero with a Thousand Faces* (New York: Meridian Books, 1956), 352.
3. Jane Tompkins, *West of Everything* (New York: Oxford University Press, 1992), 132.
4. Campbell, 337.
5. Tompkins, 117.
6. Campbell, 116.
7. Tompkins, 56.
8. Joseph M. Henderson, *Thresholds of Initiation* (Middletown, Conn.: Wesleyan University Press, 1967), 62.
9. Campbell, 344.
10. Ibid., 342.

Chapter 5

1. Jane Tompkins, *West of Everything* (New York: Oxford University Press, 1992), 137.

Chapter 6

1. Peter Bogdanovich, *The Cinema of Alfred Hitchcock* (New York: Doubleday, 1963), 141.
2. Thomas M. Leitch, *Find the Director and Other Hitchcock Games* (Athens: University of Georgia Press, 1991), 210.
3. Lesley Brill, *The Hitchcock Romance* (Princeton: Princeton University Press, 1988), 12.
4. Ibid., 9.

PART III

1. Homer, *The Odyssey*, translated by Robert Fitzgerald (Garden City, N.Y.: Anchor Books, 1963), 5.
2. Ibid., 5.
3. Ibid., 9.
4. Ibid., 11.
5. Ibid., 27.
6. Ibid., 8.
7. Ibid., 38.
8. Samuel Osherson, *Finding Our Fathers* (New York: Ballantine Books, 1986), 6.
9. Ibid., 50.
10. Homer, 295.
11. David Blankenhorn, *Fatherless America* (New York: Basic Books, 1995), 1.
12. Ibid., 2–3.

Chapter 7

1. Steven Spielberg, "Inside the Artists Studio," interviewed by James Lipton, In the Moment Productions, Ltd., 1999.
2. Ibid.
3. Steven Spielberg speaking about *E.T.*, during the 20th anniversary special on NBC, March 16, 2002.
4. Steven Spielberg, *E.T.: The Extra-Terrestrial*, 20th Anniversary DVD supplement "Evolution and Creation of E.T." Universal Studios, 2002.
5. Inez Hedges, *Breaking the Frame* (Bloomington: Indiana University Press, 1991), 109.
6. Spielberg, "Inside the Artists Studio."
7. Philip Taylor, *Steven Spielberg: The Man, His Movies and Their Meaning* (New York: The Continuum, 1999), 127.
8. Ilsa J. Bick, "The Look Back in *E.T.*," in *The Films of Steven Spielberg Critical Essays*, ed. Charles L. P. Silet (Lanham, Md.: The Scarecrow Press, 2002), 79.
9. Edward C. Whitmont, *The Symbolic Quest* (New York: Harper & Row, 1969), 240.
10. Ibid., 241.
11. Ibid., 243.
12. Eugene Monick, *Phallos: Sacred Image of the Masculine* (Toronto: Inner City Books, 1987), 9.
13. Ibid., 10.

Chapter 8

1. Samuel Osherson, *Finding Our Fathers* (New York: Ballantine Books, 1986), 206.
2. Herbert Stein, *Double Feature: Discovering Our Hidden Fantasies in Film* (New York: An [e-reads] Book, 2002), 13.
3. Osherson, 20.

Chapter 9

1. Homer, *The Odyssey*, translated by Robert Fitzgerald (Garden City, N.Y.: Anchor Books, 1963), 2.

PART IV

1. David Blankenhorn, *Fatherless America* (New York: Basic Books, 1995), 83.

Chapter 10

1. Robert Jewett and John Shelton Lawrence, *The American Monomyth* (Garden City, N.Y.: Anchor Press/Doubleday, 1977), 169–70.
2. Ibid., 140.
3. Hal Hinson, Rev. of *The Lion King*, *The Washington Post*, June 24, 1994.
4. David Blankenhorn, *Fatherless America* (New York: Basic Books, 1995), 201.
5. Ibid., 4.
6. Jewett and Lawrence, 174.
7. Blankenhorn, 222.
8. Jerome S. Bernstein, "The Decline of Masculine Rites of Passage in Our Culture: The Impact on Masculine Individuation," in *Betwixt & Between: Patterns of Masculine and Feminine Initiation*, ed. Louise Carus Mahdi, Steven Foster and Meredith Little (La Salle, Il.: Open Court, 1987), 142.
9. *The Lion King*, DVD Supplement, Disney, 2005.

10. Barbara Greenfield, "The Archetypal Masculine: Its Manifestation in Myth, and its Significance for Women," in *The Father*, ed. Andrew Samuels (New York: New York University Press, 1986), 192.
11. Robert Bly, *Iron John: A Book About Men* (Reading, Mass.: Addison-Wesley, 1990), 150.

Chapter 11

1. Hermann Melville, *Moby Dick* (New York: Holt, Rinehart and Winston, 1964), 3.
2. Edward C. Whitmont, *The Symbolic Quest* (New York: Harper & Row, 1969), 17.

Chapter 12

1. J. A. Place, *The Western Films of John Ford* (Secaucus, N.J.: The Citadel Press, 1974), 164.
2. Kathryn Kalinak, "'Typically American': Music for *The Searchers*," in The Searchers: *Essays and Reflections on John Ford's Classic Western*, ed. Arthur M. Eckstein and Peter Lehman (Detroit: Wayne State University Press, 2004), 121.
3. Ibid., 123.
4. Place, 164.
5. Kalinak, 124.
6. Arthur M. Eckstein, Introduction, in The Searchers: *Essays and Reflections on John Ford's Classic Western*, ed. Arthur M. Eckstein and Peter Lehman (Detroit: Wayne State University Press, 2004), 14–15.
7. Douglas Pye, "Miscegenation and Point of View," in The Searchers: *Essays and Reflections on John Ford's Classic Western*, ed. Arthur M. Eckstein and Peter Lehman (Detroit: Wayne State University Press, 2004), 224.
8. Samuel Osherson, *Finding Our Fathers* (New York: Ballantine Books, 1986), 206.

Selected Bibliography

Articles and Books

Bernstein, Jerome S. "The Decline of Masculine Rites of Passage in Our Culture: The Impact on Masculine Individuation," in *Betwixt & Between: Patterns of Masculine and Feminine Initiation,* edited by Louise Carus Mahdi, Steven Foster and Meredith Little, 135–58. La Salle, Il.: Open Court, 1987.

Bettleheim, Bruno. *The Uses of Enchantment.* London: Thames and Hudson, 1976.

Bick, Ilsa J. "The Look Back in *E.T.*," in *The Films of Steven Spielberg Critical Essays,* edited by Charles L. P. Silet, 71–90. Lanham, Md.: The Scarecrow Press, 2002.

Blankenhorn, David. *Fatherless America.* New York: Basic Books, 1995.

Bly, Robert. *Iron John: A Book About Men.* Reading, Mass.: Addison-Wesley, 1990.

Bogdanovich, Peter. *The Cinema of Alfred Hitchcock.* New York: Doubleday, 1963.

Brill, Lesley. *The Hitchcock Romance.* Princeton: Princeton University Press, 1988.

Campbell, Joseph. *The Hero with a Thousand Faces.* New York: Meridian Books, 1956.

_____. *Myths to Live By.* New York: Penguin Books USA Inc., 1993.

Cawelti, John G. *The Six-Gun Mystique.* Bowling Green, Oh.: Bowling Green State University Popular Press, 1984.

Eckstein, Arthur M. Introduction, in The Searchers: *Essays and Reflections on John Ford's Classic Western,* edited by Arthur M. Eckstein and Peter Lehman, 1–45. Detroit: Wayne State University Press, 2004.

Greenfield, Barbara. "The Archetypal Masculine: Its Manifestation in Myth, and its Significance for Women," in *The Father,* edited by Andrew Samuels, 187–210. New York: New York University Press, 1986.

Hedges, Inez. *Breaking the Frame.* Bloomington: Indiana University Press, 1991.

Henderson, Joseph M. *Thresholds of Initiations.* Middletown, Conn.: Wesleyan University Press, 1967.

Hillman, James. *A Blue Fire.* New York: Harper Collins, 1989.

_____. *The Dream and the Underworld.* New York: Harper & Row, 1979.

_____. "The Great Mother's son, Her Hero, and the Puer," in *Fathers and Mothers,* edited by Patricia Berry, 166–209. Dallas: Spring, 1990.

Hinson, Hal. "Rev of *The Lion King.*" *The Washington Post,* June 24, 1994.

Holtsmark, Erling B. "The *Katabasis* Theme in Modern Cinema," in *Classical Myth and Culture in the Cinema,* edited by Martin M. Winkler, 23–50. New York: Oxford University Press, 2001.

Homer. *The Odyssey,* translated by Robert Fitzgerald. Garden City, N.Y.: Anchor Books, 1963.

Jewett, Robert, and John Shelton Lawrence. *The American Monomyth.* Garden City, N.Y.: Anchor Press/Doubleday, 1977.

Joyce, James. *Ulysses.* New York: The Modern Library, 1961.

Kalinak, Kathryn. "'Typically American': Music for *The Searchers,*" in The Searchers: *Essays and Reflections on John Ford's Classic Western,* edited by Arthur M. Eckstein and Peter Lehman, 109–43. Detroit: Wayne State University Press, 2004.

Leitch, Thomas M. *Find the Director and*

Other Hitchcock Games. Athens: University of Georgia Press, 1991.

Melville, Herman. *Moby Dick*. New York: Holt, Rinehart and Winston, 1964.

Monick, Eugene. *Phallos: Sacred Image of the Masculine*. Toronto: Inner City Books, 1987.

Neumann, Erich. *The Origins and History of Consciousness*. Princeton: Princeton University Press, 1954.

Osherson, Samuel. *Finding Our Fathers*. New York: Ballantine Books, 1986.

Place, J. A. *The Western Films of John Ford*. Secaucus, N. J.: The Citadel Press, 1974.

Pye, Douglas, "Miscegenation and Point of View in *The Searchers*," in The Searchers: *Essays and Reflections on John Ford's Classic Western*, edited by Arthur M. Eckstein and Peter Lehman, 223–37. Detroit: Wayne State University Press, 2004.

Raphael, Ray. *The Men from the Boys*. Lincoln: University of Nebraska Press, 1988.

Roheim, Geza. *Fire in the Dragon*. Princeton: Princeton University Press, 1992.

Shakespeare, William. *Hamlet*, in *The Complete Plays and Poems of William Shakespeare*, 1043–179. Cambridge, Mass: The Riverside Press, 1942.

Stein, Herbert. *Double Feature: Discovering Our Hidden Fantasies in Film*. New York: An [e-reads] Book, 2002.

Steinberg, Warren. *Masculinity*. Boston: Shambhala, 1993.

Sullwold, Edith. "The Ritual-Maker Within at Adolescence," in *Betwixt & Between: Patterns of Masculine and Feminine Initiation*, edited by Louise Carus Mahdi, Steven Foster and Meredith Little, 111–31. La Salle, Il.: Open Court, 1987.

Tompkins, Jane. *West of Everything*. New York: Oxford University Press, 1992.

Truffaut, François. *Hitchcock*. Rev. ed. New York: Simon & Schuster, 1984.

Whitmont, Edward C. *The Symbolic Quest*. New York: Harper Colophon Books, 1969.

Wright, Will. *Sixguns & Society*. Los Angeles: University of California Press, 1975.

Wyly, James. *The Phallic Quest*. Toronto: Inner City Books, 1989.

Films

Allen, Woody (director), *Crimes and Misdemeanors*, DVD, MGM, 2001.

Spielberg, Steven, "Inside the Artists Studio," James Lipton, interviewer.

Spielberg, Steven, speaking about *E.T.* during the 20th anniversary special on NBC, March 16, 2002.

Spielberg, Steven, "Evolution and creation of E.T." in *E.T.: The Extra-Terrestrial*, 20th Anniversary DVD supplement, Universal Studios, 2002.

The Lion King, DVD Supplement, Disney, 2005.

Index